SWAMP THING

THE DEAD DON'T SLEEP

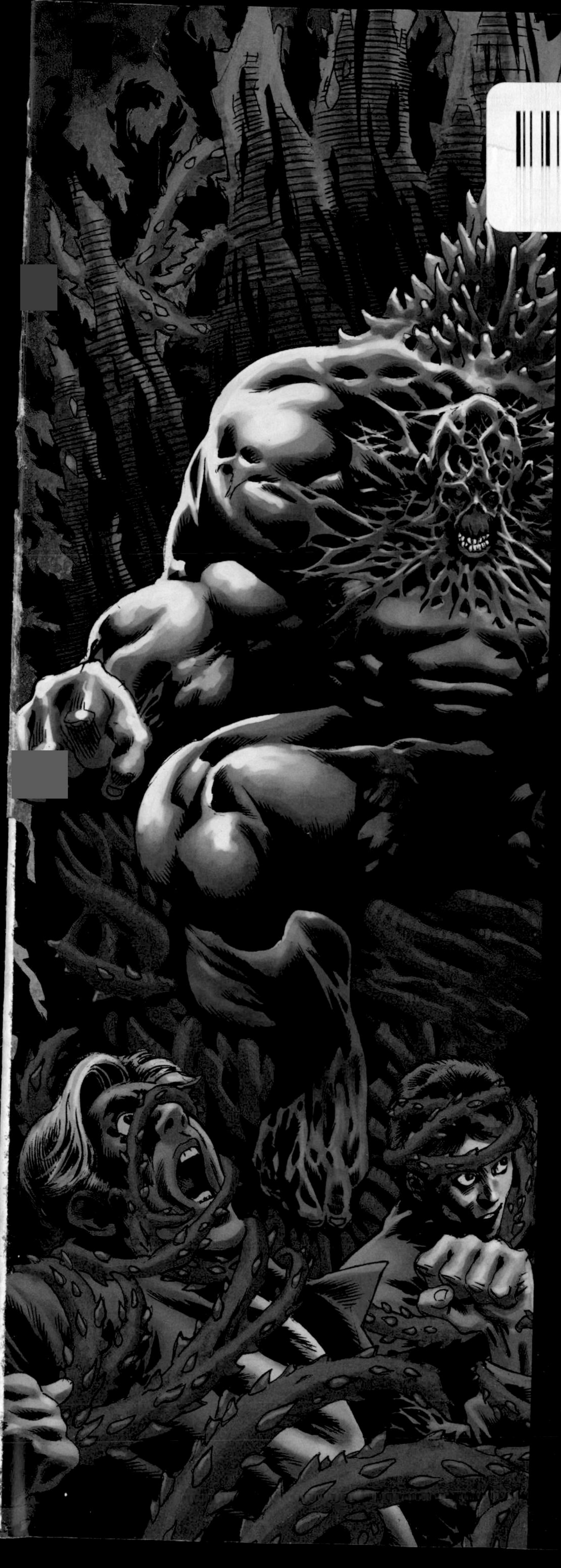

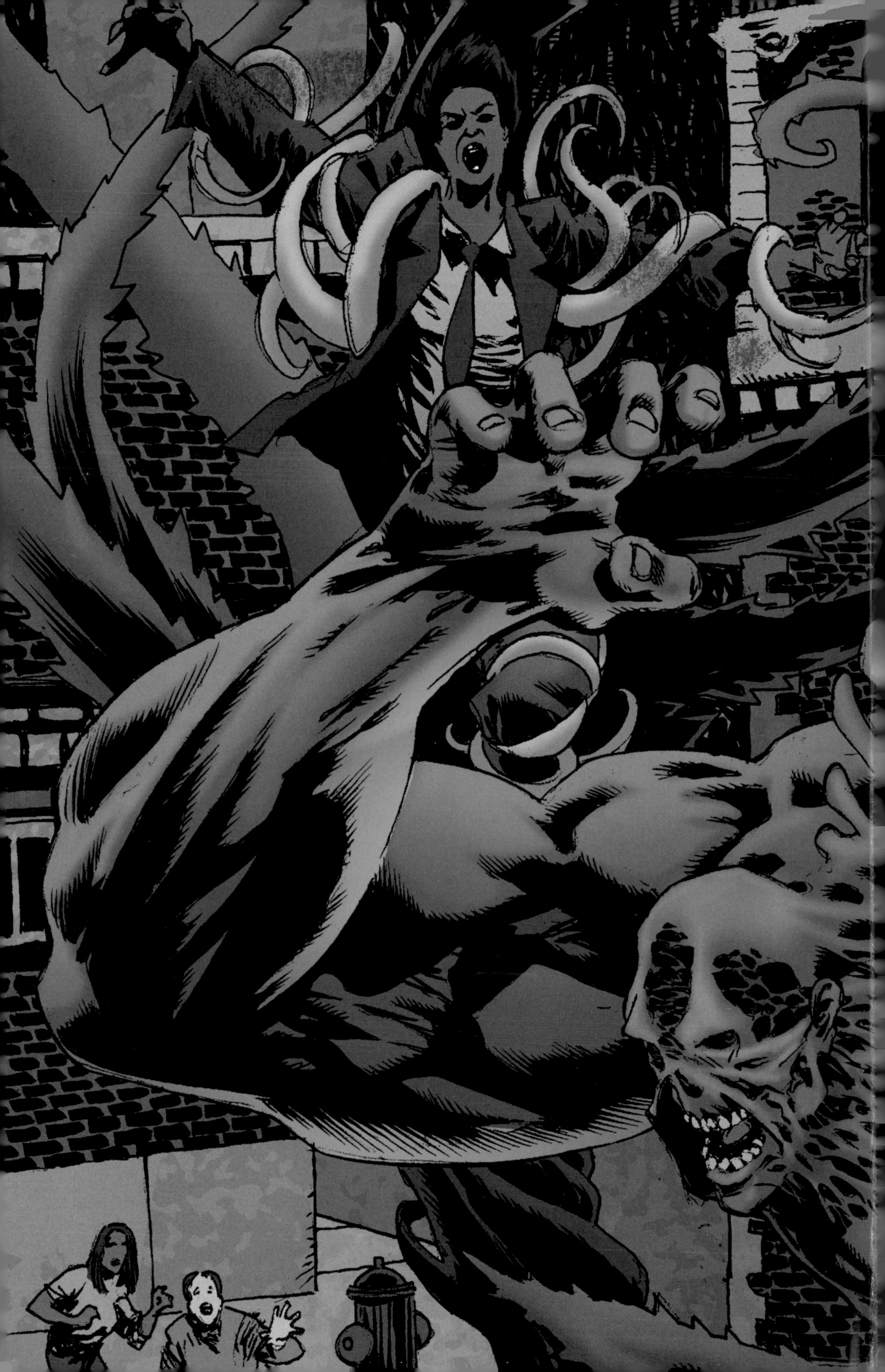

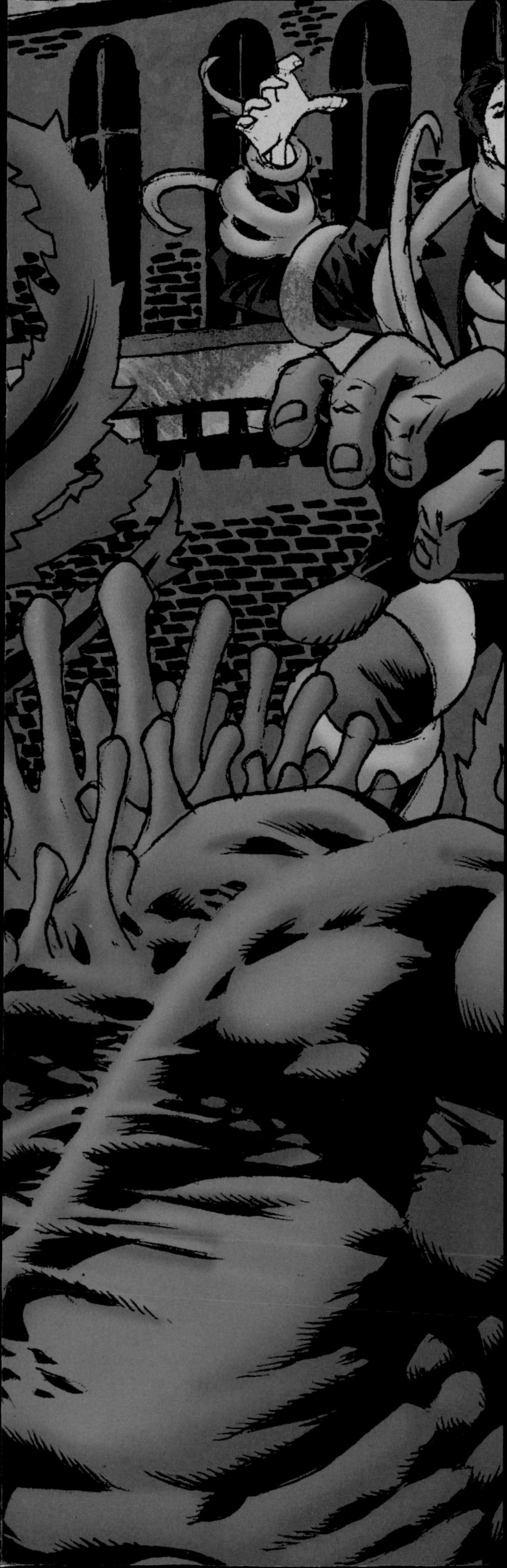

SWAMP THING

THE DEAD DON'T SLEEP

WRITTEN BY
LEN WEIN

ART BY
KELLEY JONES

COLOR BY
MICHELLE MADSEN

LETTERS BY
ROB LEIGH

COVER ART & ORIGINAL SERIES COVERS
KELLEY JONES with CHRIS SOTOMAYOR

SWAMP THING CREATED BY
LEN WEIN and BERNIE WRIGHTSON

ZATANNA CREATED BY
GARDNER FOX and MURPHY ANDERSON

REBECCA TAYLOR Editor – Original Series
JEB WOODARD Group Editor – Collected Editions
SCOTT NYBAKKEN Editor – Collected Edition
STEVE COOK Design Director – Books
DAMIAN RYLAND Publication Design

BOB HARRAS Senior VP – Editor-in-Chief, DC Comics

DIANE NELSON President
DAN DIDIO and JIM LEE Co-Publishers
GEOFF JOHNS Chief Creative Officer
AMIT DESAI Senior VP – Marketing & Global Franchise Management
NAIRI GARDINER Senior VP – Finance
SAM ADES VP – Digital Marketing
BOBBIE CHASE VP – Talent Development
MARK CHIARELLO Senior VP – Art, Design & Collected Editions
JOHN CUNNINGHAM VP – Content Strategy
ANNE DEPIES VP – Strategy Planning & Reporting
DON FALLETTI VP – Manufacturing Operations
LAWRENCE GANEM VP – Editorial Administration & Talent Relations
ALISON GILL Senior VP – Manufacturing & Operations
HANK KANALZ Senior VP – Editorial Strategy & Administration
JAY KOGAN VP – Legal Affairs
DEREK MADDALENA Senior VP – Sales & Business Development
JACK MAHAN VP – Business Affairs
DAN MIRON VP – Sales Planning & Trade Development
NICK NAPOLITANO VP – Manufacturing Administration
CAROL ROEDER VP – Marketing
EDDIE SCANNELL VP – Mass Account & Digital Sales
COURTNEY SIMMONS Senior VP – Publicity & Communications
JIM (SKI) SOKOLOWSKI VP – Comic Book Specialty & Newsstand Sales
SANDY YI Senior VP – Global Franchise Management

SWAMP THING: THE DEAD DON'T SLEEP

DC Comics, 2900 West Alameda Ave., Burbank, CA 91505
Printed by RR Donnelley, Salem, VA, USA. 9/2/16. First Printing.
ISBN: 978-1-4012-7001-8

Library of Congress Cataloging-in-Publication Data is available.

PEFC Certified

Printed on paper from
sustainably managed
forests and controlled
sources

PEFC

PEFC/29-31-75   www.pefc.org

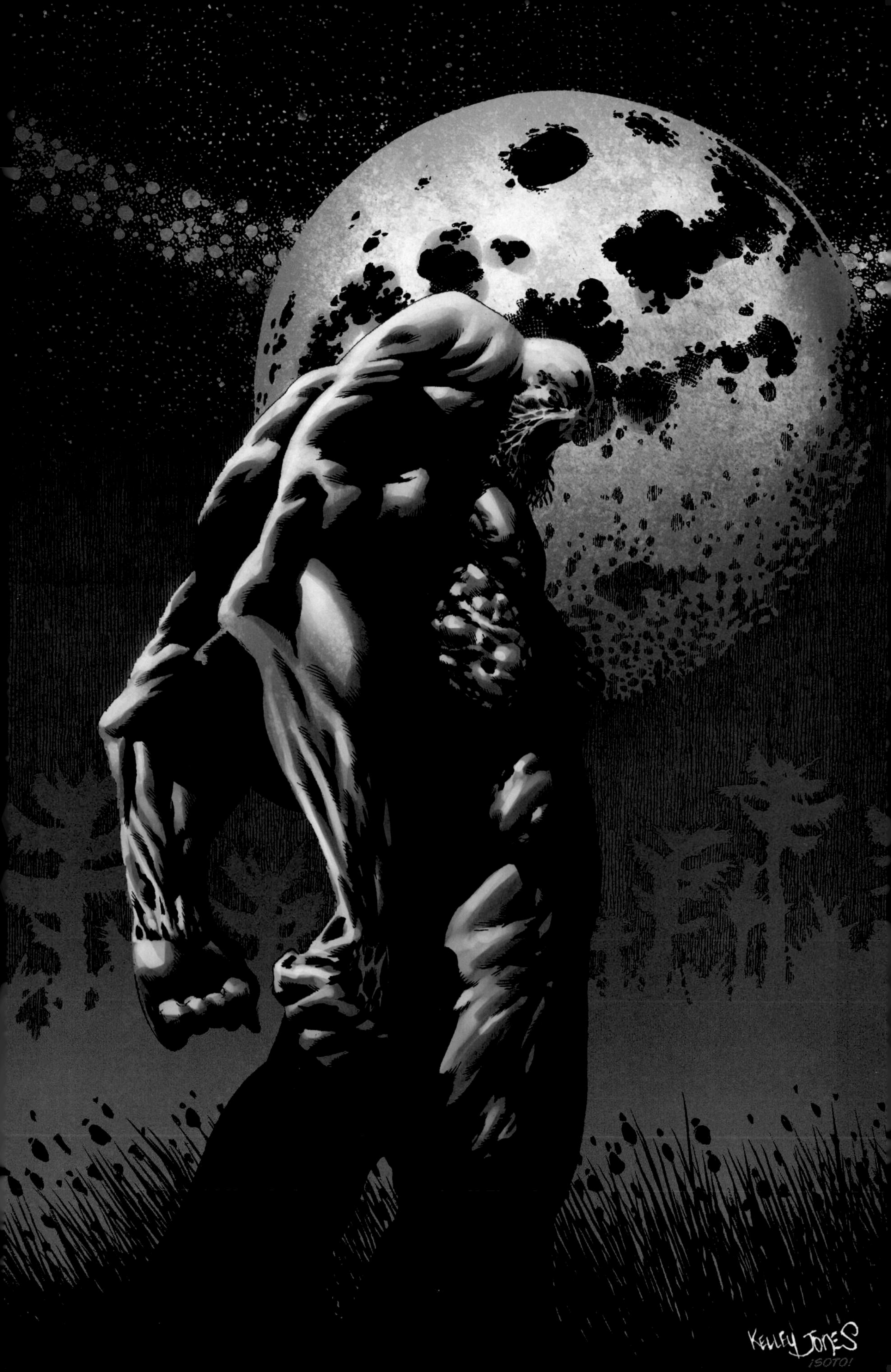
KELLEY JONES
¡SOTO!

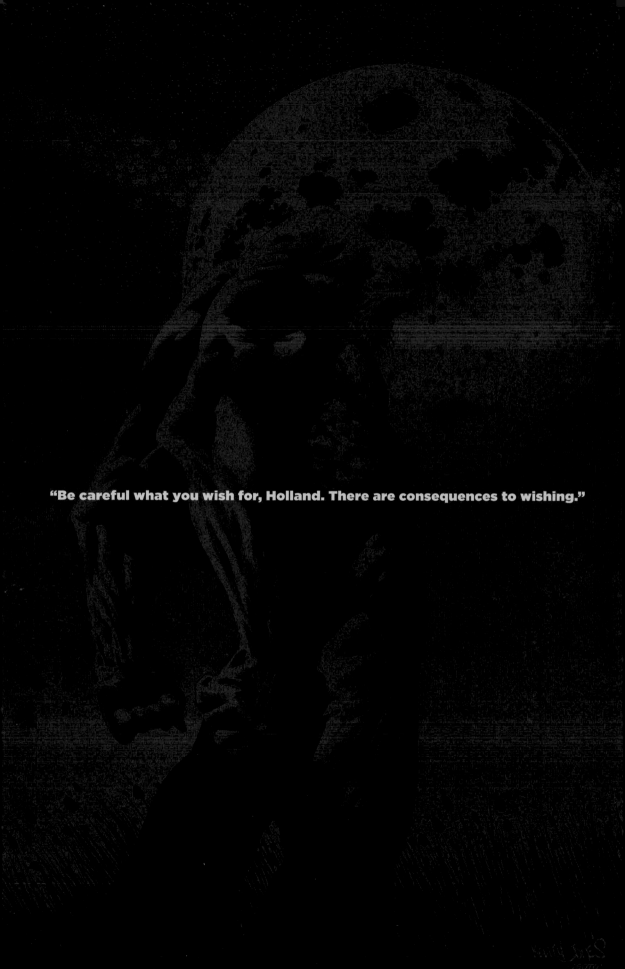

"Be careful what you wish for, Holland. There are consequences to wishing."

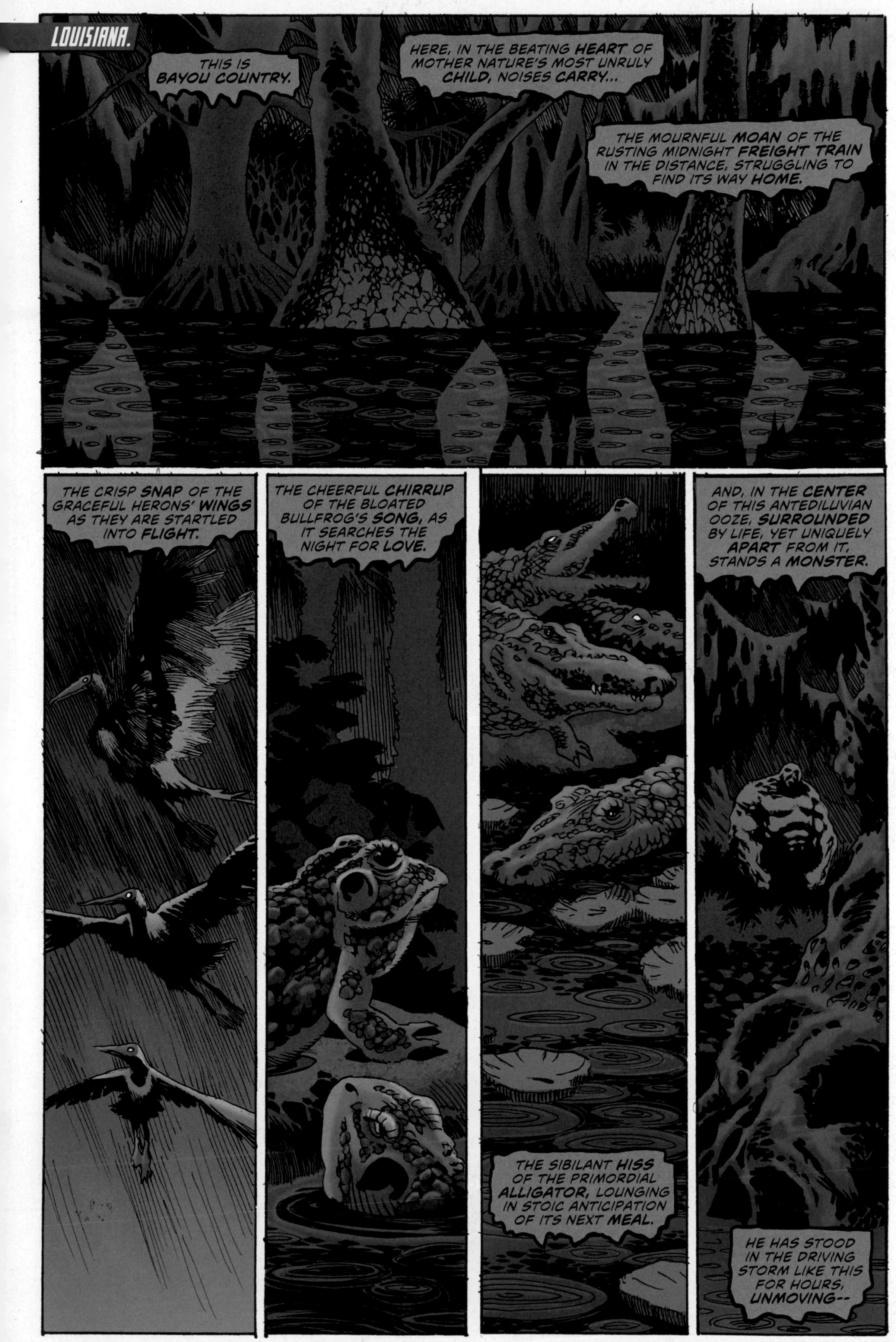
LOUISIANA.
THIS IS BAYOU COUNTRY.
HERE, IN THE BEATING HEART OF MOTHER NATURE'S MOST UNRULY CHILD, NOISES CARRY...
THE MOURNFUL MOAN OF THE RUSTING MIDNIGHT FREIGHT TRAIN IN THE DISTANCE, STRUGGLING TO FIND ITS WAY HOME.
THE CRISP SNAP OF THE GRACEFUL HERONS' WINGS AS THEY ARE STARTLED INTO FLIGHT.
THE CHEERFUL CHIRRUP OF THE BLOATED BULLFROG'S SONG, AS IT SEARCHES THE NIGHT FOR LOVE.
THE SIBILANT HISS OF THE PRIMORDIAL ALLIGATOR, LOUNGING IN STOIC ANTICIPATION OF ITS NEXT MEAL.
AND, IN THE CENTER OF THIS ANTEDILUVIAN OOZE, SURROUNDED BY LIFE, YET UNIQUELY APART FROM IT, STANDS A MONSTER.
HE HAS STOOD IN THE DRIVING STORM LIKE THIS FOR HOURS, UNMOVING--

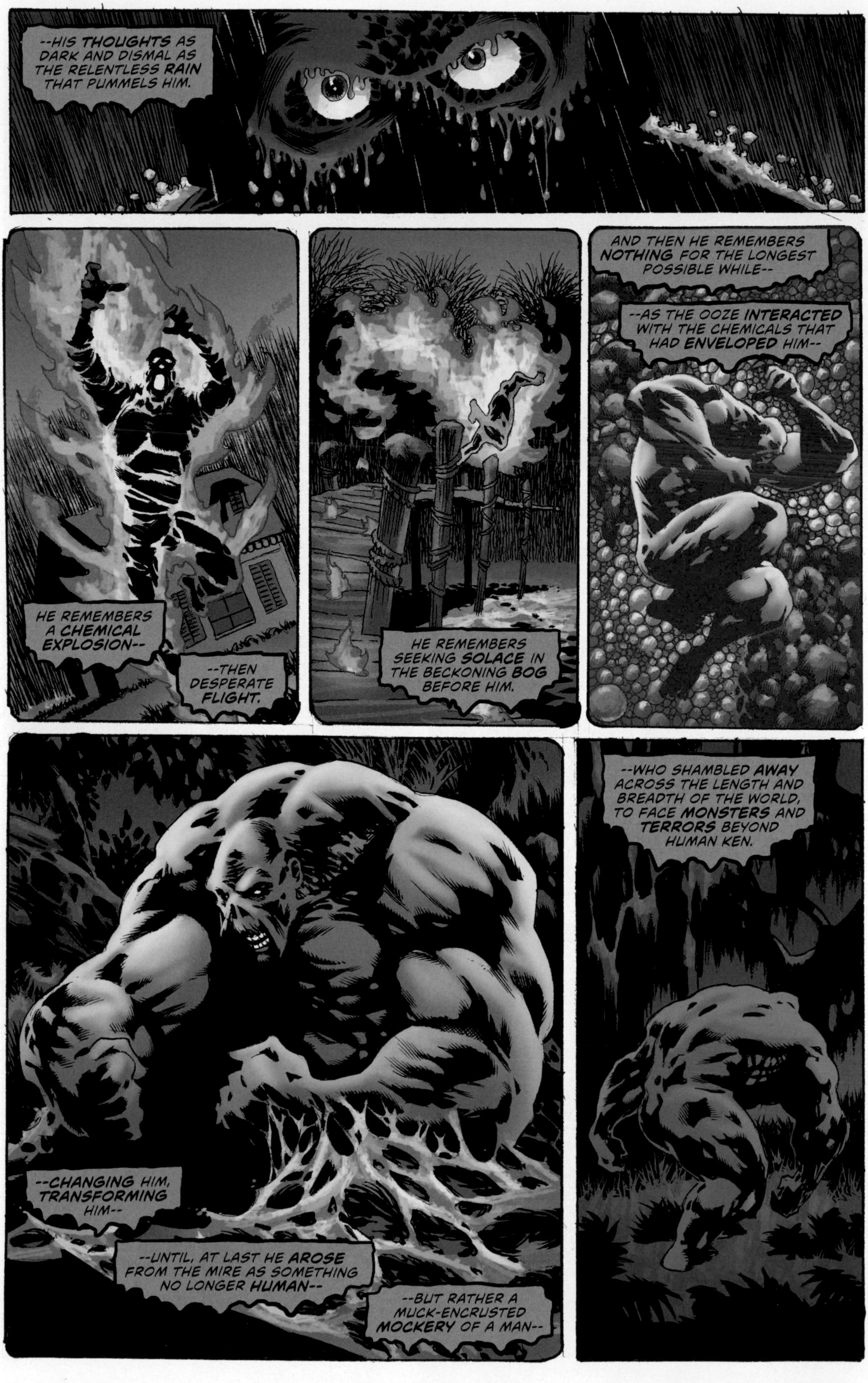
--HIS THOUGHTS AS DARK AND DISMAL AS THE RELENTLESS RAIN THAT PUMMELS HIM.
HE REMEMBERS A CHEMICAL EXPLOSION--
--THEN DESPERATE FLIGHT.
HE REMEMBERS SEEKING SOLACE IN THE BECKONING BOG BEFORE HIM.
AND THEN HE REMEMBERS NOTHING FOR THE LONGEST POSSIBLE WHILE--
--AS THE OOZE INTERACTED WITH THE CHEMICALS THAT HAD ENVELOPED HIM--
--CHANGING HIM, TRANSFORMING HIM--
--UNTIL, AT LAST HE AROSE FROM THE MIRE AS SOMETHING NO LONGER HUMAN--
--BUT RATHER A MUCK-ENCRUSTED MOCKERY OF A MAN--
--WHO SHAMBLED AWAY ACROSS THE LENGTH AND BREADTH OF THE WORLD, TO FACE MONSTERS AND TERRORS BEYOND HUMAN KEN.

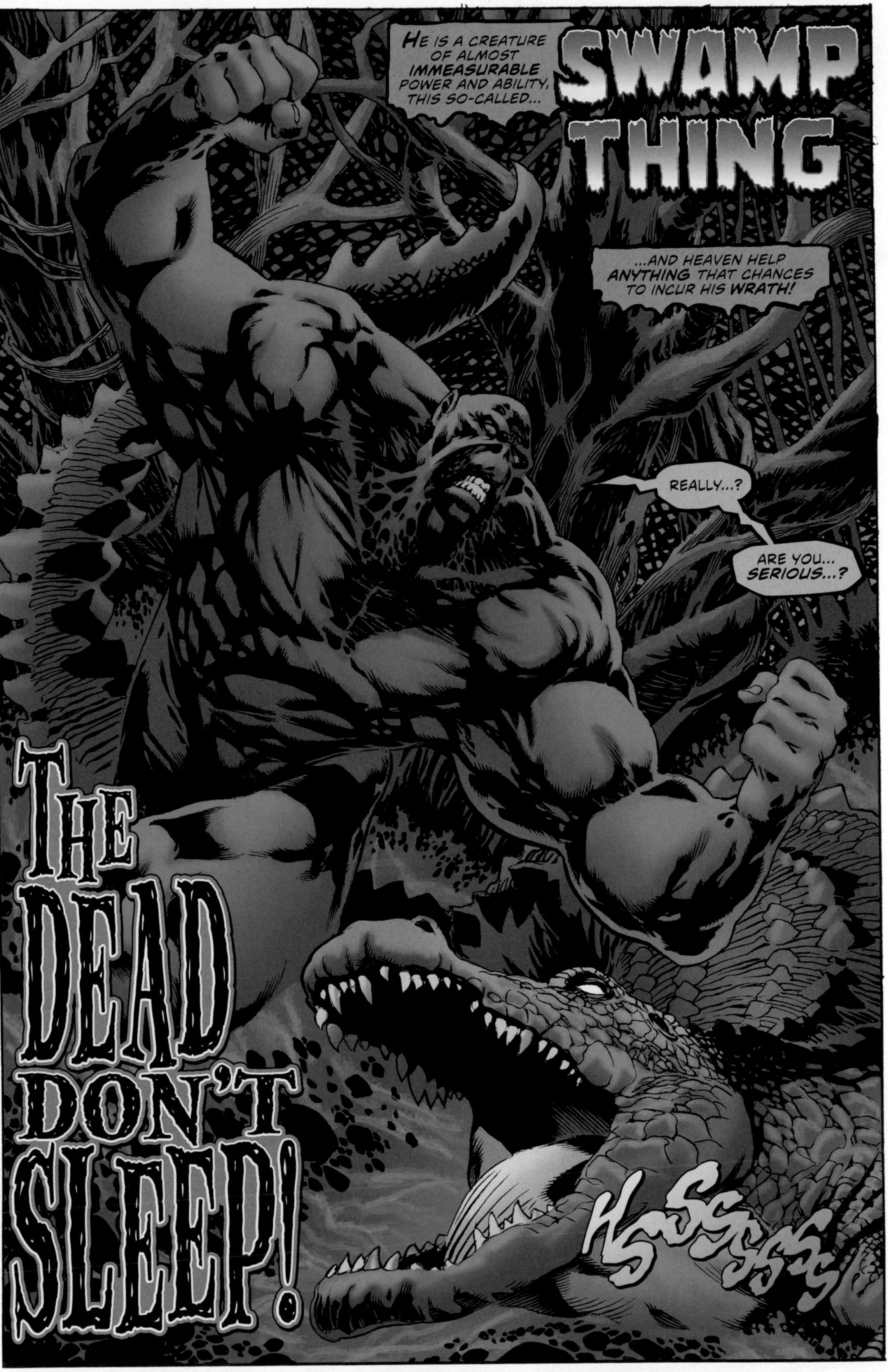
HE IS A CREATURE OF ALMOST IMMEASURABLE POWER AND ABILITY, THIS SO-CALLED...
SWAMP THING
...AND HEAVEN HELP ANYTHING THAT CHANCES TO INCUR HIS WRATH!
REALLY...?
ARE YOU... SERIOUS...?
THE DEAD DON'T SLEEP!
HSSSSSS

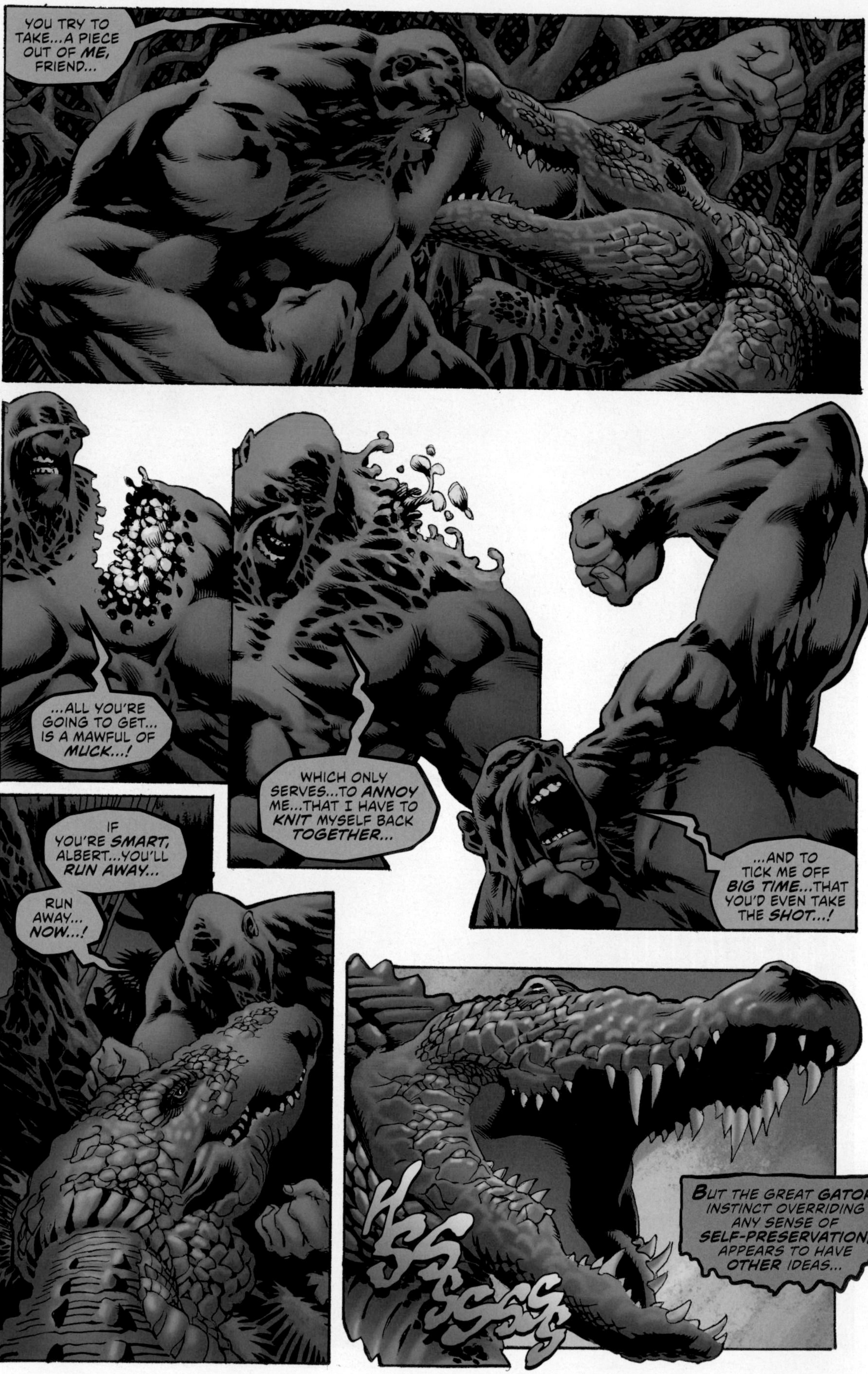
YOU TRY TO TAKE...A PIECE OUT OF ME, FRIEND...
...ALL YOU'RE GOING TO GET... IS A MAWFUL OF MUCK...!
WHICH ONLY SERVES...TO ANNOY ME...THAT I HAVE TO KNIT MYSELF BACK TOGETHER...
...AND TO TICK ME OFF BIG TIME...THAT YOU'D EVEN TAKE THE SHOT...!
IF YOU'RE SMART, ALBERT...YOU'LL RUN AWAY...
RUN AWAY... NOW...!
HSSSSSSS
BUT THE GREAT GATOR, INSTINCT OVERRIDING ANY SENSE OF SELF-PRESERVATION, APPEARS TO HAVE OTHER IDEAS...

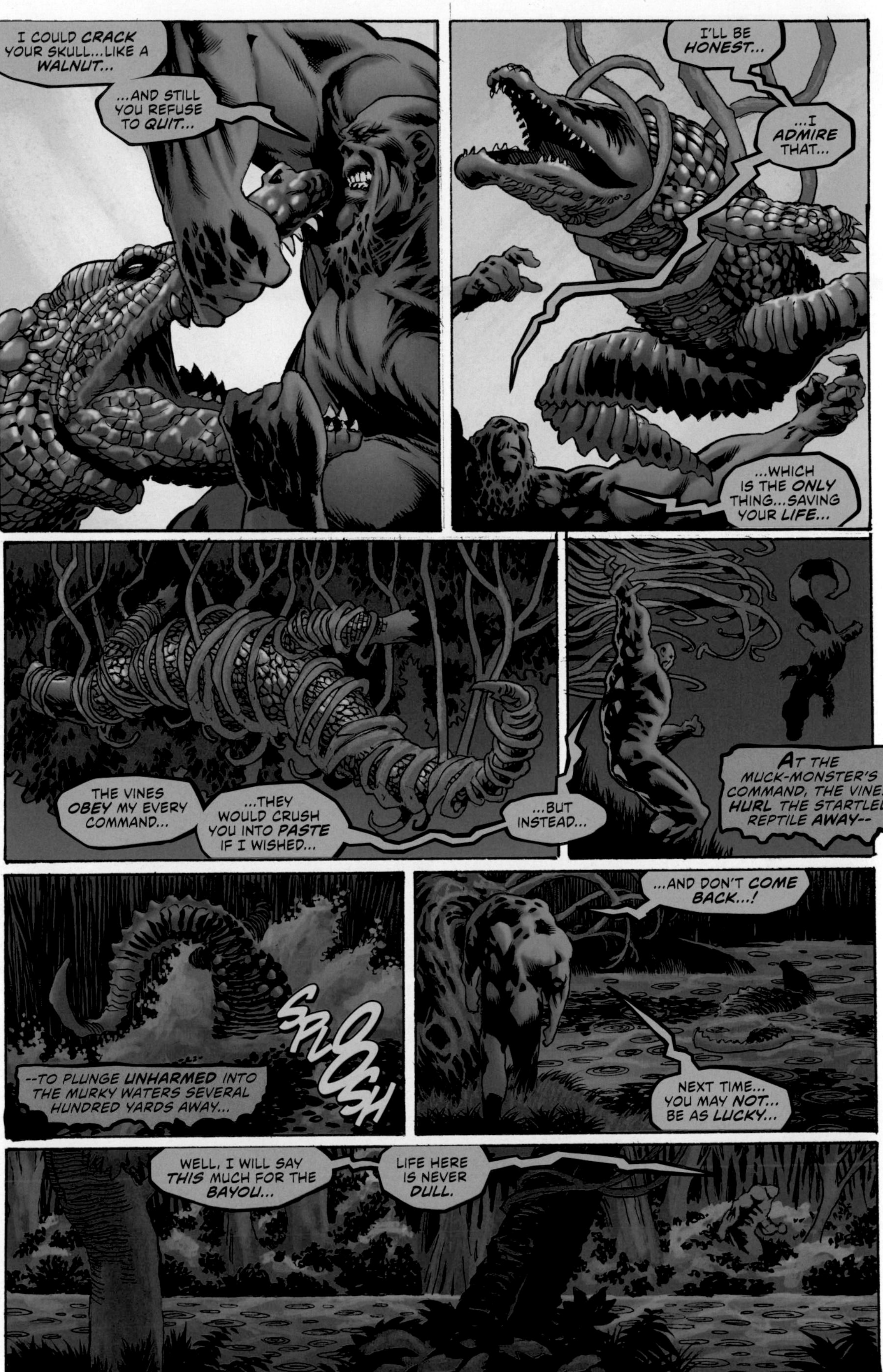
I COULD CRACK YOUR SKULL...LIKE A WALNUT...
...AND STILL YOU REFUSE TO QUIT...
I'LL BE HONEST...
...I ADMIRE THAT...
...WHICH IS THE ONLY THING...SAVING YOUR LIFE...
THE VINES OBEY MY EVERY COMMAND...
...THEY WOULD CRUSH YOU INTO PASTE IF I WISHED...
...BUT INSTEAD...
AT THE MUCK-MONSTER'S COMMAND, THE VINES HURL THE STARTLED REPTILE AWAY--
SPLOOSH
--TO PLUNGE UNHARMED INTO THE MURKY WATERS SEVERAL HUNDRED YARDS AWAY...
...AND DON'T COME BACK...!
NEXT TIME... YOU MAY NOT... BE AS LUCKY...
WELL, I WILL SAY THIS MUCH FOR THE BAYOU...
LIFE HERE IS NEVER DULL.

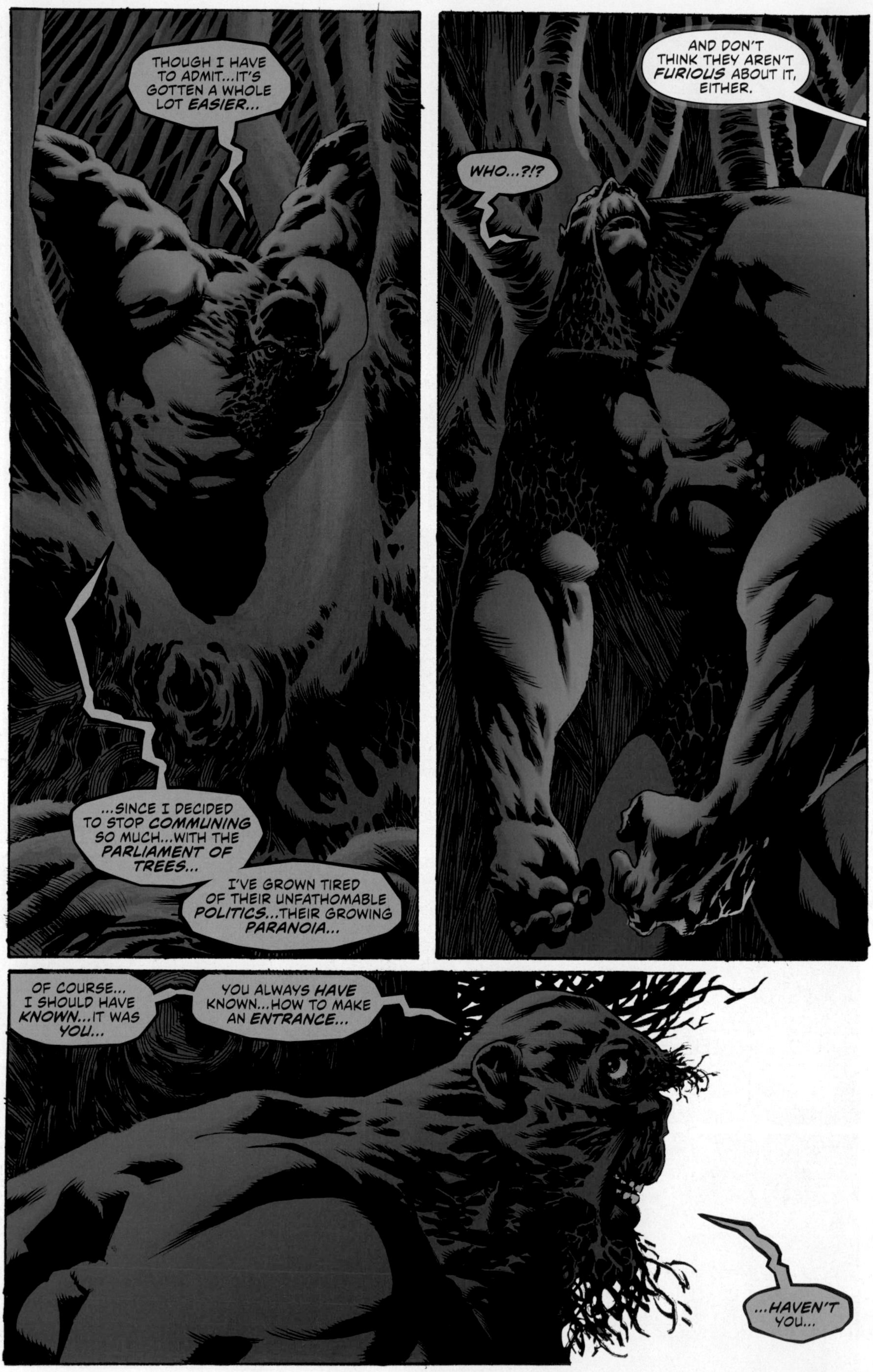
THOUGH I HAVE TO ADMIT...IT'S GOTTEN A WHOLE LOT EASIER...
...SINCE I DECIDED TO STOP COMMUNING SO MUCH...WITH THE PARLIAMENT OF TREES...
I'VE GROWN TIRED OF THEIR UNFATHOMABLE POLITICS...THEIR GROWING PARANOIA...
AND DON'T THINK THEY AREN'T FURIOUS ABOUT IT, EITHER.
WHO...?!?
OF COURSE... I SHOULD HAVE KNOWN...IT WAS YOU...
YOU ALWAYS HAVE KNOWN...HOW TO MAKE AN ENTRANCE...
...HAVEN'T YOU...

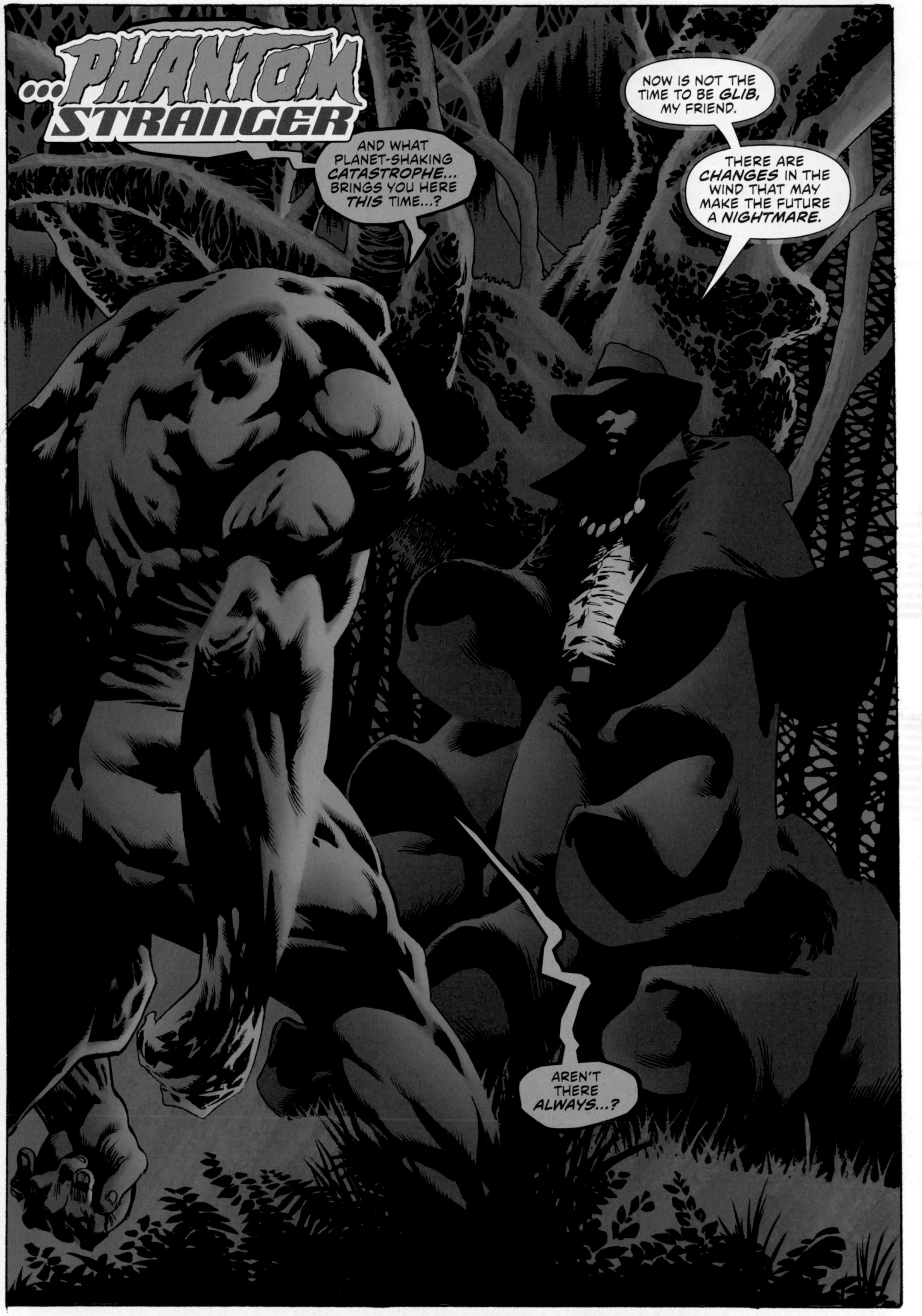
...PHANTOM STRANGER
AND WHAT PLANET-SHAKING CATASTROPHE... BRINGS YOU HERE THIS TIME...?
NOW IS NOT THE TIME TO BE GLIB, MY FRIEND.
THERE ARE CHANGES IN THE WIND THAT MAY MAKE THE FUTURE A NIGHTMARE.
AREN'T THERE ALWAYS...?

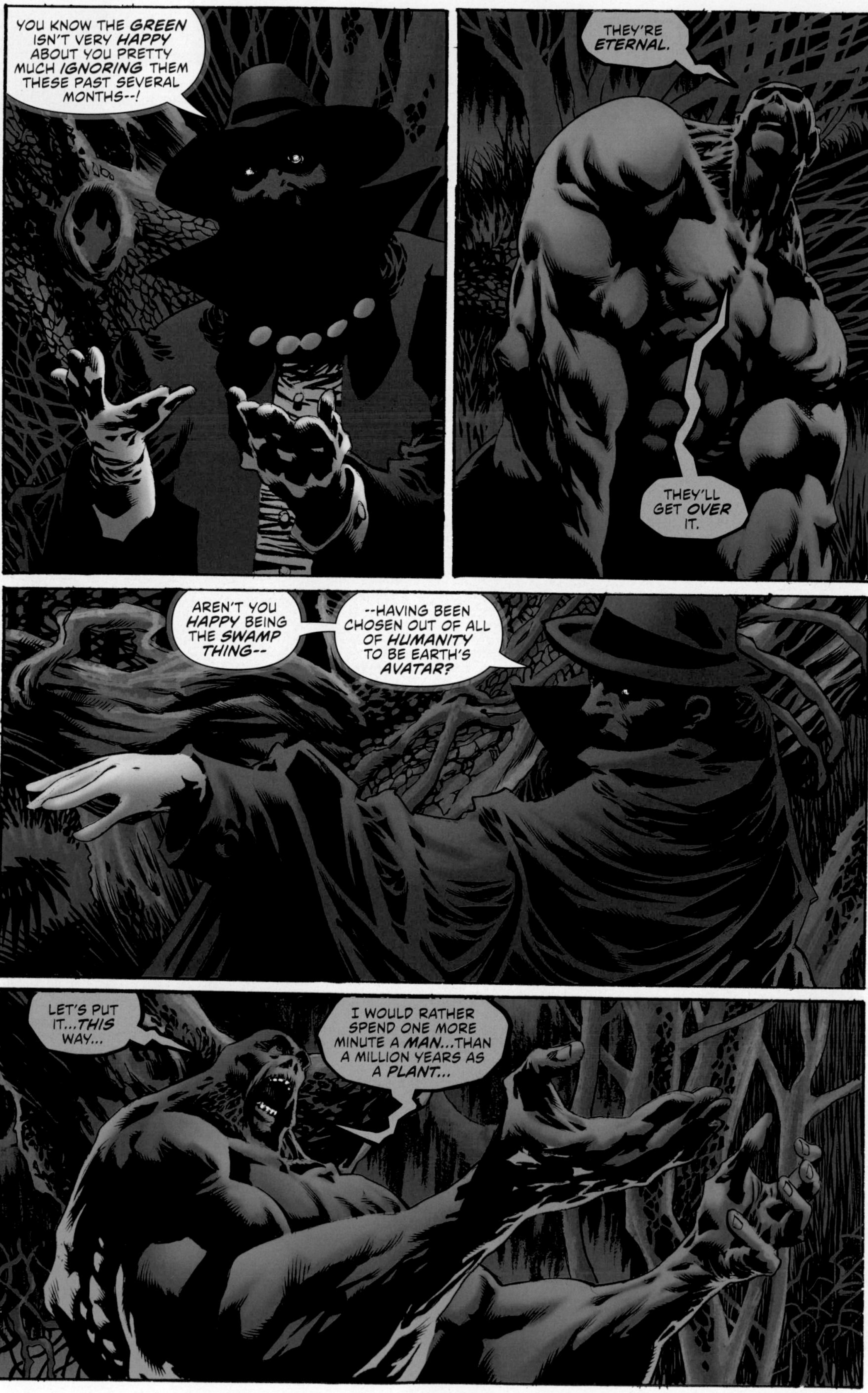
YOU KNOW THE GREEN ISN'T VERY HAPPY ABOUT YOU PRETTY MUCH IGNORING THEM THESE PAST SEVERAL MONTHS--!
THEY'RE ETERNAL.
THEY'LL GET OVER IT.
AREN'T YOU HAPPY BEING THE SWAMP THING--
--HAVING BEEN CHOSEN OUT OF ALL OF HUMANITY TO BE EARTH'S AVATAR?
LET'S PUT IT...THIS WAY...
I WOULD RATHER SPEND ONE MORE MINUTE A MAN...THAN A MILLION YEARS AS A PLANT...

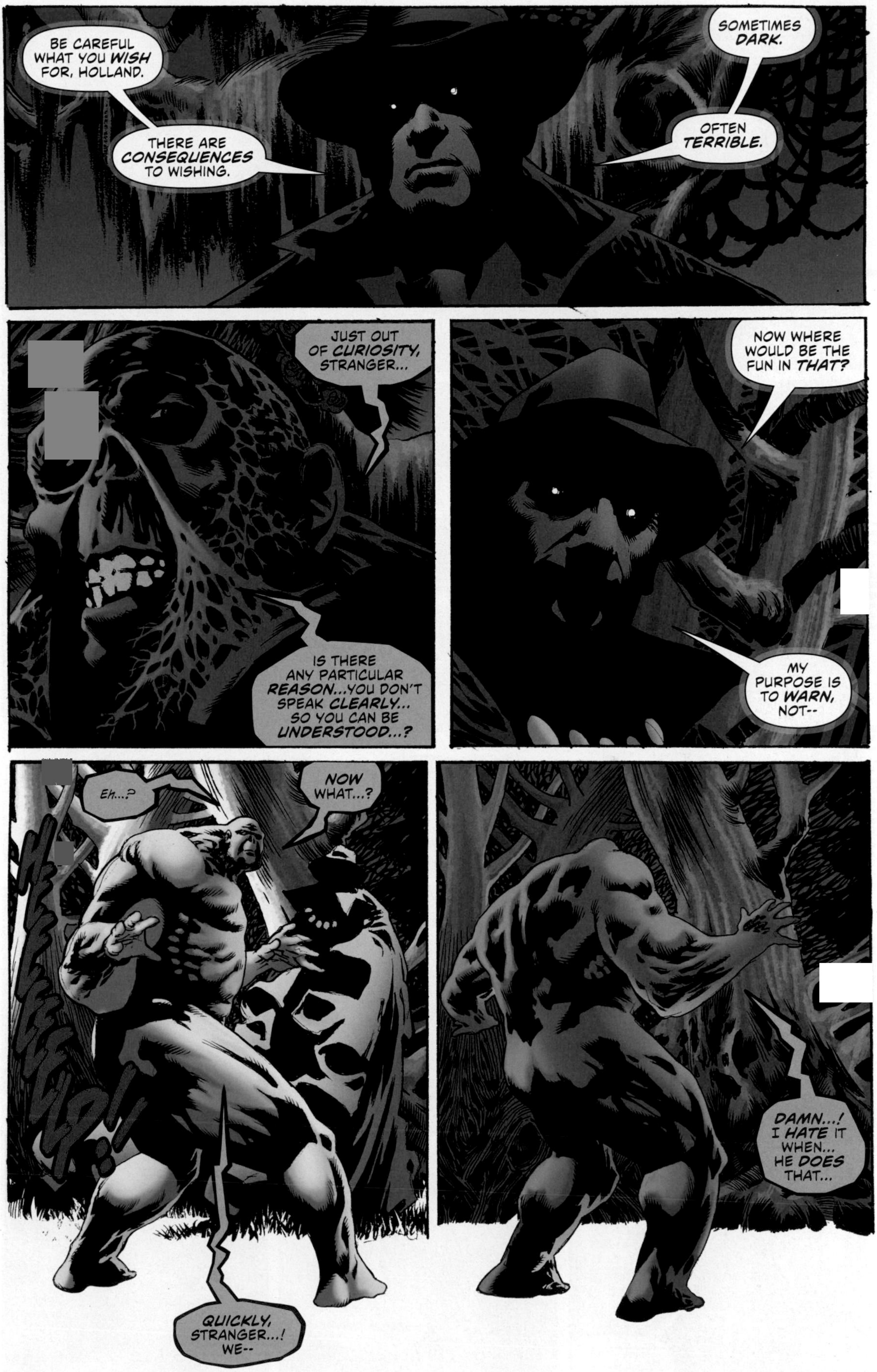
BE CAREFUL WHAT YOU WISH FOR, HOLLAND.
THERE ARE CONSEQUENCES TO WISHING.
SOMETIMES DARK.
OFTEN TERRIBLE.
JUST OUT OF CURIOSITY, STRANGER...
IS THERE ANY PARTICULAR REASON...YOU DON'T SPEAK CLEARLY... SO YOU CAN BE UNDERSTOOD...?
NOW WHERE WOULD BE THE FUN IN THAT?
MY PURPOSE IS TO WARN, NOT--
Eh...?
NOW WHAT...?
QUICKLY, STRANGER...! WE--
DAMN...! I HATE IT WHEN... HE DOES THAT...

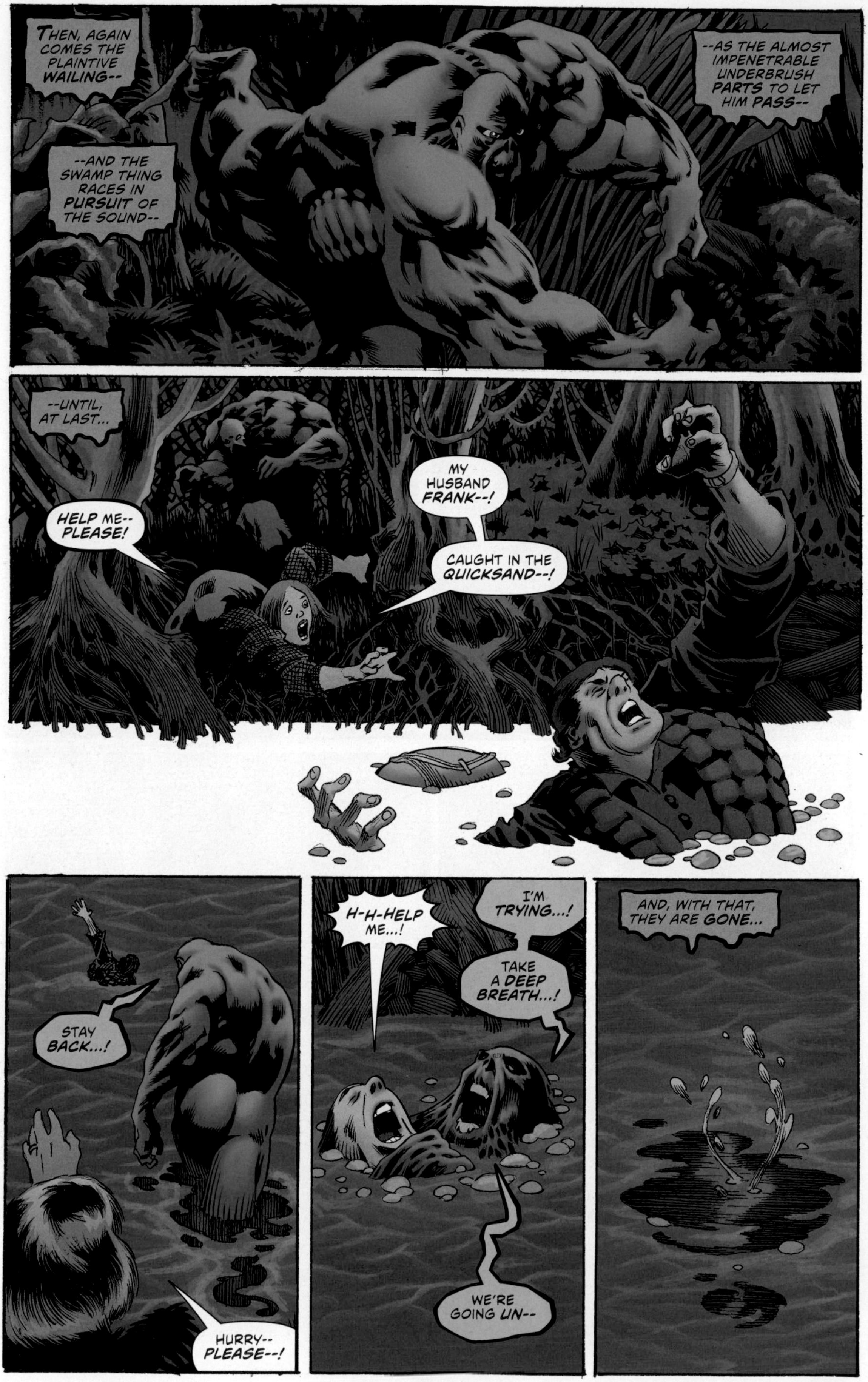
THEN, AGAIN COMES THE PLAINTIVE WAILING--
--AND THE SWAMP THING RACES IN PURSUIT OF THE SOUND--
--AS THE ALMOST IMPENETRABLE UNDERBRUSH PARTS TO LET HIM PASS--
--UNTIL, AT LAST...
HELP ME-- PLEASE!
MY HUSBAND FRANK--!
CAUGHT IN THE QUICKSAND--!
STAY BACK...!
HURRY-- PLEASE--!
H-H-HELP ME...!
I'M TRYING...!
TAKE A DEEP BREATH...!
WE'RE GOING UN--
AND, WITH THAT, THEY ARE GONE...

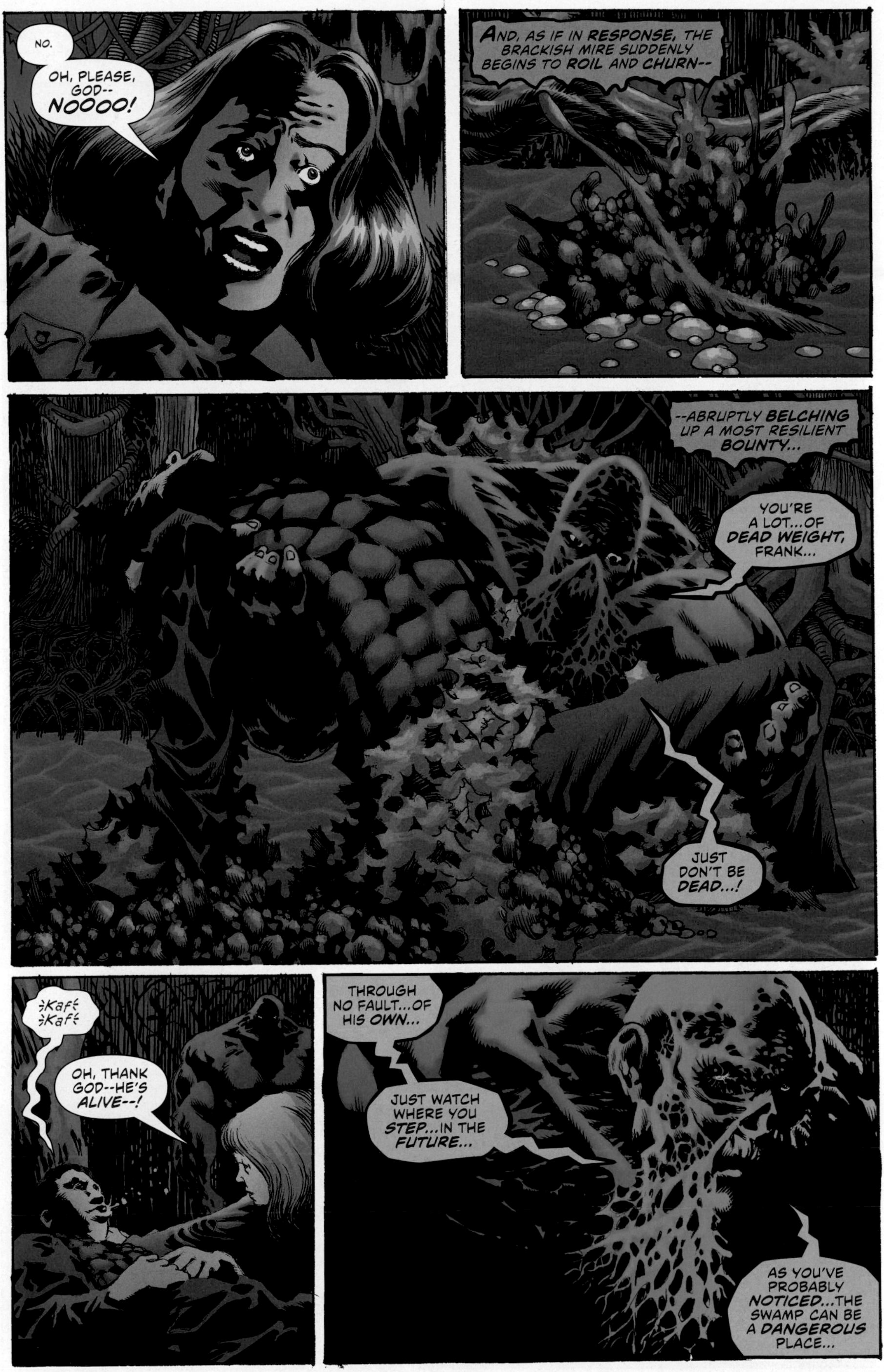
NO.
OH, PLEASE, GOD-- NOOOO!
AND, AS IF IN RESPONSE, THE BRACKISH MIRE SUDDENLY BEGINS TO ROIL AND CHURN--
--ABRUPTLY BELCHING UP A MOST RESILIENT BOUNTY...
YOU'RE A LOT...OF DEAD WEIGHT, FRANK...
JUST DON'T BE DEAD...!
KAF KAF
OH, THANK GOD--HE'S ALIVE--!
THROUGH NO FAULT...OF HIS OWN...
JUST WATCH WHERE YOU STEP...IN THE FUTURE...
AS YOU'VE PROBABLY NOTICED...THE SWAMP CAN BE A DANGEROUS PLACE...

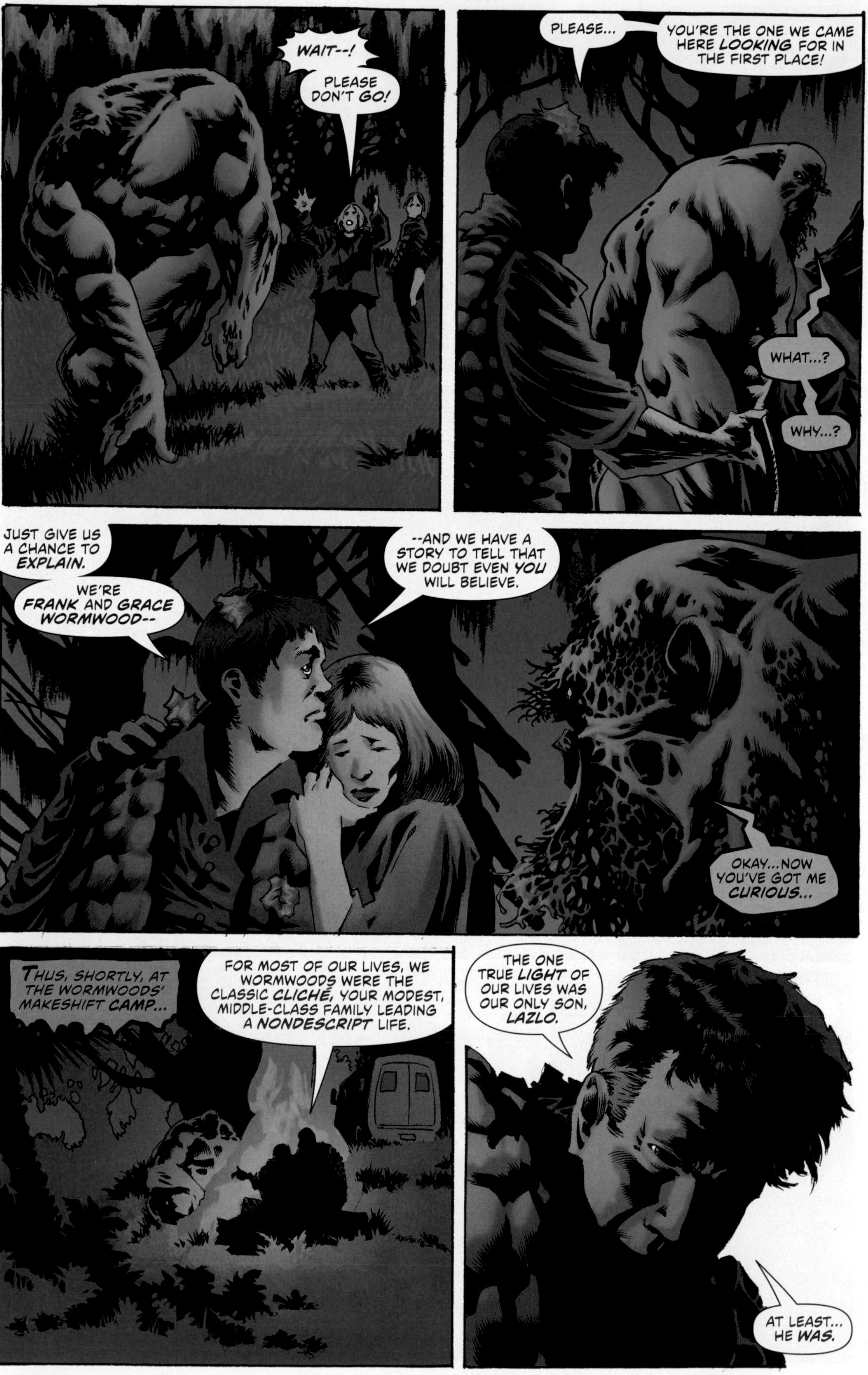

WAIT--!
PLEASE DON'T GO!
PLEASE...
YOU'RE THE ONE WE CAME HERE LOOKING FOR IN THE FIRST PLACE!
WHAT...?
WHY...?
JUST GIVE US A CHANCE TO EXPLAIN.
WE'RE FRANK AND GRACE WORMWOOD--
--AND WE HAVE A STORY TO TELL THAT WE DOUBT EVEN YOU WILL BELIEVE.
OKAY...NOW YOU'VE GOT ME CURIOUS...
THUS, SHORTLY, AT THE WORMWOODS' MAKESHIFT CAMP...
FOR MOST OF OUR LIVES, WE WORMWOODS WERE THE CLASSIC CLICHE, YOUR MODEST, MIDDLE-CLASS FAMILY LEADING A NONDESCRIPT LIFE.
THE ONE TRUE LIGHT OF OUR LIVES WAS OUR ONLY SON, LAZLO.
AT LEAST... HE WAS.

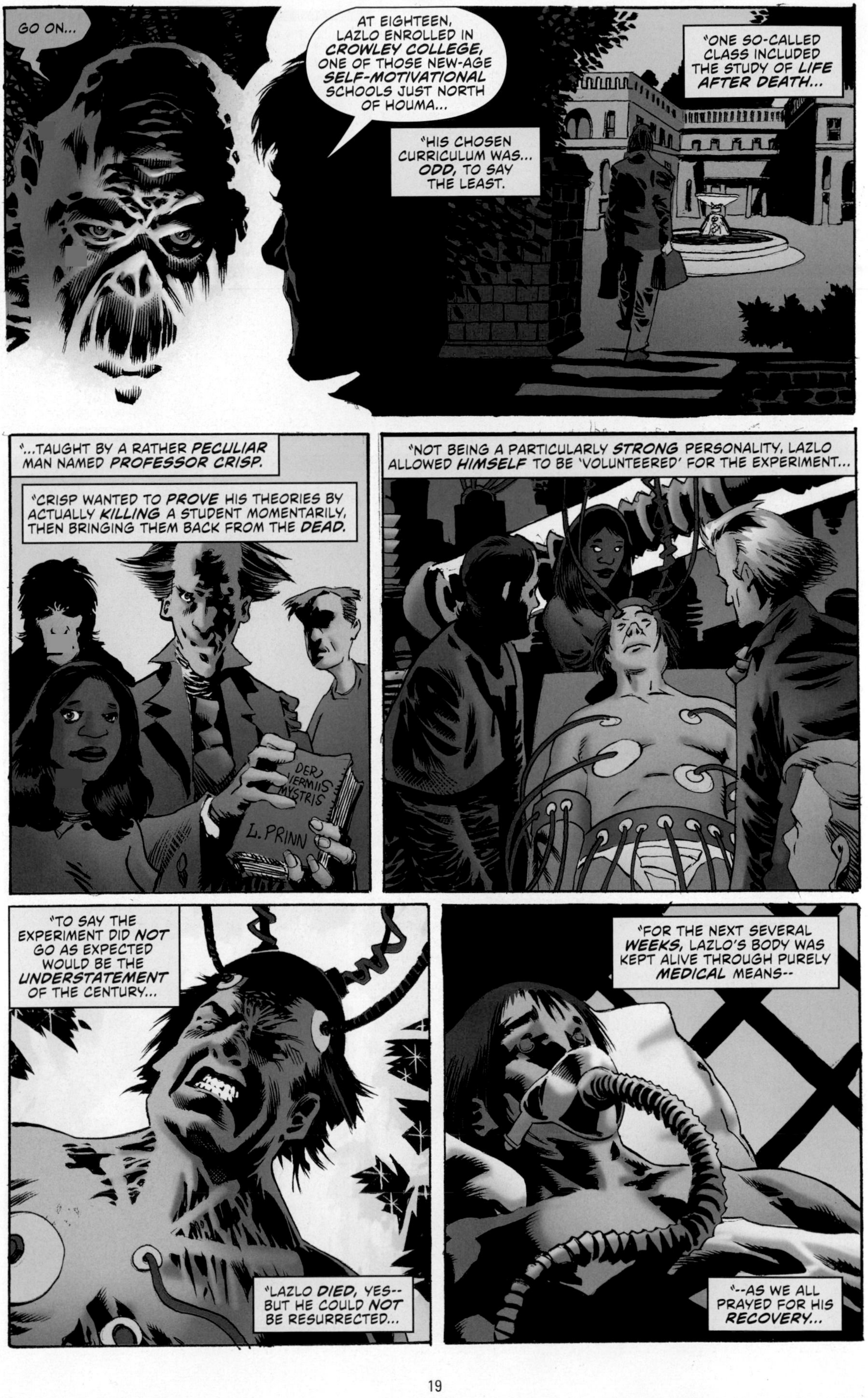
GO ON...
AT EIGHTEEN, LAZLO ENROLLED IN CROWLEY COLLEGE, ONE OF THOSE NEW-AGE SELF-MOTIVATIONAL SCHOOLS JUST NORTH OF HOUMA...
"HIS CHOSEN CURRICULUM WAS... ODD, TO SAY THE LEAST.
"ONE SO-CALLED CLASS INCLUDED THE STUDY OF LIFE AFTER DEATH...
"...TAUGHT BY A RATHER PECULIAR MAN NAMED PROFESSOR CRISP.
"CRISP WANTED TO PROVE HIS THEORIES BY ACTUALLY KILLING A STUDENT MOMENTARILY, THEN BRINGING THEM BACK FROM THE DEAD.
DE VERMIIS MYSTRIS
L. PRINN
"NOT BEING A PARTICULARLY STRONG PERSONALITY, LAZLO ALLOWED HIMSELF TO BE 'VOLUNTEERED' FOR THE EXPERIMENT...
"TO SAY THE EXPERIMENT DID NOT GO AS EXPECTED WOULD BE THE UNDERSTATEMENT OF THE CENTURY...
"LAZLO DIED, YES-- BUT HE COULD NOT BE RESURRECTED...
"FOR THE NEXT SEVERAL WEEKS, LAZLO'S BODY WAS KEPT ALIVE THROUGH PURELY MEDICAL MEANS--
"--AS WE ALL PRAYED FOR HIS RECOVERY...

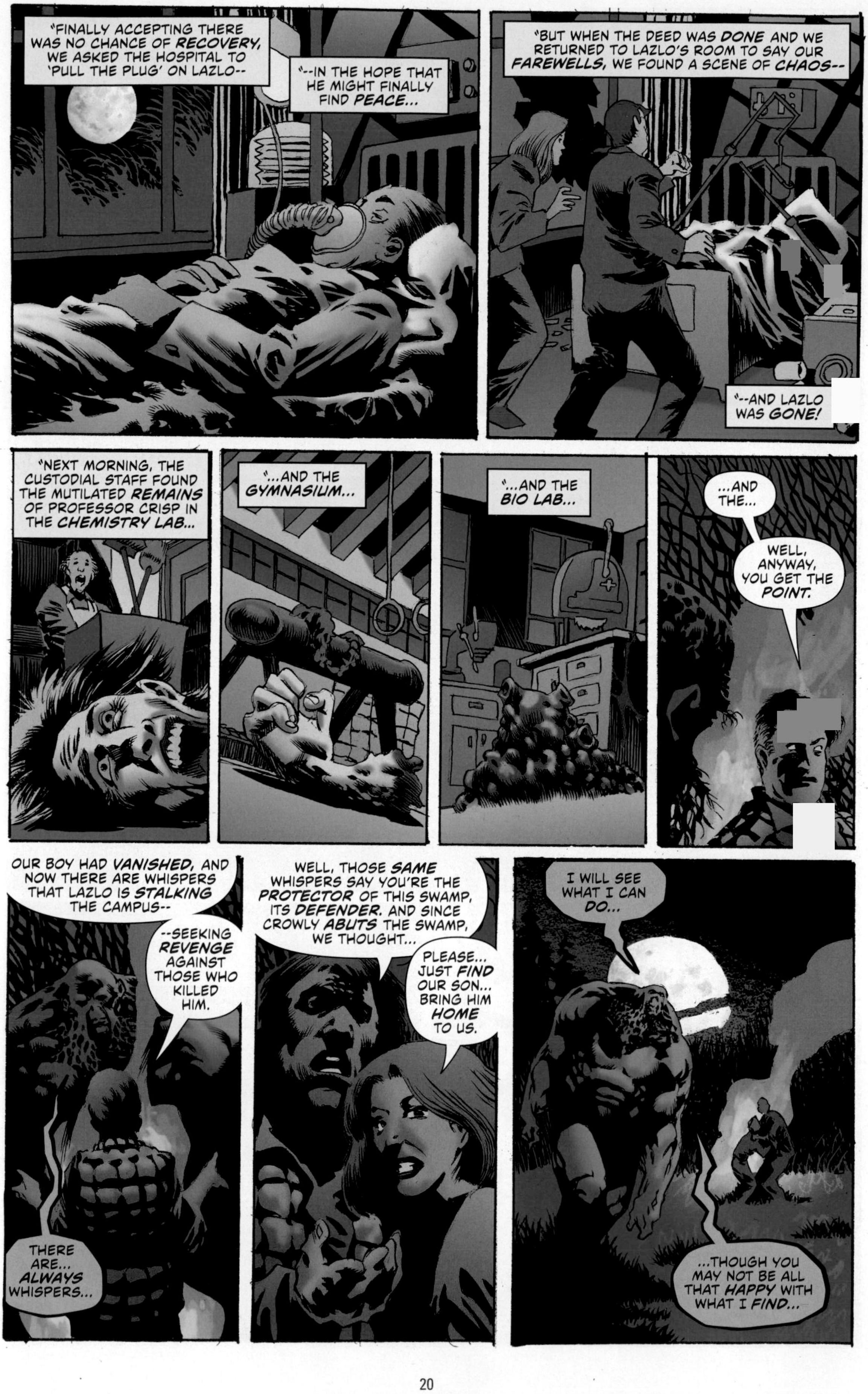
"FINALLY ACCEPTING THERE WAS NO CHANCE OF RECOVERY, WE ASKED THE HOSPITAL TO 'PULL THE PLUG' ON LAZLO--
"--IN THE HOPE THAT HE MIGHT FINALLY FIND PEACE...
"BUT WHEN THE DEED WAS DONE AND WE RETURNED TO LAZLO'S ROOM TO SAY OUR FAREWELLS, WE FOUND A SCENE OF CHAOS--
"--AND LAZLO WAS GONE!
"NEXT MORNING, THE CUSTODIAL STAFF FOUND THE MUTILATED REMAINS OF PROFESSOR CRISP IN THE CHEMISTRY LAB...
"...AND THE GYMNASIUM...
"...AND THE BIO LAB...
...AND THE...
WELL, ANYWAY, YOU GET THE POINT.
OUR BOY HAD VANISHED, AND NOW THERE ARE WHISPERS THAT LAZLO IS STALKING THE CAMPUS--
--SEEKING REVENGE AGAINST THOSE WHO KILLED HIM.
THERE ARE... ALWAYS WHISPERS...
WELL, THOSE SAME WHISPERS SAY YOU'RE THE PROTECTOR OF THIS SWAMP, ITS DEFENDER. AND SINCE CROWLY ABUTS THE SWAMP, WE THOUGHT...
PLEASE... JUST FIND OUR SON... BRING HIM HOME TO US.
I WILL SEE WHAT I CAN DO...
...THOUGH YOU MAY NOT BE ALL THAT HAPPY WITH WHAT I FIND...

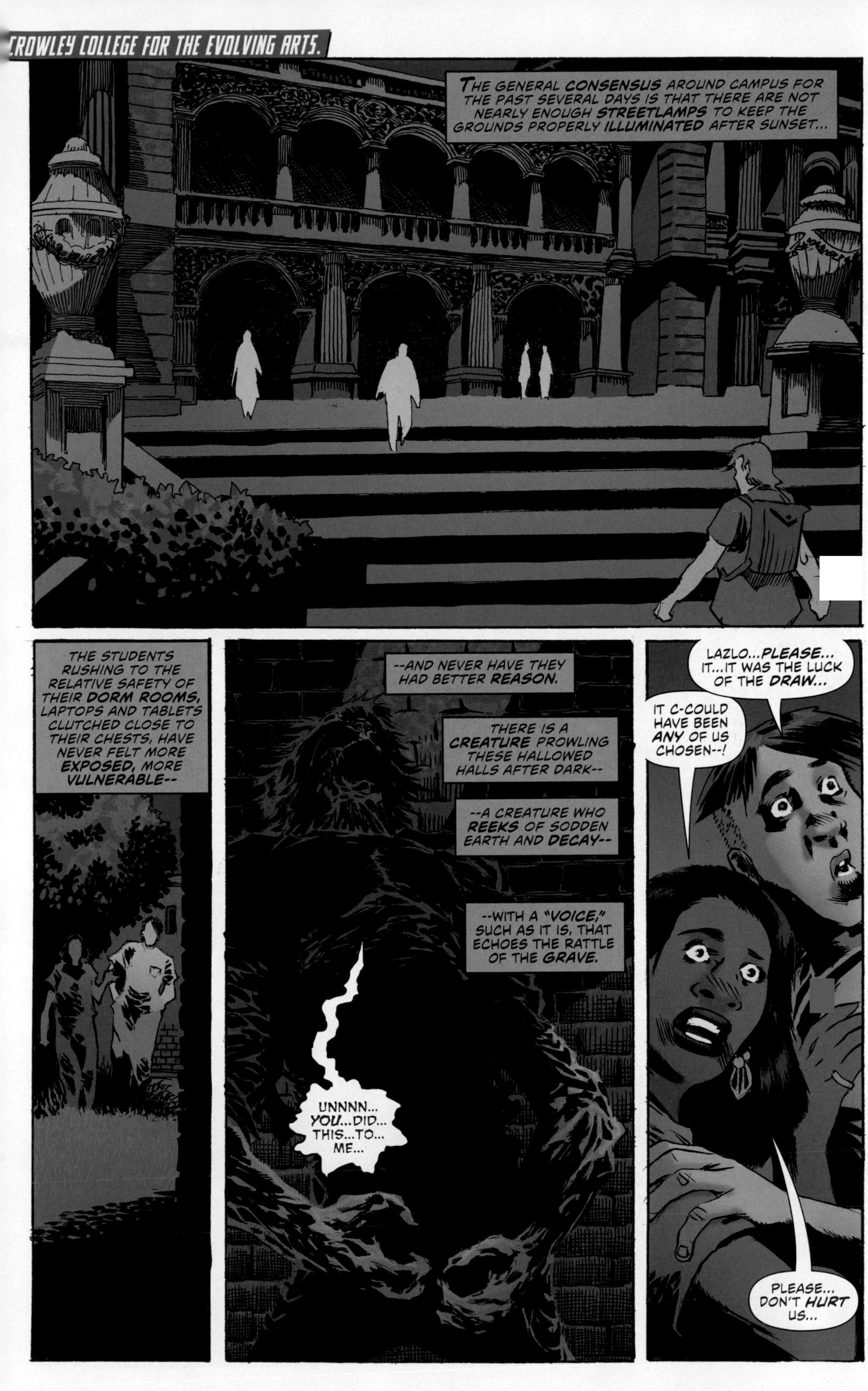
CROWLEY COLLEGE FOR THE EVOLVING ARTS.
THE GENERAL CONSENSUS AROUND CAMPUS FOR THE PAST SEVERAL DAYS IS THAT THERE ARE NOT NEARLY ENOUGH STREETLAMPS TO KEEP THE GROUNDS PROPERLY ILLUMINATED AFTER SUNSET...
THE STUDENTS RUSHING TO THE RELATIVE SAFETY OF THEIR DORM ROOMS, LAPTOPS AND TABLETS CLUTCHED CLOSE TO THEIR CHESTS, HAVE NEVER FELT MORE EXPOSED, MORE VULNERABLE--
--AND NEVER HAVE THEY HAD BETTER REASON.
THERE IS A CREATURE PROWLING THESE HALLOWED HALLS AFTER DARK--
--A CREATURE WHO REEKS OF SODDEN EARTH AND DECAY--
--WITH A "VOICE," SUCH AS IT IS, THAT ECHOES THE RATTLE OF THE GRAVE.
UNNNN... YOU...DID... THIS...TO... ME...
LAZLO...PLEASE... IT...IT WAS THE LUCK OF THE DRAW...
IT C-COULD HAVE BEEN ANY OF US CHOSEN--!
PLEASE... DON'T HURT US...

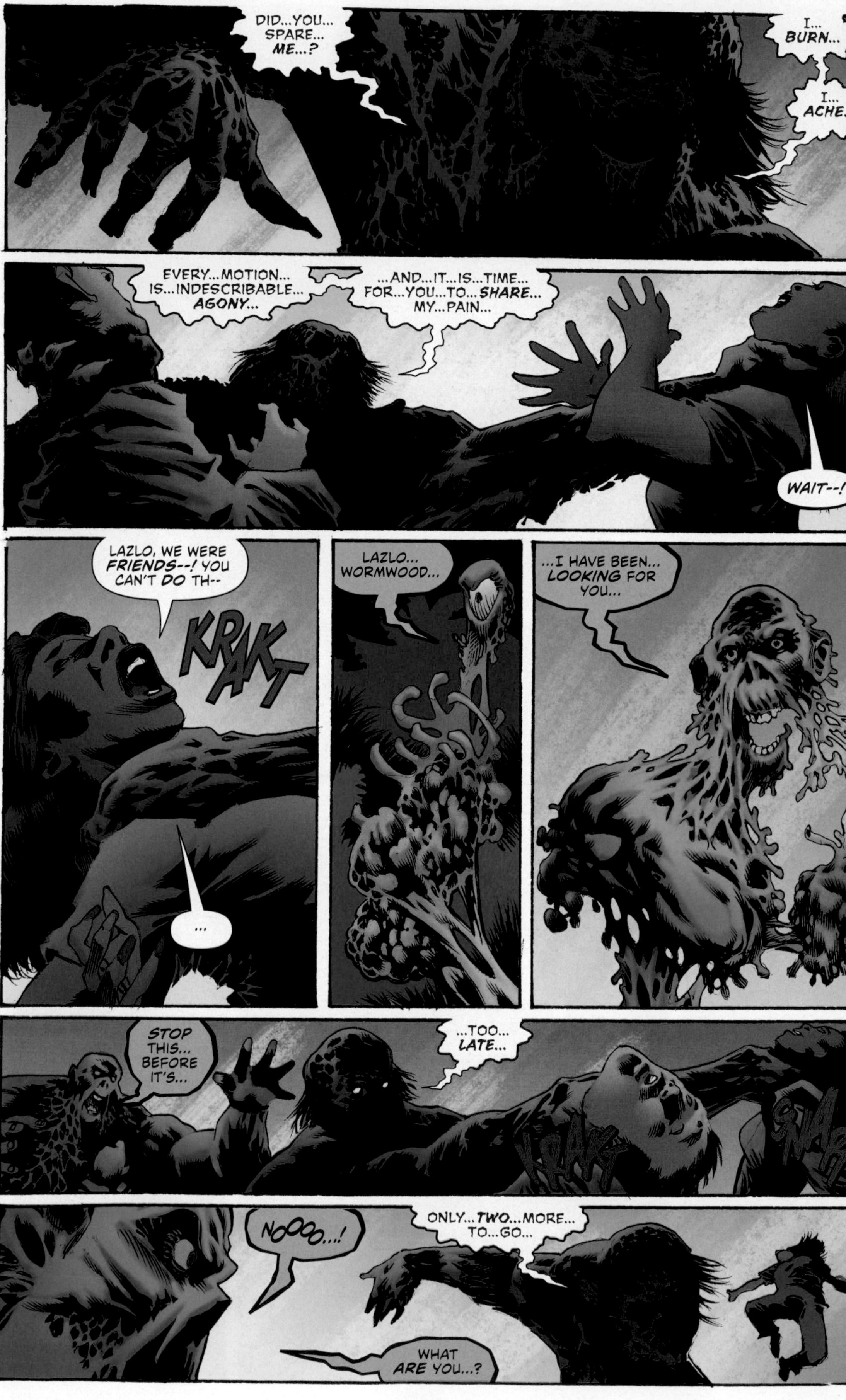
DID...YOU... SPARE... ME...?
I... BURN...
I... ACHE...
EVERY...MOTION... IS...INDESCRIBABLE... AGONY...
...AND...IT...IS...TIME... FOR...YOU...TO...SHARE... MY...PAIN...
WAIT--!
LAZLO, WE WERE FRIENDS--! YOU CAN'T DO TH--
KRAKT
...
LAZLO... WORMWOOD...
...I HAVE BEEN... LOOKING FOR YOU...
STOP THIS... BEFORE IT'S...
...TOO... LATE...
NOOOO...!
ONLY...TWO...MORE... TO...GO...
WHAT ARE YOU...?

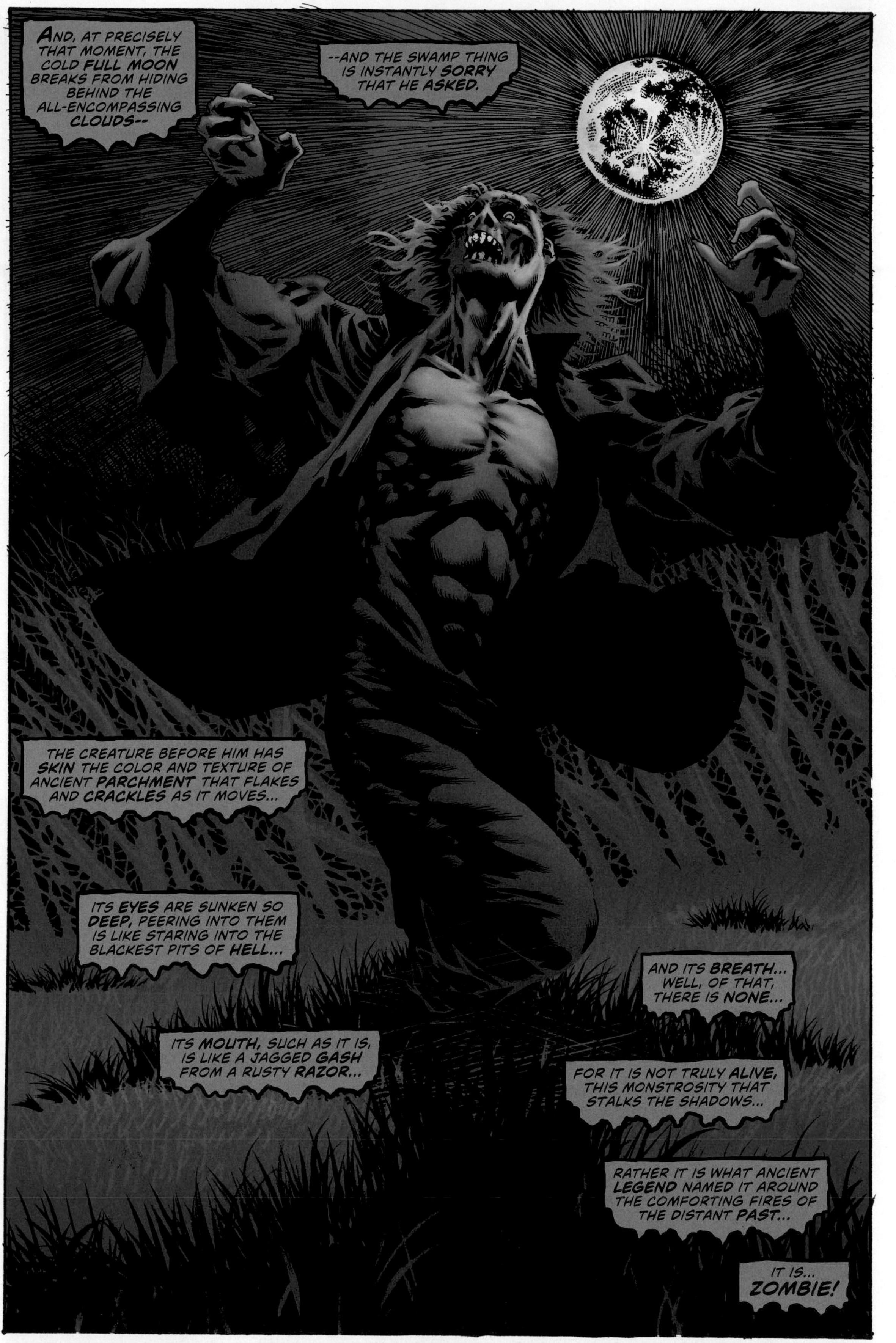
AND, AT PRECISELY THAT MOMENT, THE COLD FULL MOON BREAKS FROM HIDING BEHIND THE ALL-ENCOMPASSING CLOUDS--
--AND THE SWAMP THING IS INSTANTLY SORRY THAT HE ASKED.
THE CREATURE BEFORE HIM HAS SKIN THE COLOR AND TEXTURE OF ANCIENT PARCHMENT THAT FLAKES AND CRACKLES AS IT MOVES...
ITS EYES ARE SUNKEN SO DEEP, PEERING INTO THEM IS LIKE STARING INTO THE BLACKEST PITS OF HELL...
ITS MOUTH, SUCH AS IT IS, IS LIKE A JAGGED GASH FROM A RUSTY RAZOR...
AND ITS BREATH... WELL, OF THAT, THERE IS NONE...
FOR IT IS NOT TRULY ALIVE, THIS MONSTROSITY THAT STALKS THE SHADOWS...
RATHER IT IS WHAT ANCIENT LEGEND NAMED IT AROUND THE COMFORTING FIRES OF THE DISTANT PAST...
IT IS... ZOMBIE!

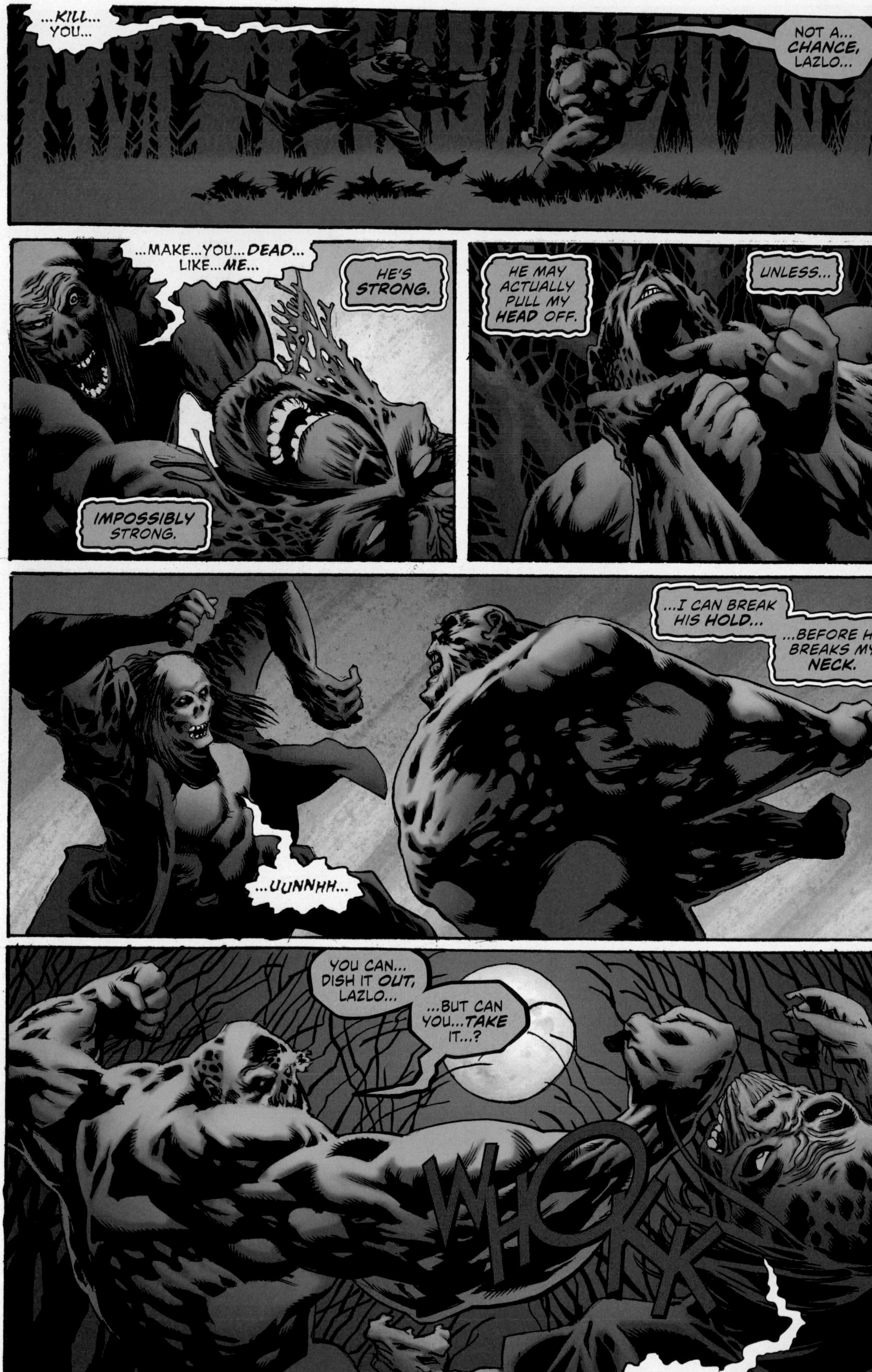
...KILL... YOU...
NOT A... CHANCE, LAZLO...
...MAKE...YOU...DEAD... LIKE...ME...
HE'S STRONG.
IMPOSSIBLY STRONG.
HE MAY ACTUALLY PULL MY HEAD OFF.
UNLESS...
...I CAN BREAK HIS HOLD...
...BEFORE HE BREAKS MY NECK.
...UUNNHH...
YOU CAN... DISH IT OUT, LAZLO...
...BUT CAN YOU...TAKE IT...?
WHOKK
...HHHKKK...

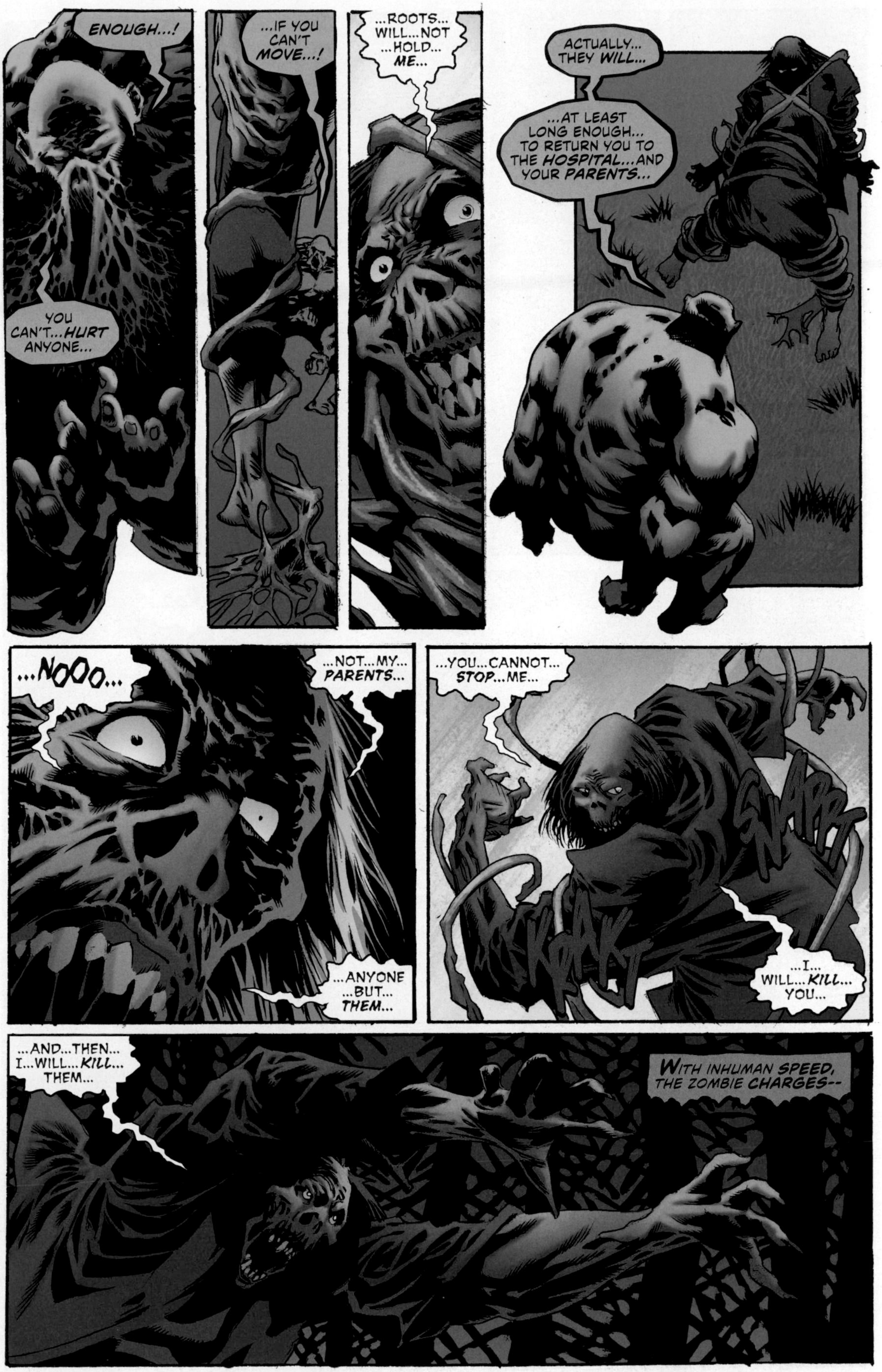
ENOUGH...!
YOU CAN'T...HURT ANYONE...
...IF YOU CAN'T MOVE...!
...ROOTS... WILL...NOT ...HOLD... ME...
ACTUALLY... THEY WILL...
...AT LEAST LONG ENOUGH... TO RETURN YOU TO THE HOSPITAL...AND YOUR PARENTS...
...NOOO...
...NOT...MY... PARENTS...
...ANYONE ...BUT... THEM...
...YOU...CANNOT... STOP...ME...
...I... WILL...KILL... YOU...
...AND...THEN... I...WILL...KILL... THEM...
WITH INHUMAN SPEED, THE ZOMBIE CHARGES--

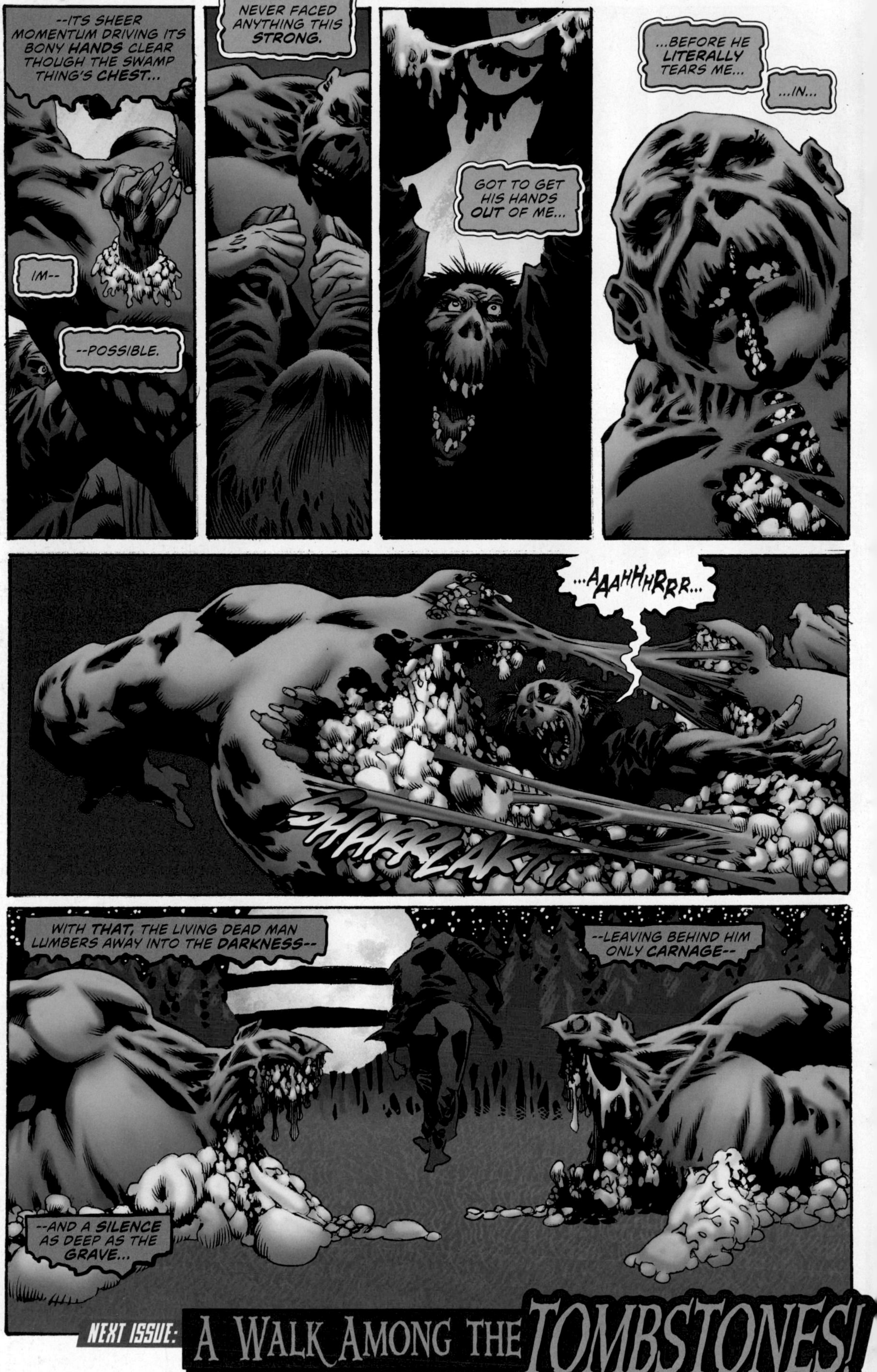

--ITS SHEER MOMENTUM DRIVING ITS BONY HANDS CLEAR THOUGH THE SWAMP THING'S CHEST...
IM--
--POSSIBLE.
NEVER FACED ANYTHING THIS STRONG.
GOT TO GET HIS HANDS OUT OF ME...
...BEFORE HE LITERALLY TEARS ME...
...IN...
...AAAHHHRRRR...
SHHRLAKTTT
WITH THAT, THE LIVING DEAD MAN LUMBERS AWAY INTO THE DARKNESS--
--LEAVING BEHIND HIM ONLY CARNAGE--
--AND A SILENCE AS DEEP AS THE GRAVE...
NEXT ISSUE: A WALK AMONG THE TOMBSTONES!

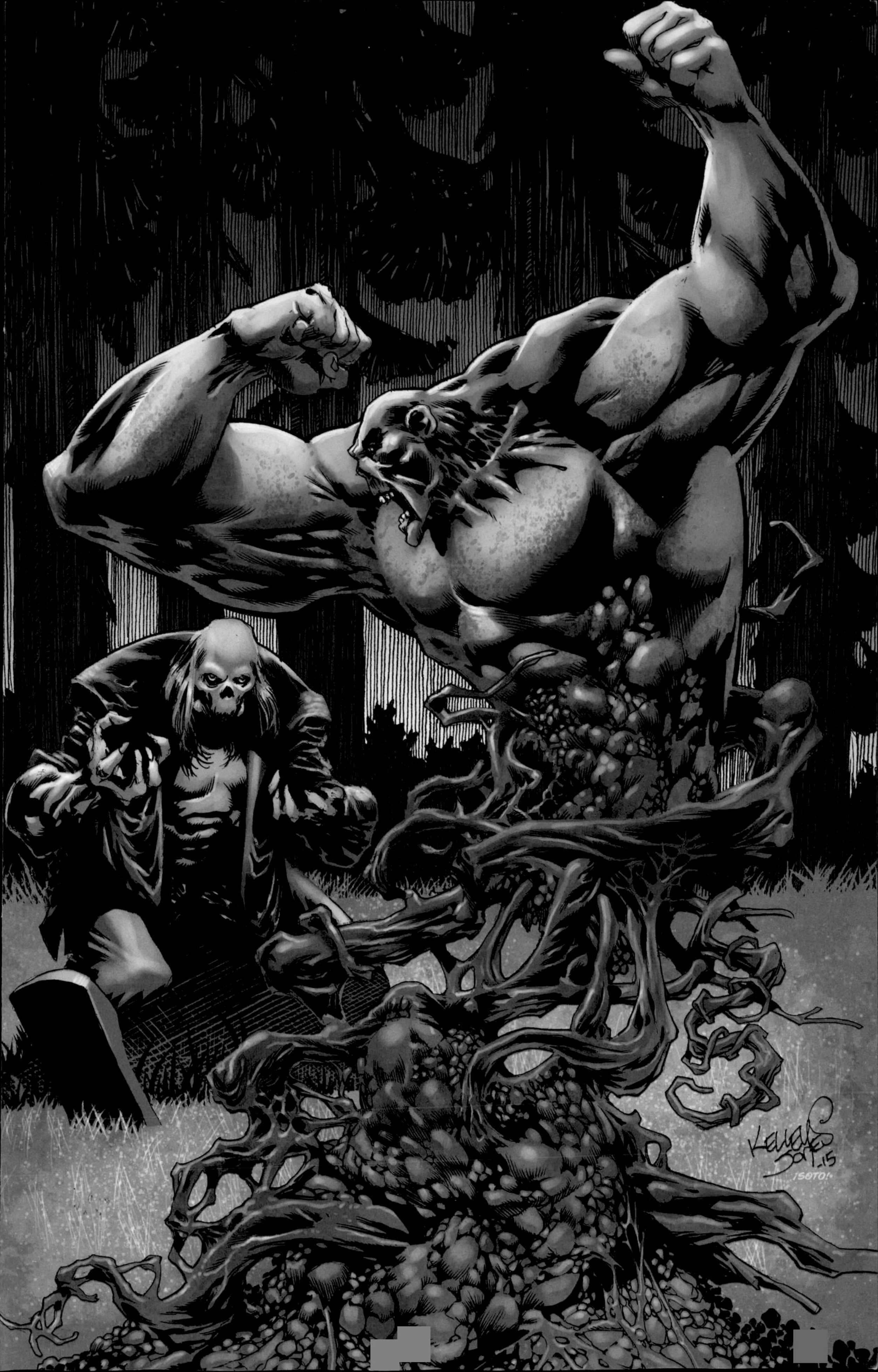

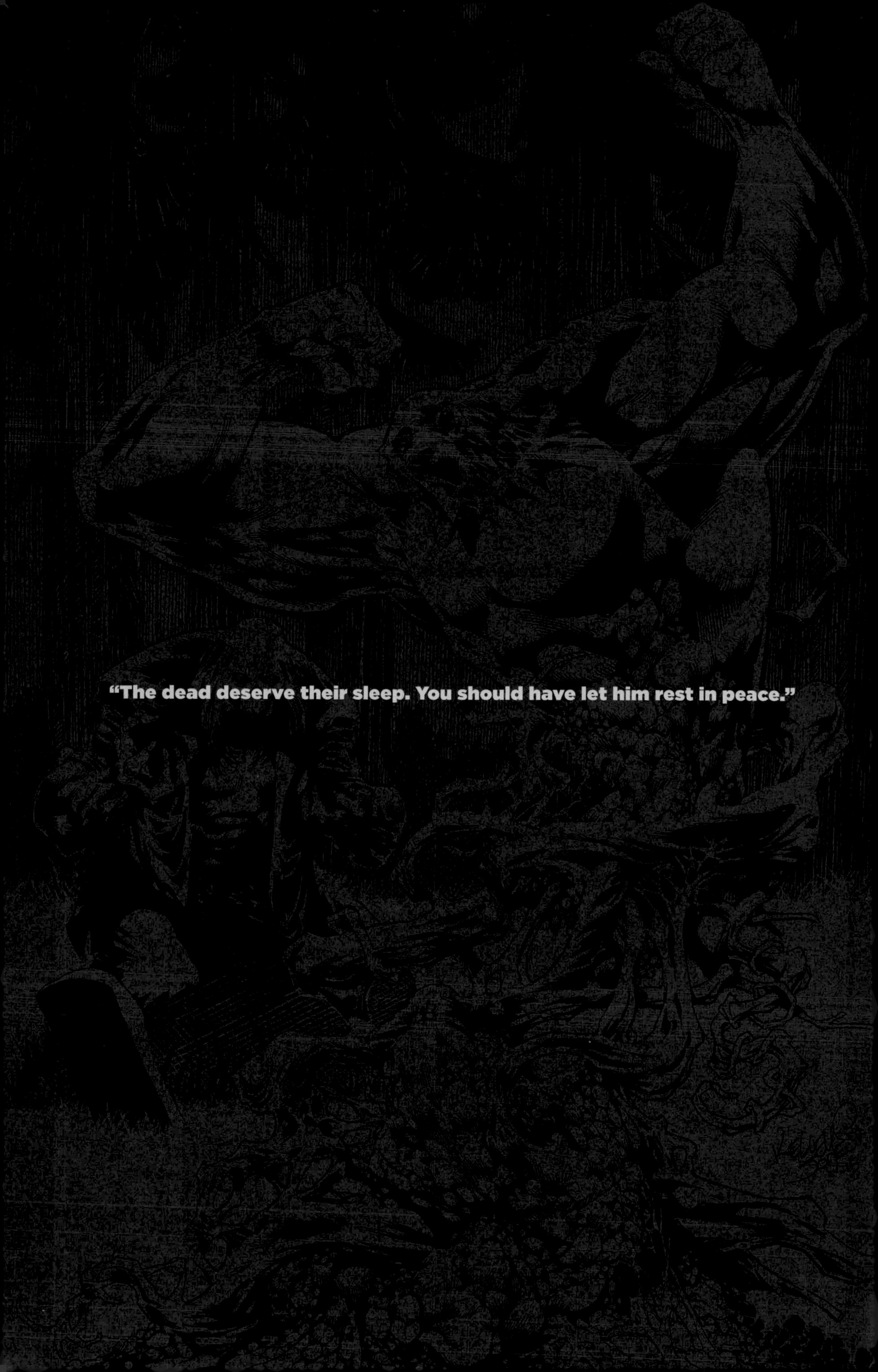
"The dead deserve their sleep. You should have let him rest in peace."

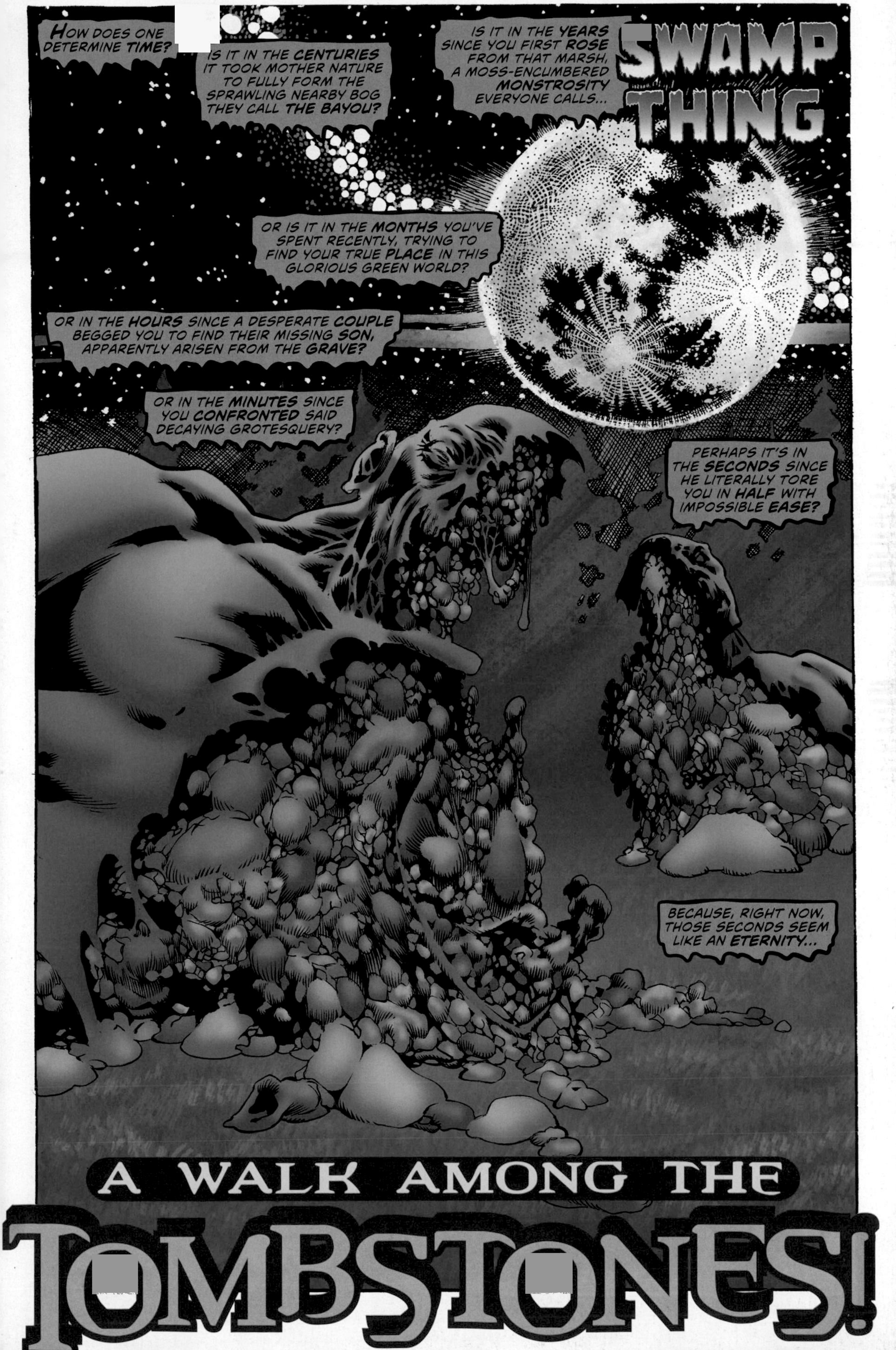
HOW DOES ONE DETERMINE TIME?
IS IT IN THE CENTURIES IT TOOK MOTHER NATURE TO FULLY FORM THE SPRAWLING NEARBY BOG THEY CALL THE BAYOU?
IS IT IN THE YEARS SINCE YOU FIRST ROSE FROM THAT MARSH, A MOSS-ENCUMBERED MONSTROSITY EVERYONE CALLS...
SWAMP THING
OR IS IT IN THE MONTHS YOU'VE SPENT RECENTLY, TRYING TO FIND YOUR TRUE PLACE IN THIS GLORIOUS GREEN WORLD?
OR IN THE HOURS SINCE A DESPERATE COUPLE BEGGED YOU TO FIND THEIR MISSING SON, APPARENTLY ARISEN FROM THE GRAVE?
OR IN THE MINUTES SINCE YOU CONFRONTED SAID DECAYING GROTESQUERY?
PERHAPS IT'S IN THE SECONDS SINCE HE LITERALLY TORE YOU IN HALF WITH IMPOSSIBLE EASE?
BECAUSE, RIGHT NOW, THOSE SECONDS SEEM LIKE AN ETERNITY...
A WALK AMONG THE
TOMBSTONES!

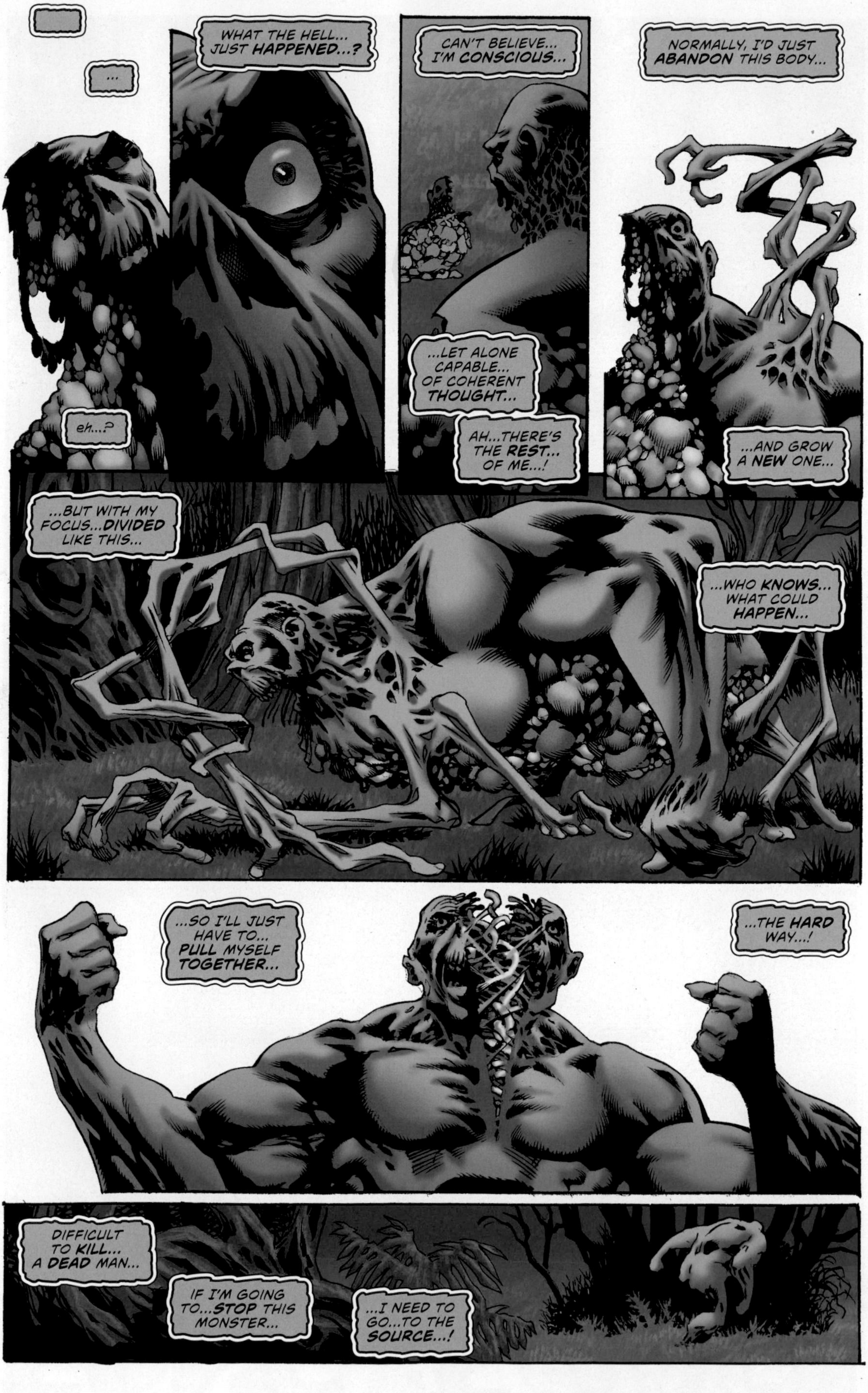
...
eh...?
WHAT THE HELL... JUST HAPPENED...?
CAN'T BELIEVE... I'M CONSCIOUS...
...LET ALONE CAPABLE... OF COHERENT THOUGHT...
AH...THERE'S THE REST... OF ME...!
NORMALLY, I'D JUST ABANDON THIS BODY...
...AND GROW A NEW ONE...
...BUT WITH MY FOCUS...DIVIDED LIKE THIS...
...WHO KNOWS... WHAT COULD HAPPEN...
...SO I'LL JUST HAVE TO... PULL MYSELF TOGETHER...
...THE HARD WAY...!
DIFFICULT TO KILL... A DEAD MAN...
IF I'M GOING TO...STOP THIS MONSTER...
...I NEED TO GO...TO THE SOURCE...!

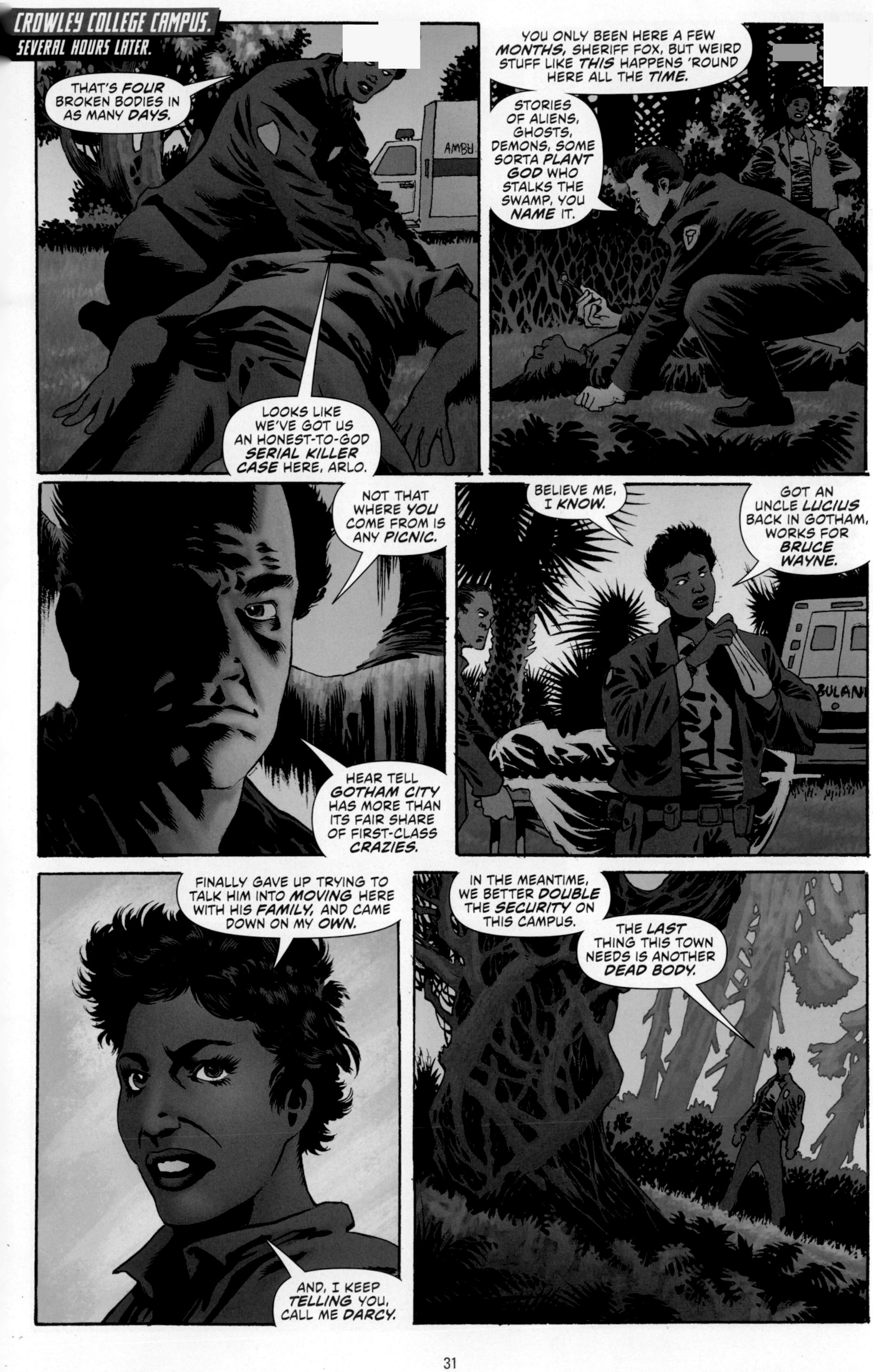
CROWLEY COLLEGE CAMPUS.
SEVERAL HOURS LATER.
THAT'S FOUR BROKEN BODIES IN AS MANY DAYS.
LOOKS LIKE WE'VE GOT US AN HONEST-TO-GOD SERIAL KILLER CASE HERE, ARLO.
YOU ONLY BEEN HERE A FEW MONTHS, SHERIFF FOX, BUT WEIRD STUFF LIKE THIS HAPPENS 'ROUND HERE ALL THE TIME.
STORIES OF ALIENS, GHOSTS, DEMONS, SOME SORTA PLANT GOD WHO STALKS THE SWAMP, YOU NAME IT.
NOT THAT WHERE YOU COME FROM IS ANY PICNIC.
HEAR TELL GOTHAM CITY HAS MORE THAN ITS FAIR SHARE OF FIRST-CLASS CRAZIES.
BELIEVE ME, I KNOW.
GOT AN UNCLE LUCIUS BACK IN GOTHAM, WORKS FOR BRUCE WAYNE.
FINALLY GAVE UP TRYING TO TALK HIM INTO MOVING HERE WITH HIS FAMILY, AND CAME DOWN ON MY OWN.
AND, I KEEP TELLING YOU, CALL ME DARCY.
IN THE MEANTIME, WE BETTER DOUBLE THE SECURITY ON THIS CAMPUS.
THE LAST THING THIS TOWN NEEDS IS ANOTHER DEAD BODY.

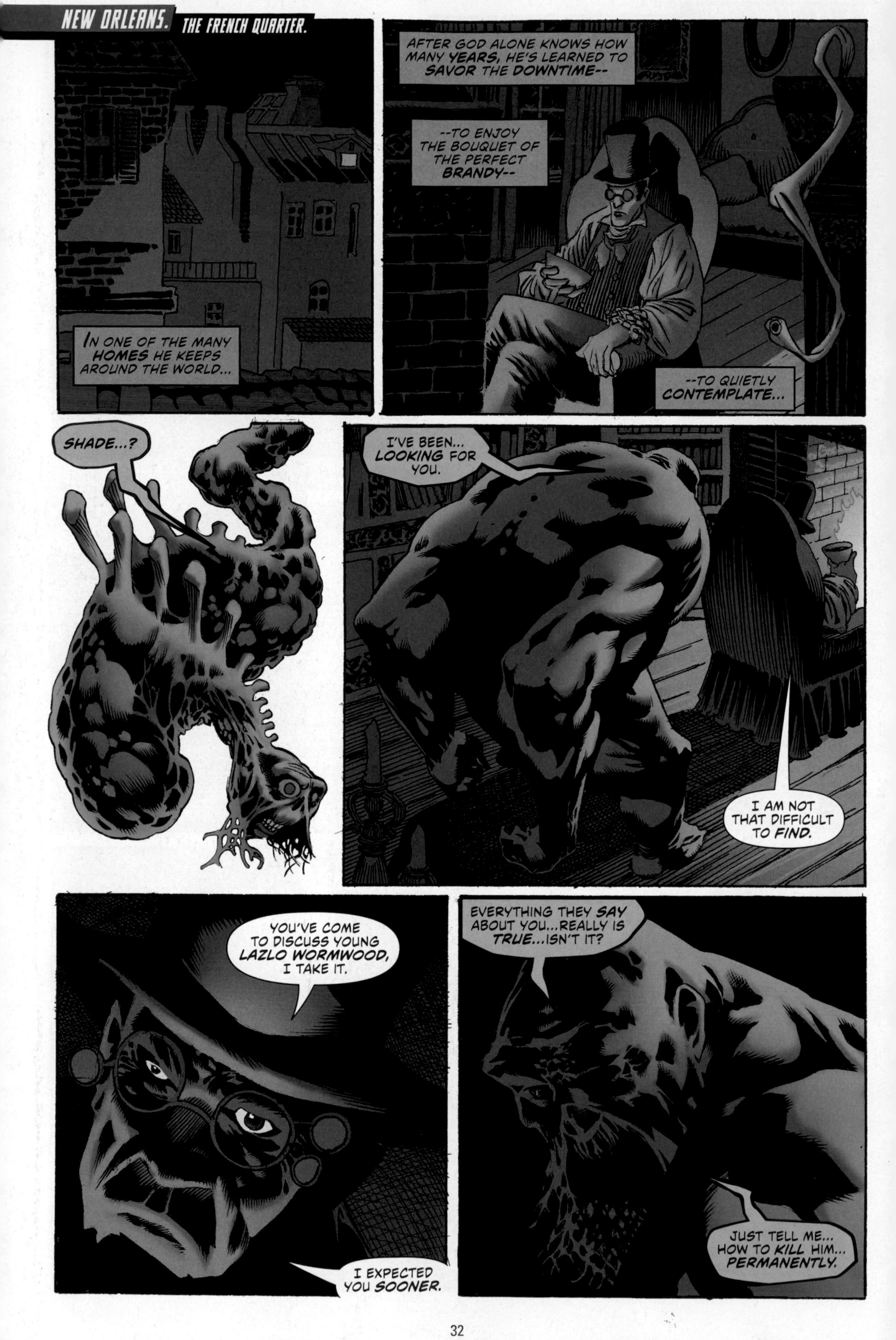
NEW ORLEANS.
THE FRENCH QUARTER.
IN ONE OF THE MANY HOMES HE KEEPS AROUND THE WORLD...
AFTER GOD ALONE KNOWS HOW MANY YEARS, HE'S LEARNED TO SAVOR THE DOWNTIME--
--TO ENJOY THE BOUQUET OF THE PERFECT BRANDY--
--TO QUIETLY CONTEMPLATE...
SHADE...?
I'VE BEEN... LOOKING FOR YOU.
I AM NOT THAT DIFFICULT TO FIND.
YOU'VE COME TO DISCUSS YOUNG LAZLO WORMWOOD, I TAKE IT.
I EXPECTED YOU SOONER.
EVERYTHING THEY SAY ABOUT YOU...REALLY IS TRUE...ISN'T IT?
JUST TELL ME... HOW TO KILL HIM... PERMANENTLY.

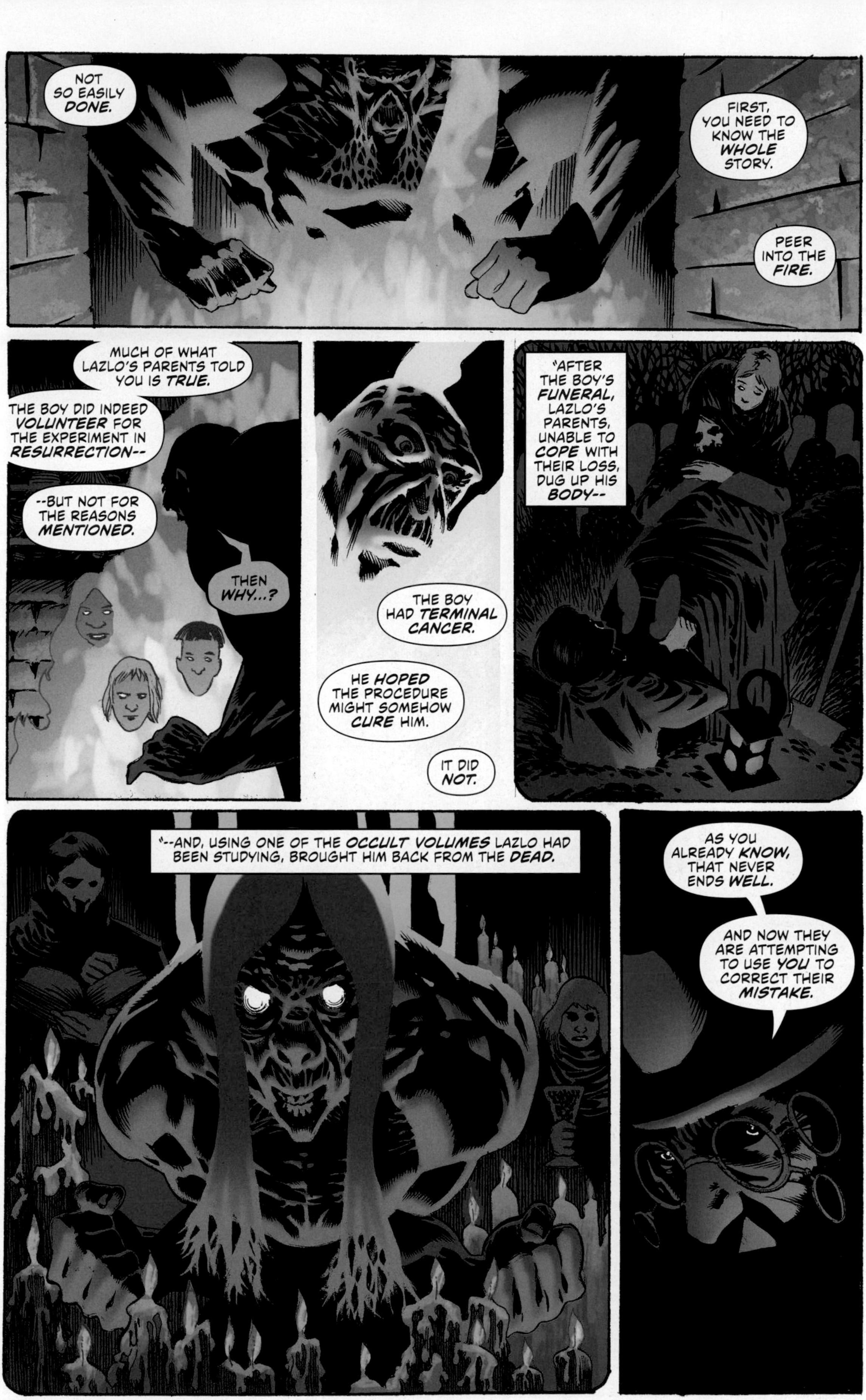
NOT SO EASILY DONE.
FIRST, YOU NEED TO KNOW THE WHOLE STORY.
PEER INTO THE FIRE.
MUCH OF WHAT LAZLO'S PARENTS TOLD YOU IS TRUE.
THE BOY DID INDEED VOLUNTEER FOR THE EXPERIMENT IN RESURRECTION--
--BUT NOT FOR THE REASONS MENTIONED.
THEN WHY...?
THE BOY HAD TERMINAL CANCER.
HE HOPED THE PROCEDURE MIGHT SOMEHOW CURE HIM.
IT DID NOT.
"AFTER THE BOY'S FUNERAL, LAZLO'S PARENTS, UNABLE TO COPE WITH THEIR LOSS, DUG UP HIS BODY--
"--AND, USING ONE OF THE OCCULT VOLUMES LAZLO HAD BEEN STUDYING, BROUGHT HIM BACK FROM THE DEAD.
AS YOU ALREADY KNOW, THAT NEVER ENDS WELL.
AND NOW THEY ARE ATTEMPTING TO USE YOU TO CORRECT THEIR MISTAKE.

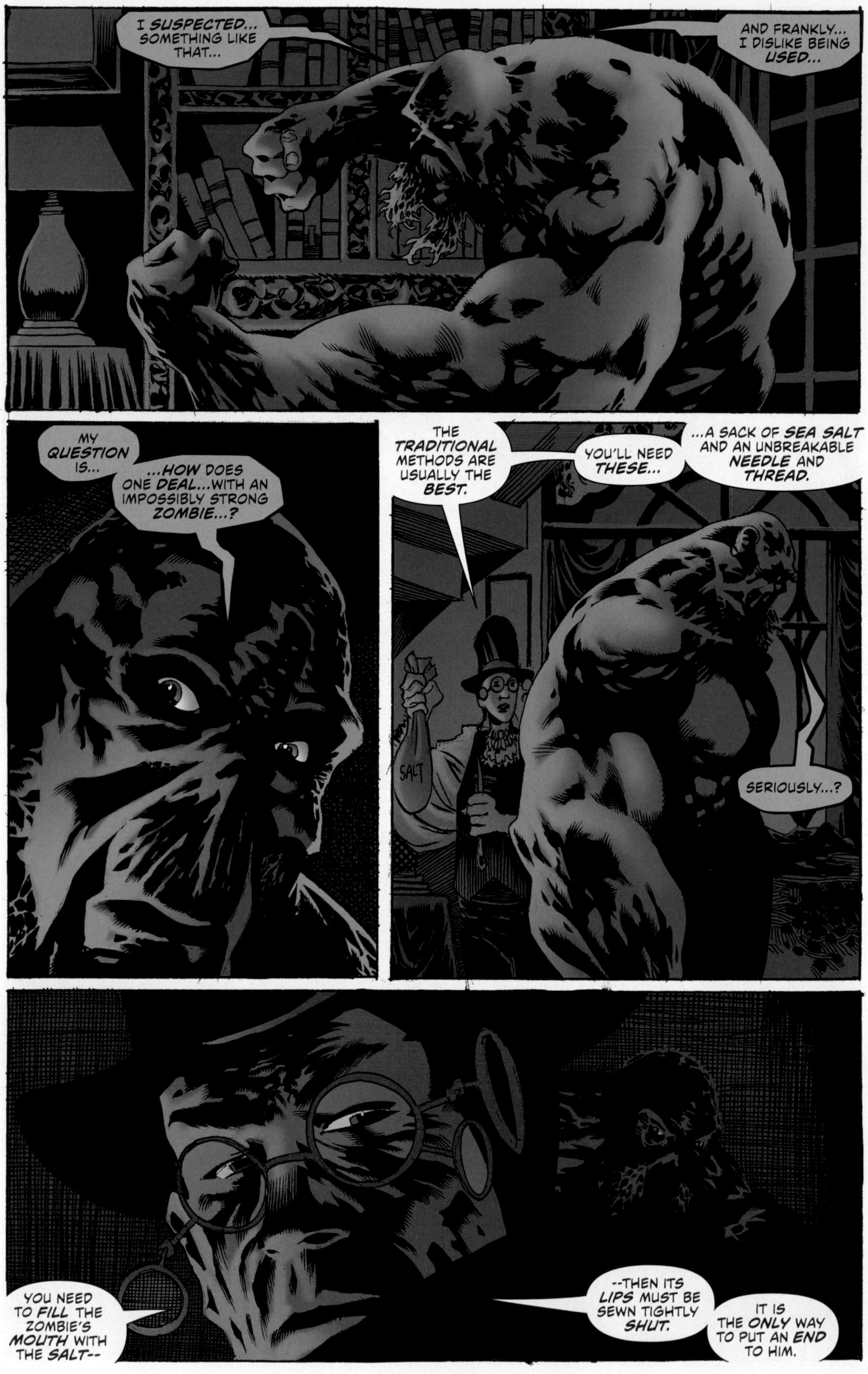
I SUSPECTED... SOMETHING LIKE THAT...
AND FRANKLY... I DISLIKE BEING USED...
MY QUESTION IS...
...HOW DOES ONE DEAL...WITH AN IMPOSSIBLY STRONG ZOMBIE...?
THE TRADITIONAL METHODS ARE USUALLY THE BEST.
YOU'LL NEED THESE...
...A SACK OF SEA SALT AND AN UNBREAKABLE NEEDLE AND THREAD.
SALT
SERIOUSLY...?
YOU NEED TO FILL THE ZOMBIE'S MOUTH WITH THE SALT--
--THEN ITS LIPS MUST BE SEWN TIGHTLY SHUT.
IT IS THE ONLY WAY TO PUT AN END TO HIM.

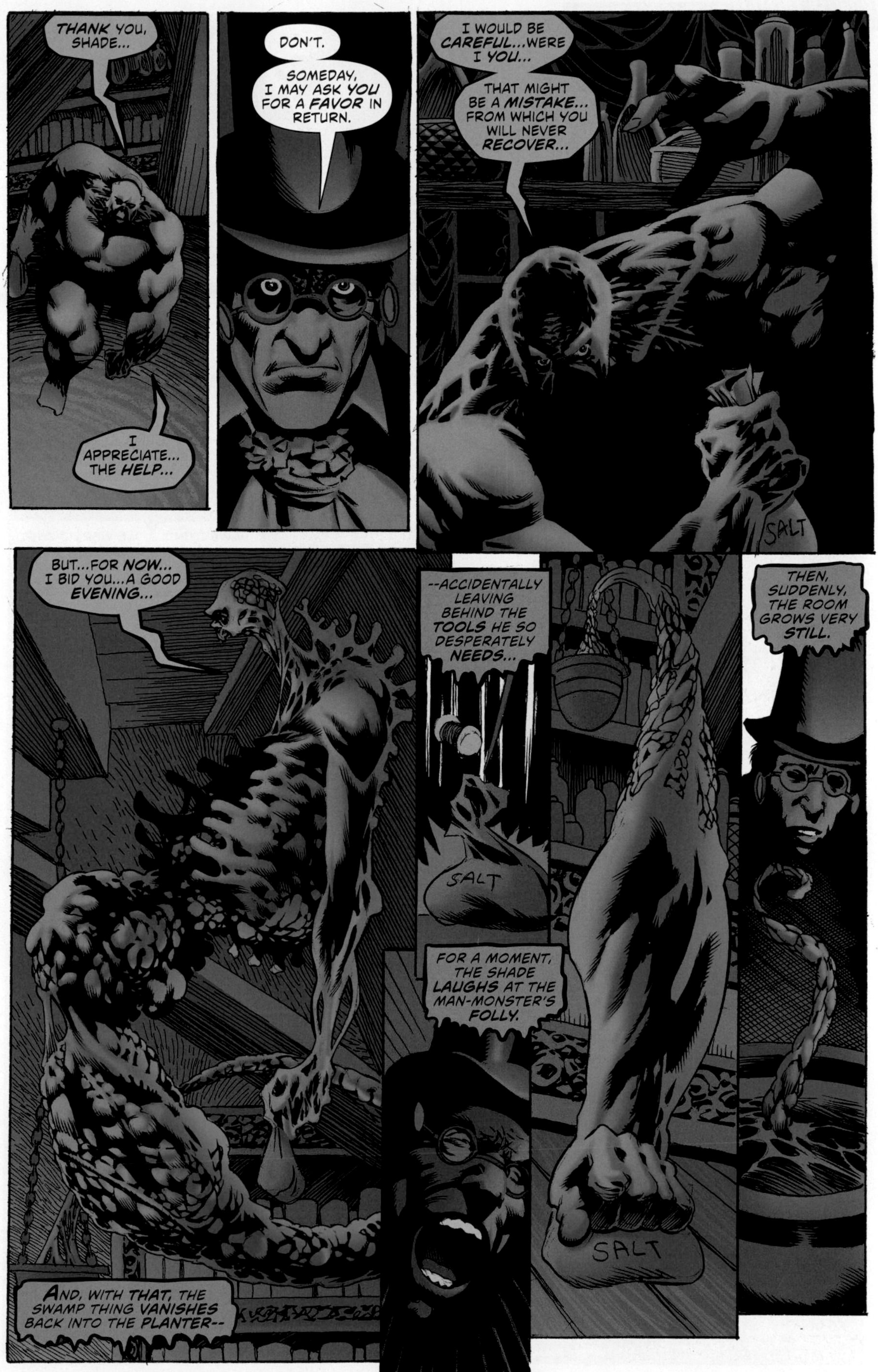
THANK YOU, SHADE...
I APPRECIATE... THE HELP...
DON'T.
SOMEDAY, I MAY ASK YOU FOR A FAVOR IN RETURN.
I WOULD BE CAREFUL...WERE I YOU...
THAT MIGHT BE A MISTAKE... FROM WHICH YOU WILL NEVER RECOVER...
SALT
BUT...FOR NOW... I BID YOU...A GOOD EVENING...
AND, WITH THAT, THE SWAMP THING VANISHES BACK INTO THE PLANTER--
--ACCIDENTALLY LEAVING BEHIND THE TOOLS HE SO DESPERATELY NEEDS...
SALT
FOR A MOMENT, THE SHADE LAUGHS AT THE MAN-MONSTER'S FOLLY.
SALT
THEN, SUDDENLY, THE ROOM GROWS VERY STILL.

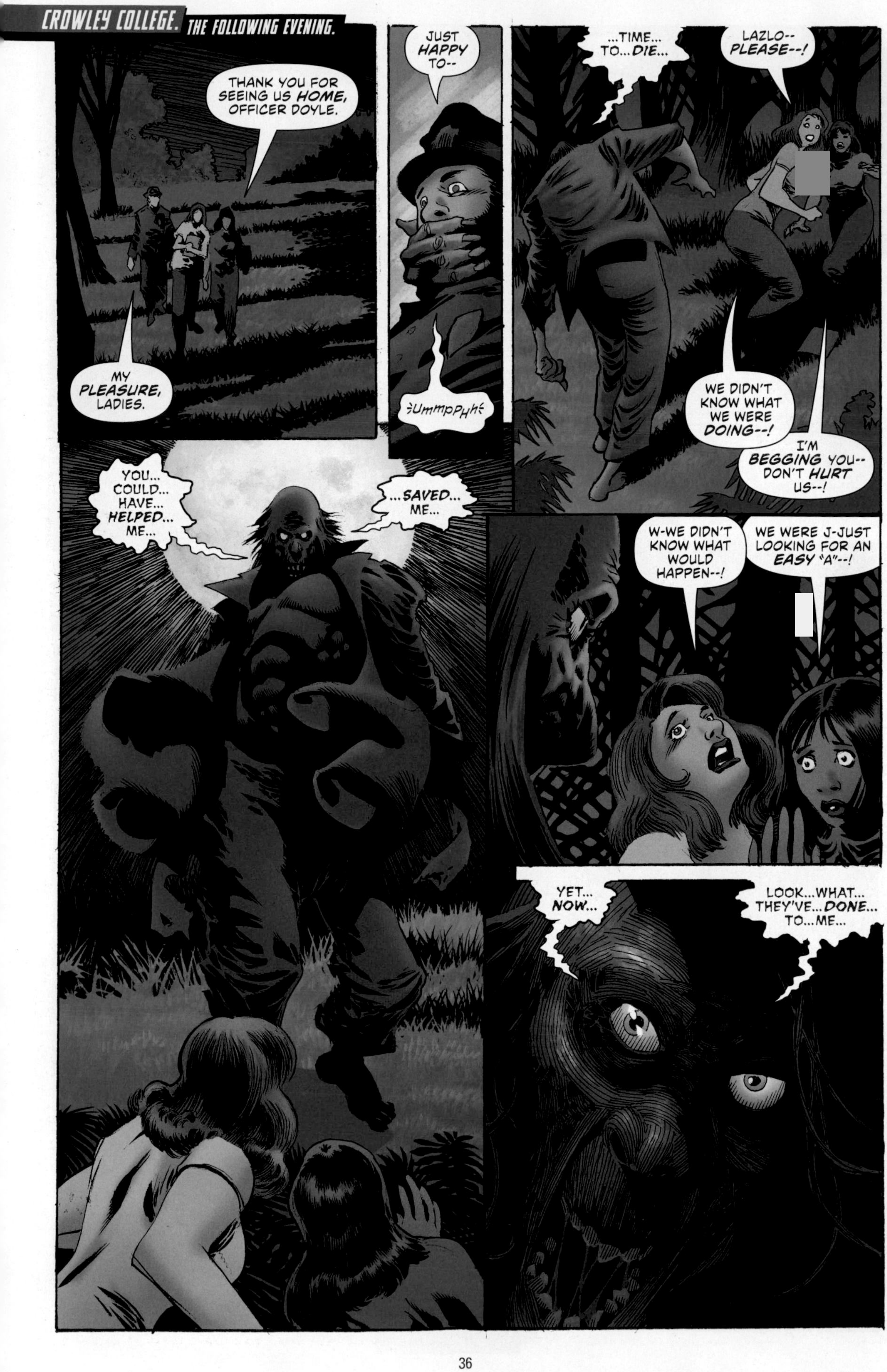
CROWLEY COLLEGE. THE FOLLOWING EVENING.
THANK YOU FOR SEEING US HOME, OFFICER DOYLE.
MY PLEASURE, LADIES.
JUST HAPPY TO--
UmmpPH
...TIME... TO...DIE...
LAZLO-- PLEASE--!
WE DIDN'T KNOW WHAT WE WERE DOING--!
I'M BEGGING YOU-- DON'T HURT US--!
YOU... COULD... HAVE... HELPED... ME...
...SAVED... ME...
W-WE DIDN'T KNOW WHAT WOULD HAPPEN--!
WE WERE J-JUST LOOKING FOR AN EASY "A"--!
YET... NOW...
LOOK...WHAT... THEY'VE...DONE... TO...ME...

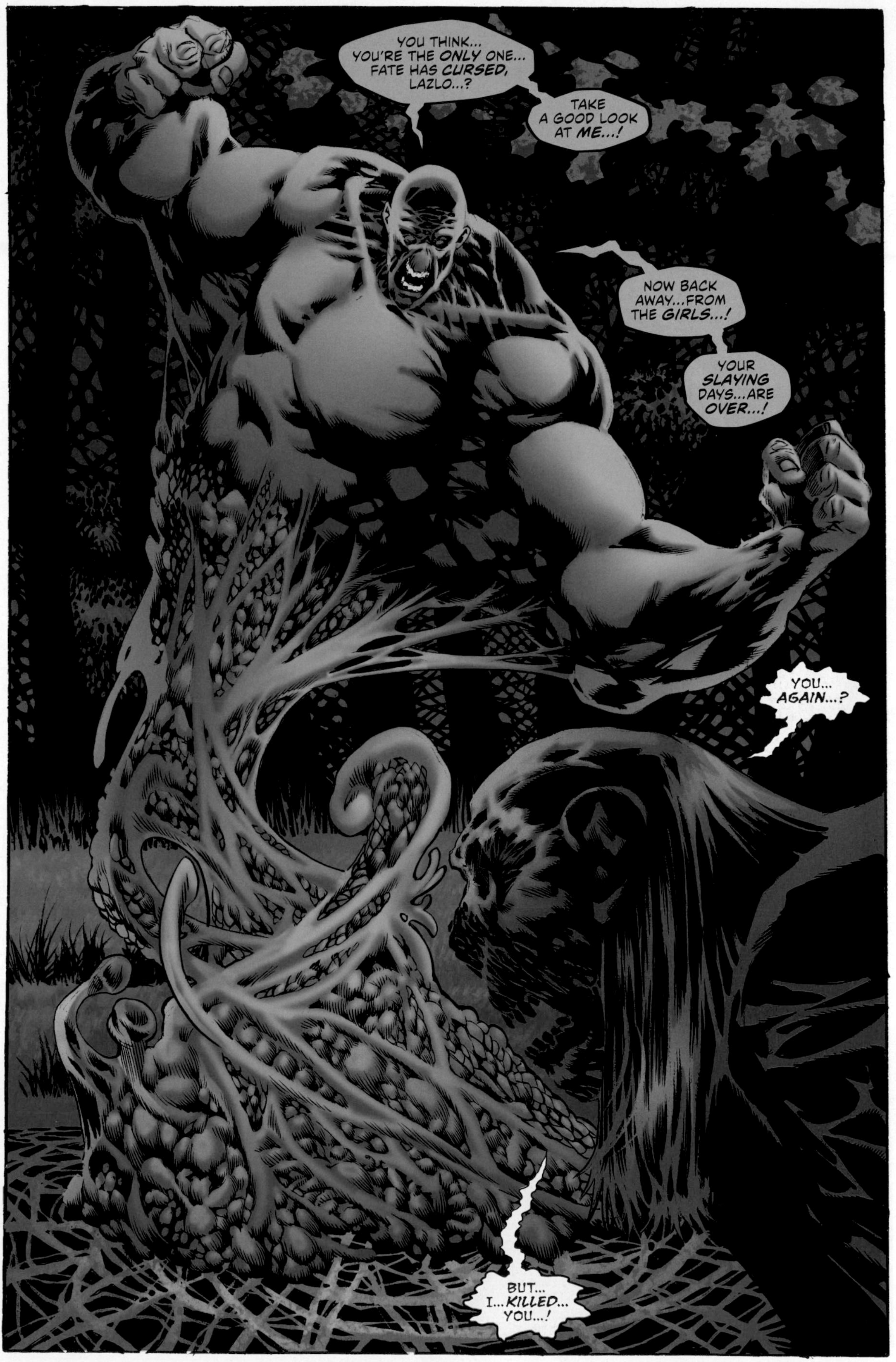
YOU THINK... YOU'RE THE ONLY ONE... FATE HAS CURSED, LAZLO...?
TAKE A GOOD LOOK AT ME...!
NOW BACK AWAY...FROM THE GIRLS...!
YOUR SLAYING DAYS...ARE OVER...!
YOU... AGAIN...?
BUT... I...KILLED... YOU...!

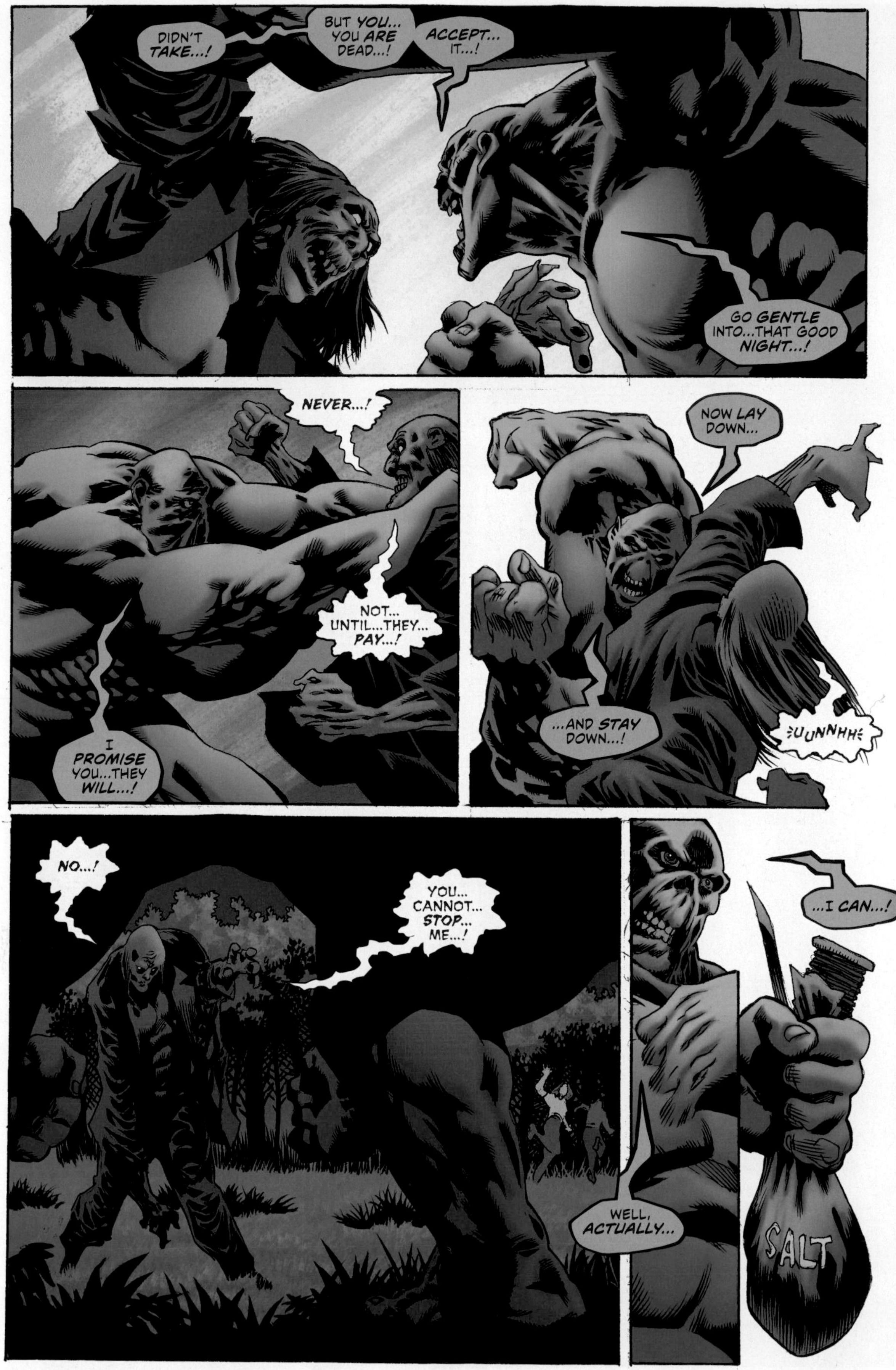
DIDN'T TAKE...!
BUT YOU... YOU ARE DEAD...!
ACCEPT... IT...!
GO GENTLE INTO...THAT GOOD NIGHT...!
NEVER...!
NOT... UNTIL...THEY... PAY...!
I PROMISE YOU...THEY WILL...!
NOW LAY DOWN...
...AND STAY DOWN...!
UUNNHH
NO...!
YOU... CANNOT... STOP... ME...!
WELL, ACTUALLY...
...I CAN...!
SALT

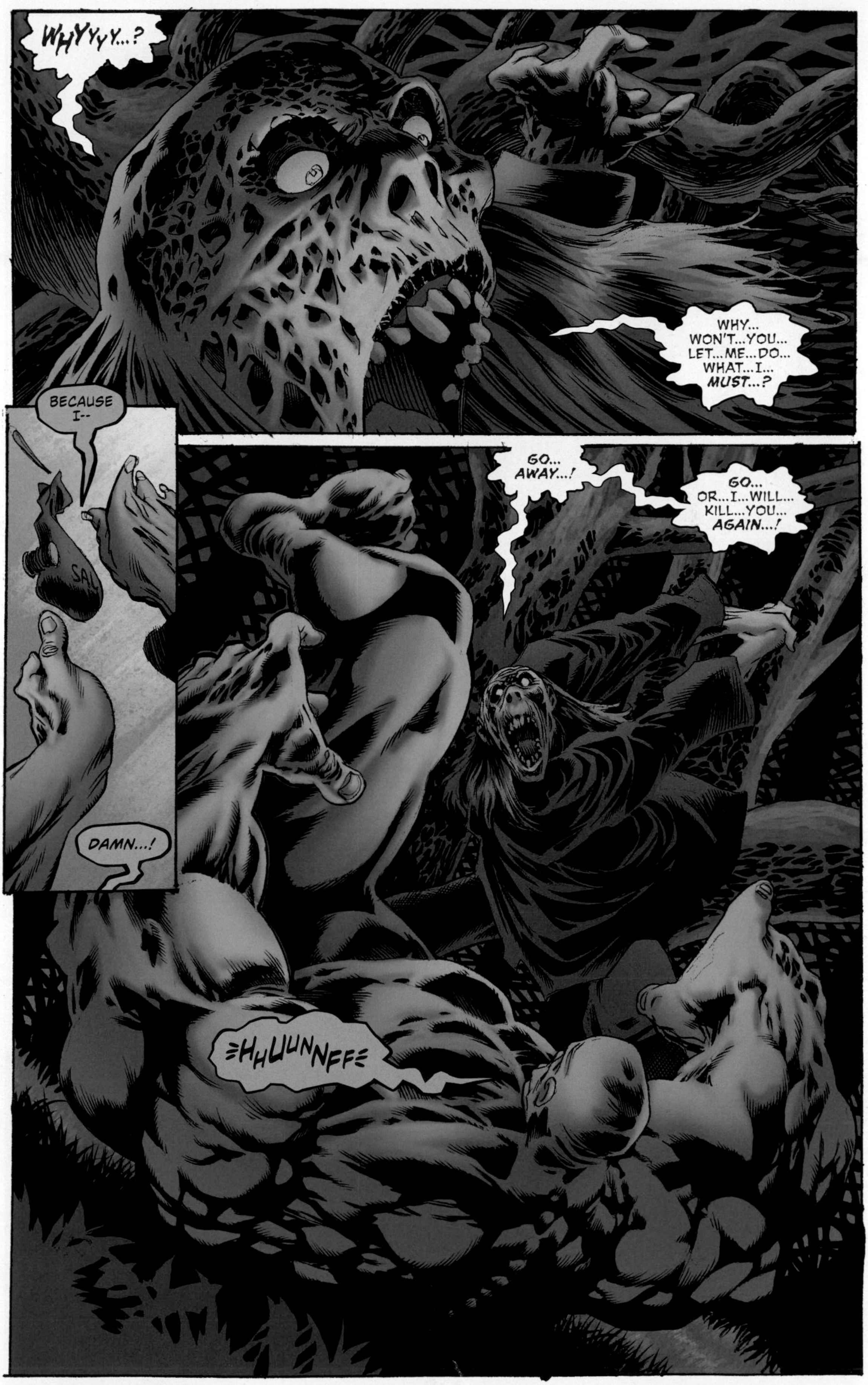
WHYYYY...?
WHY... WON'T...YOU... LET...ME...DO... WHAT...I... MUST...?
BECAUSE I--
SAL
DAMN...!
GO... AWAY...!
GO... OR...I...WILL... KILL...YOU... AGAIN...!
HHUUNNFF

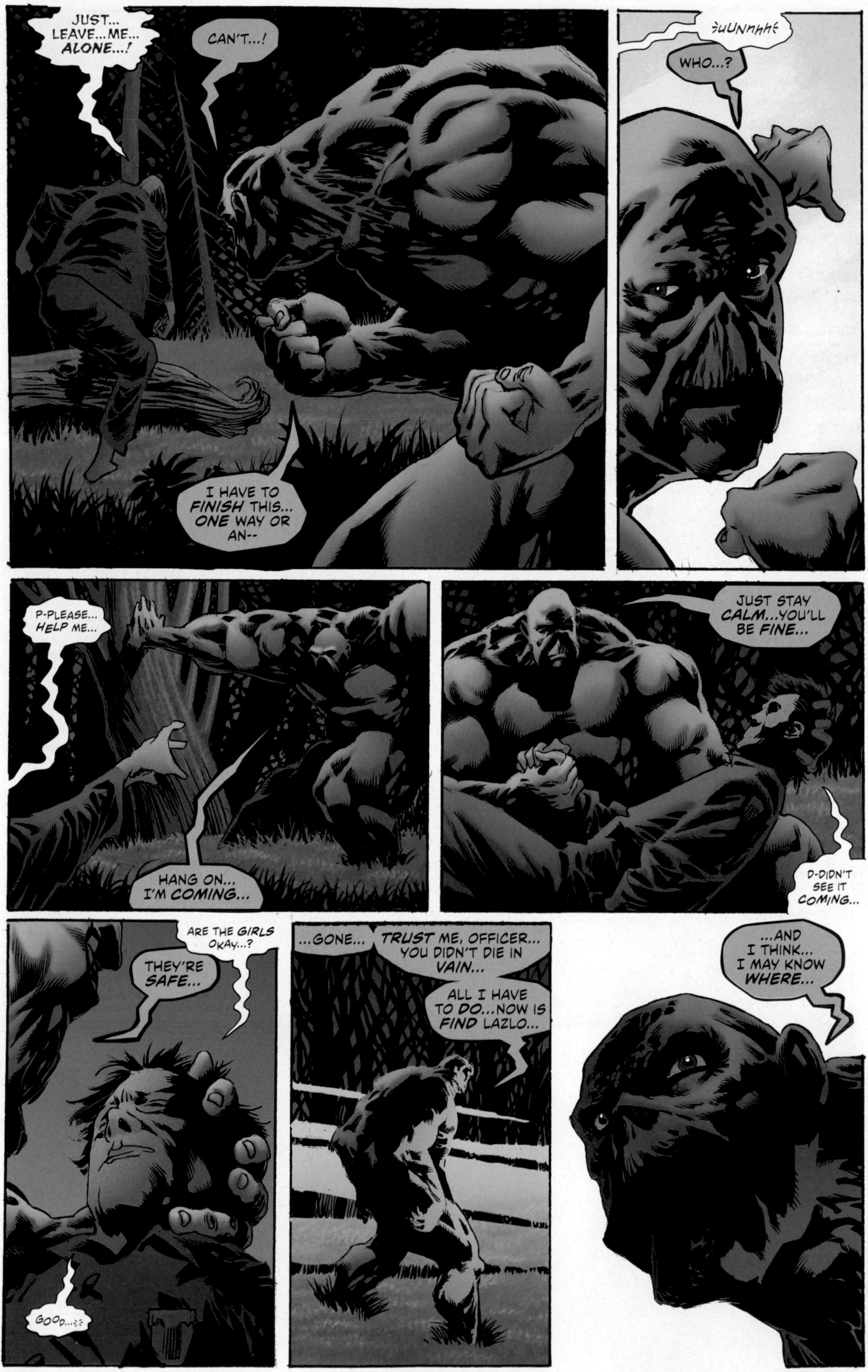
JUST... LEAVE...ME... ALONE...!
CAN'T...!
I HAVE TO FINISH THIS... ONE WAY OR AN--
uUNhhh
WHO...?
P-PLEASE... HELP ME...
HANG ON... I'M COMING...
JUST STAY CALM...YOU'LL BE FINE...
D-DIDN'T SEE IT COMING...
ARE THE GIRLS OKAY...?
THEY'RE SAFE...
GOOD...
...GONE...
TRUST ME, OFFICER... YOU DIDN'T DIE IN VAIN...
ALL I HAVE TO DO...NOW IS FIND LAZLO...
...AND I THINK... I MAY KNOW WHERE...

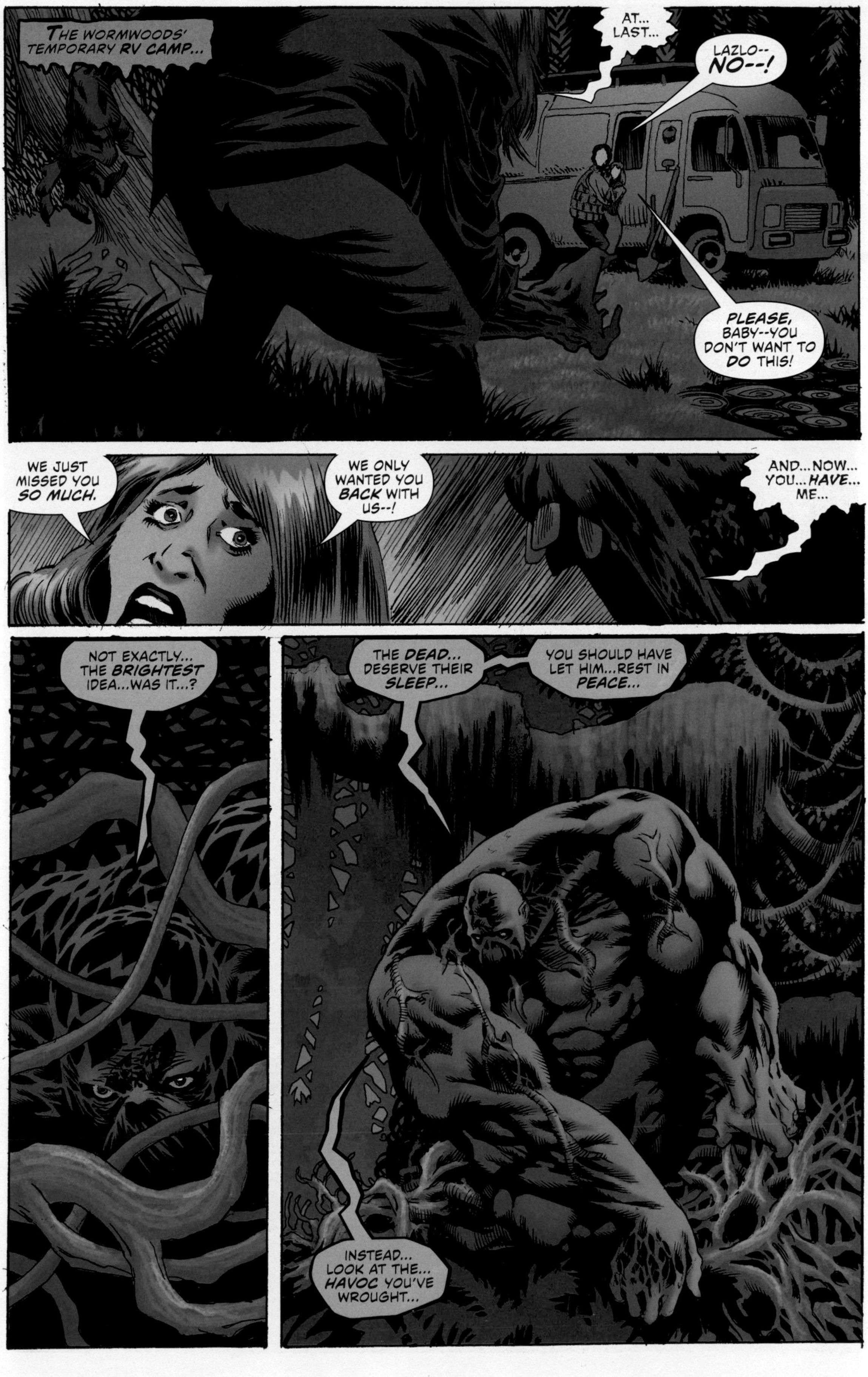
THE WORMWOODS' TEMPORARY RV CAMP...
AT... LAST...
LAZLO-- NO--!
PLEASE, BABY--YOU DON'T WANT TO DO THIS!
WE JUST MISSED YOU SO MUCH.
WE ONLY WANTED YOU BACK WITH US--!
AND...NOW... YOU...HAVE... ME...
NOT EXACTLY... THE BRIGHTEST IDEA...WAS IT...?
THE DEAD... DESERVE THEIR SLEEP...
YOU SHOULD HAVE LET HIM...REST IN PEACE...
INSTEAD... LOOK AT THE... HAVOC YOU'VE WROUGHT...

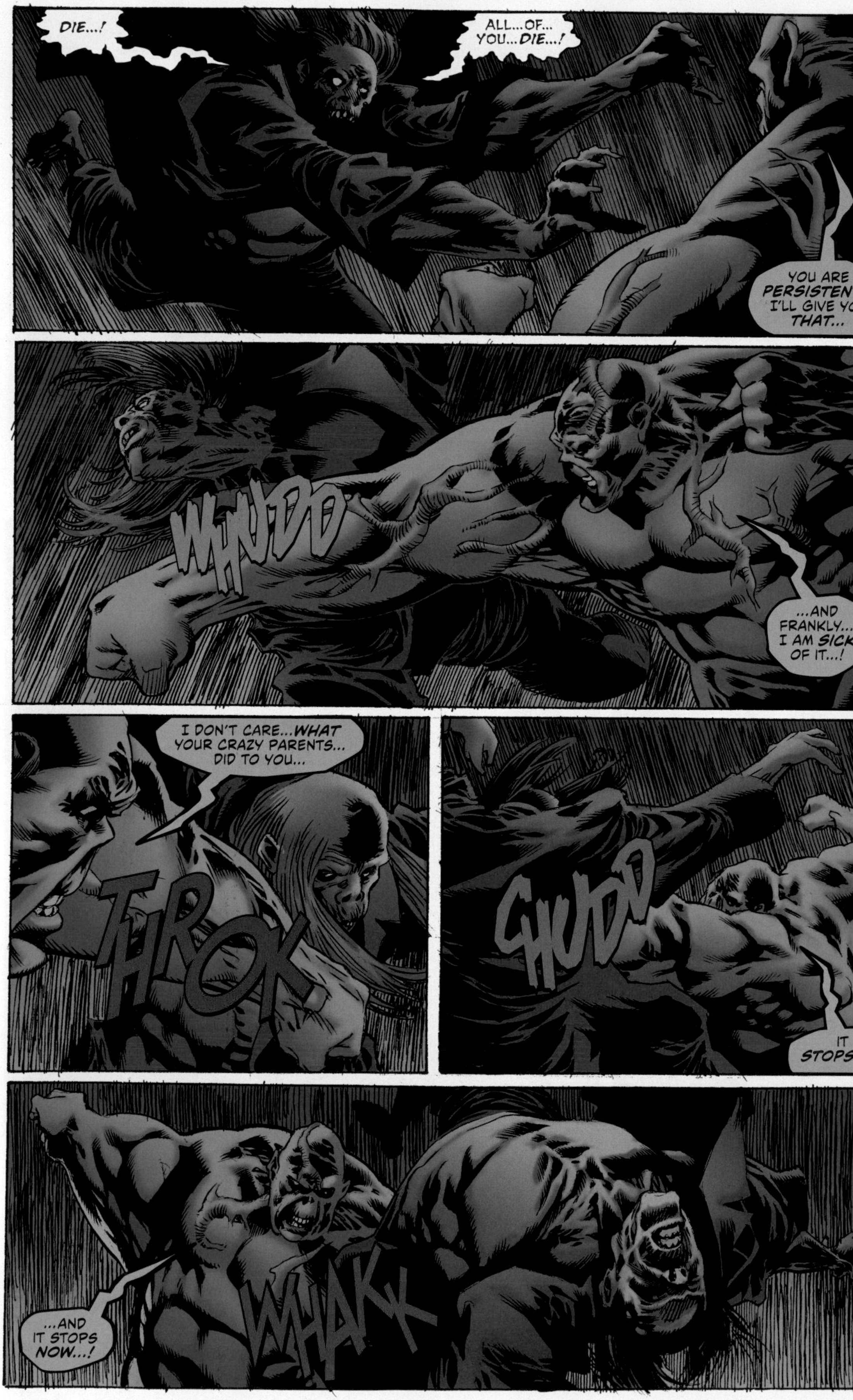

DIE...!
ALL...OF... YOU...DIE...!
YOU ARE PERSISTENT... I'LL GIVE YOU THAT...
WHUDD
...AND FRANKLY... I AM SICK OF IT...!
I DON'T CARE...WHAT YOUR CRAZY PARENTS... DID TO YOU...
THROK
CHUDD
IT STOPS...
WHAKK
...AND IT STOPS NOW...!

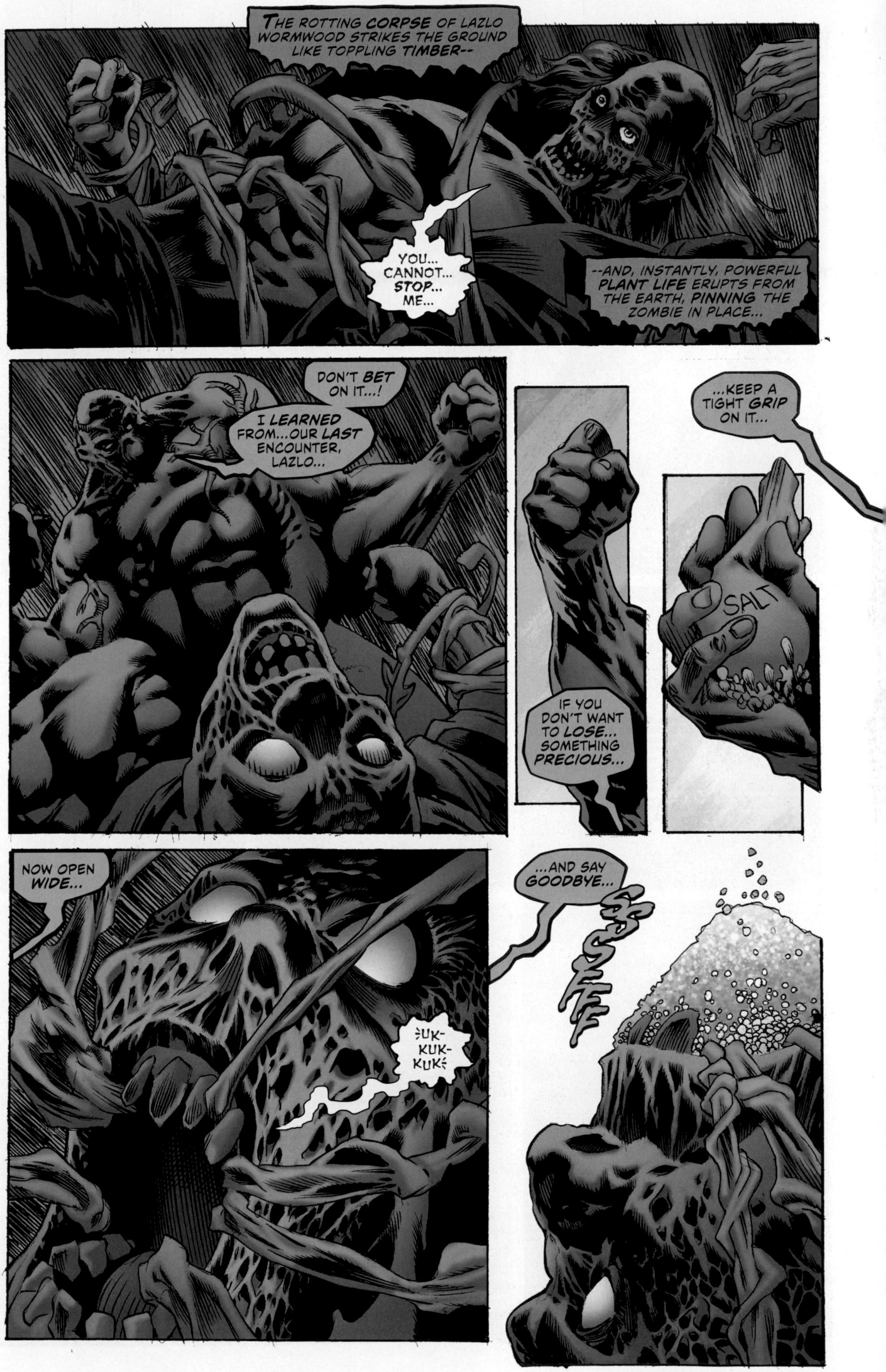

THE ROTTING CORPSE OF LAZLO WORMWOOD STRIKES THE GROUND LIKE TOPPLING TIMBER--
YOU... CANNOT... STOP... ME...
--AND, INSTANTLY, POWERFUL PLANT LIFE ERUPTS FROM THE EARTH, PINNING THE ZOMBIE IN PLACE...
DON'T BET ON IT...!
I LEARNED FROM...OUR LAST ENCOUNTER, LAZLO...
...KEEP A TIGHT GRIP ON IT...
SALT
IF YOU DON'T WANT TO LOSE... SOMETHING PRECIOUS...
NOW OPEN WIDE...
UK-KUK-KUK
...AND SAY GOODBYE...

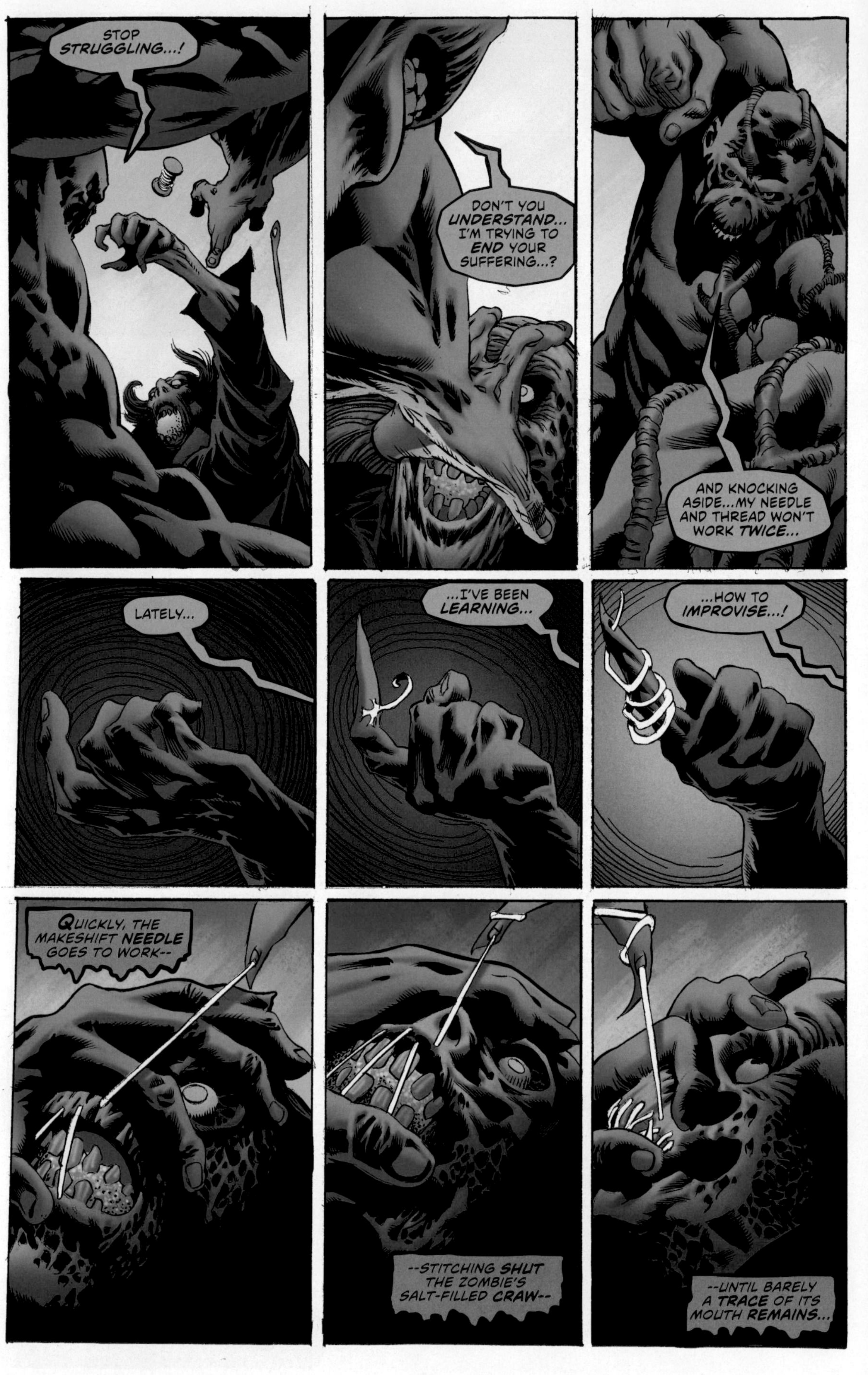
STOP STRUGGLING...!
DON'T YOU UNDERSTAND... I'M TRYING TO END YOUR SUFFERING...?
AND KNOCKING ASIDE...MY NEEDLE AND THREAD WON'T WORK TWICE...
LATELY...
...I'VE BEEN LEARNING...
...HOW TO IMPROVISE...!
QUICKLY, THE MAKESHIFT NEEDLE GOES TO WORK--
--STITCHING SHUT THE ZOMBIE'S SALT-FILLED CRAW--
--UNTIL BARELY A TRACE OF ITS MOUTH REMAINS...

AND YET, INCREDIBLY, IMPOSSIBLY, THE UNDEAD CREATURE BURSTS FREE OF ITS BONDS--

HOW...?

--AND STAGGERS FORWARD, STEP BY EXCRUCIATING STEP--

--PAST THE ASTONISHED SWAMP THING--

--AND TOWARD THE TERRIFIED SOURCE OF ITS PAIN--

--PUSHING ITSELF BEYOND ALL HUMAN COMPREHENSION--

--FOOT BY DRAGGING FOOT--

--HUNGRY FOR RIGHTEOUS VENGEANCE--

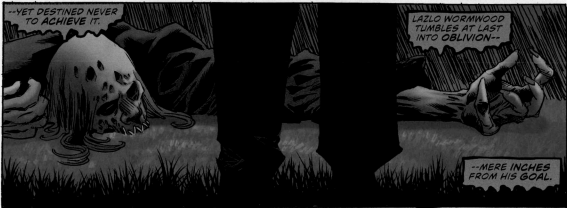

--YET DESTINED NEVER TO ACHIEVE IT.

LAZLO WORMWOOD TUMBLES AT LAST INTO OBLIVION--

--MERE INCHES FROM HIS GOAL.

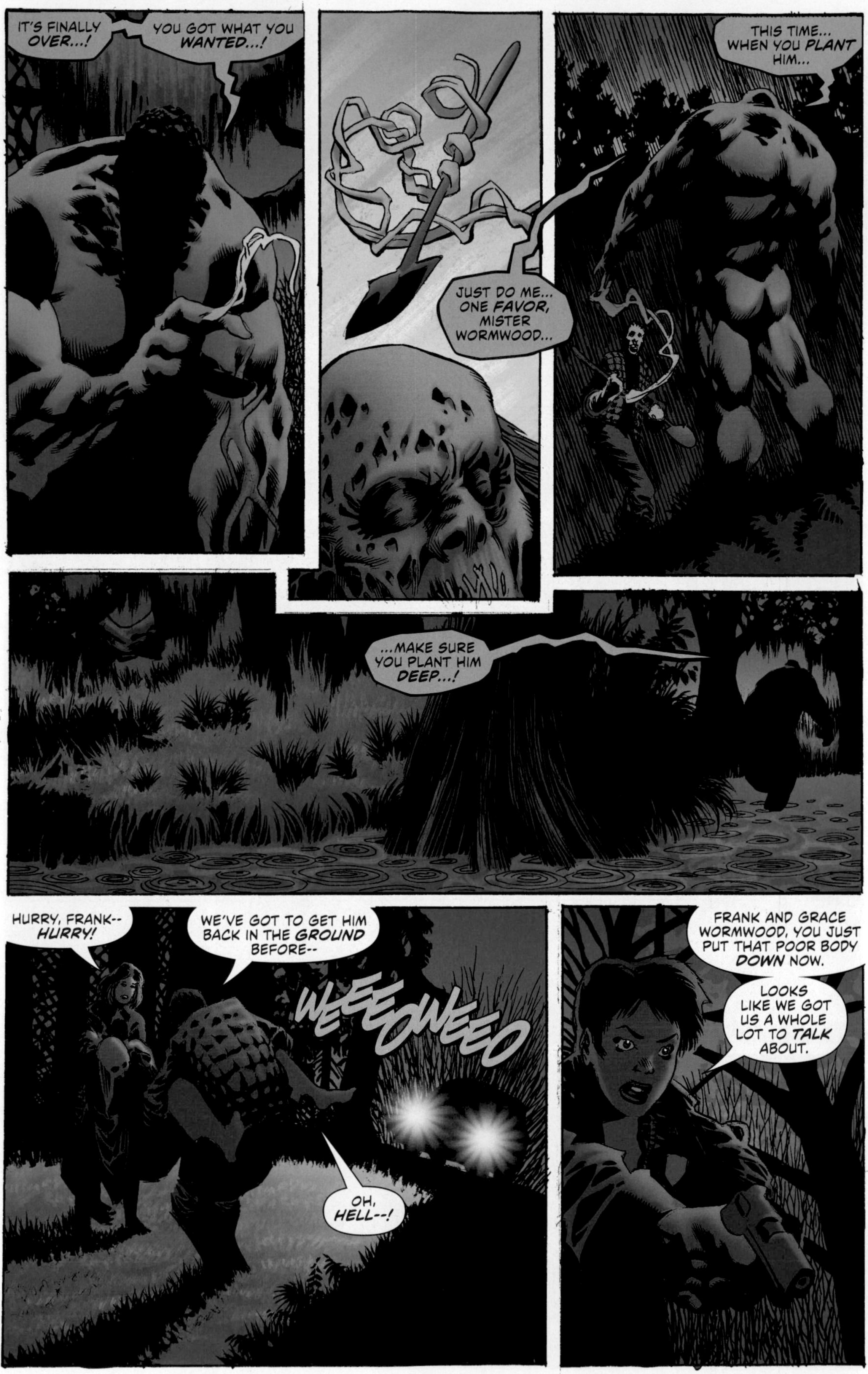

IT'S FINALLY OVER...!
YOU GOT WHAT YOU WANTED...!
JUST DO ME... ONE FAVOR, MISTER WORMWOOD...
THIS TIME... WHEN YOU PLANT HIM...
...MAKE SURE YOU PLANT HIM DEEP...!
HURRY, FRANK-- HURRY!
WE'VE GOT TO GET HIM BACK IN THE GROUND BEFORE--
WEEEOWEEEO
OH, HELL--!
FRANK AND GRACE WORMWOOD, YOU JUST PUT THAT POOR BODY DOWN NOW.
LOOKS LIKE WE GOT US A WHOLE LOT TO TALK ABOUT.

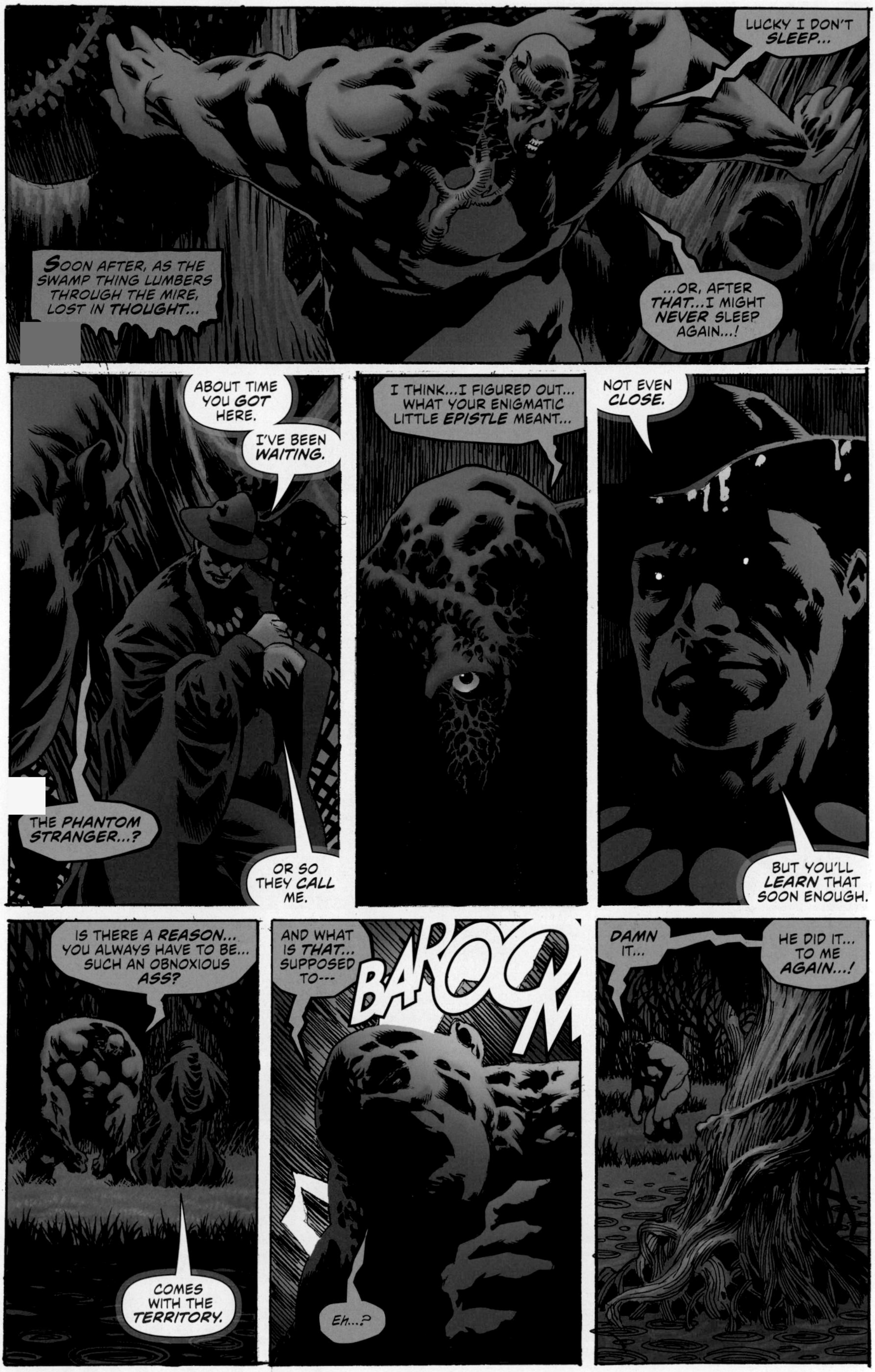
SOON AFTER, AS THE SWAMP THING LUMBERS THROUGH THE MIRE, LOST IN THOUGHT...
LUCKY I DON'T SLEEP...
...OR, AFTER THAT...I MIGHT NEVER SLEEP AGAIN...!
ABOUT TIME YOU GOT HERE.
I'VE BEEN WAITING.
THE PHANTOM STRANGER...?
OR SO THEY CALL ME.
I THINK...I FIGURED OUT... WHAT YOUR ENIGMATIC LITTLE EPISTLE MEANT...
NOT EVEN CLOSE.
BUT YOU'LL LEARN THAT SOON ENOUGH.
IS THERE A REASON... YOU ALWAYS HAVE TO BE... SUCH AN OBNOXIOUS ASS?
COMES WITH THE TERRITORY.
AND WHAT IS THAT... SUPPOSED TO---
BAROOM
Eh...?
DAMN IT...
HE DID IT... TO ME AGAIN...!

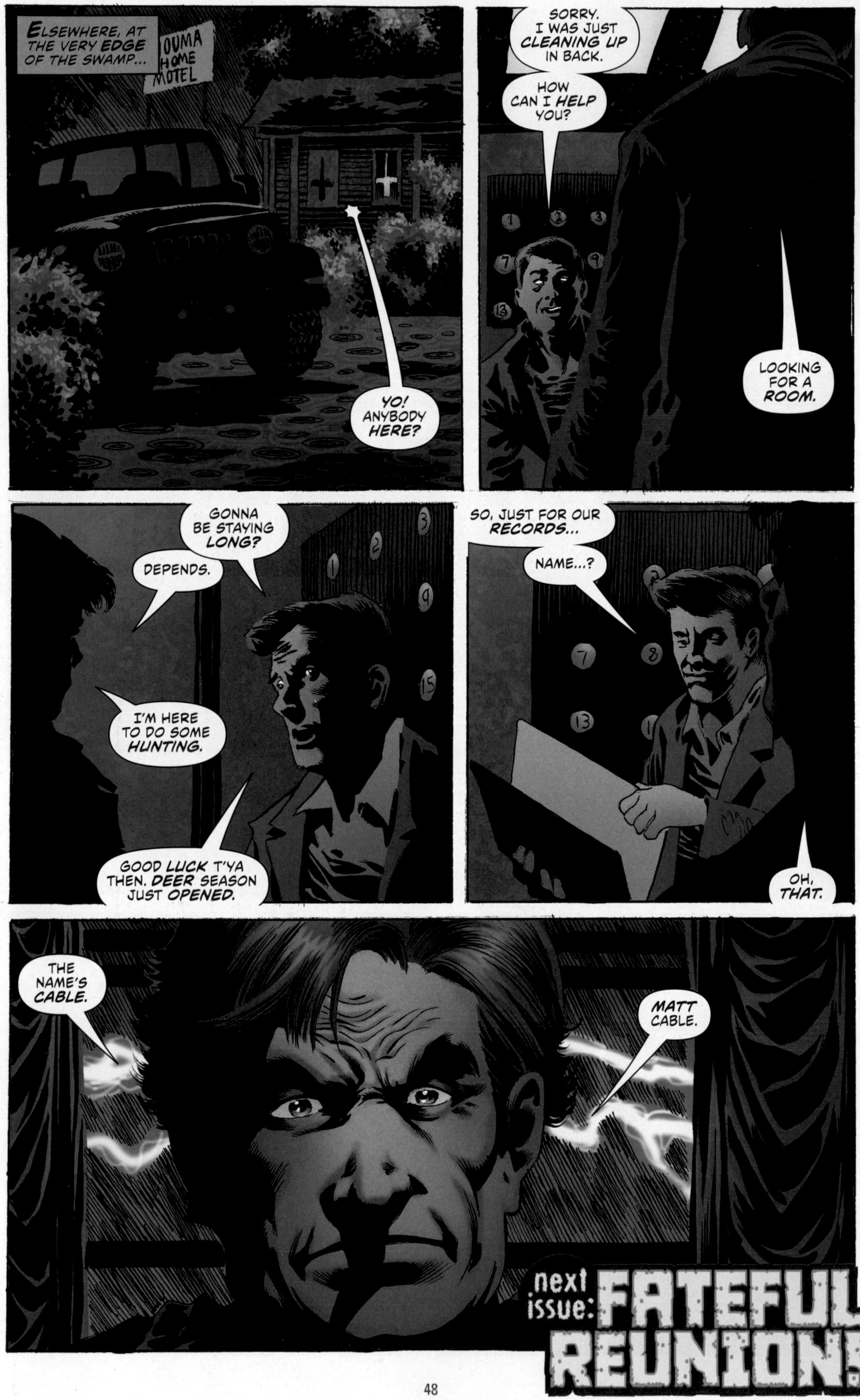
ELSEWHERE, AT THE VERY EDGE OF THE SWAMP...
OUMA HOME MOTEL
YO! ANYBODY HERE?
SORRY. I WAS JUST CLEANING UP IN BACK.
HOW CAN I HELP YOU?
LOOKING FOR A ROOM.
GONNA BE STAYING LONG?
DEPENDS.
I'M HERE TO DO SOME HUNTING.
GOOD LUCK T'YA THEN. DEER SEASON JUST OPENED.
SO, JUST FOR OUR RECORDS...
NAME...?
OH, THAT.
THE NAME'S CABLE.
MATT CABLE.
next issue: FATEFUL REUNION!

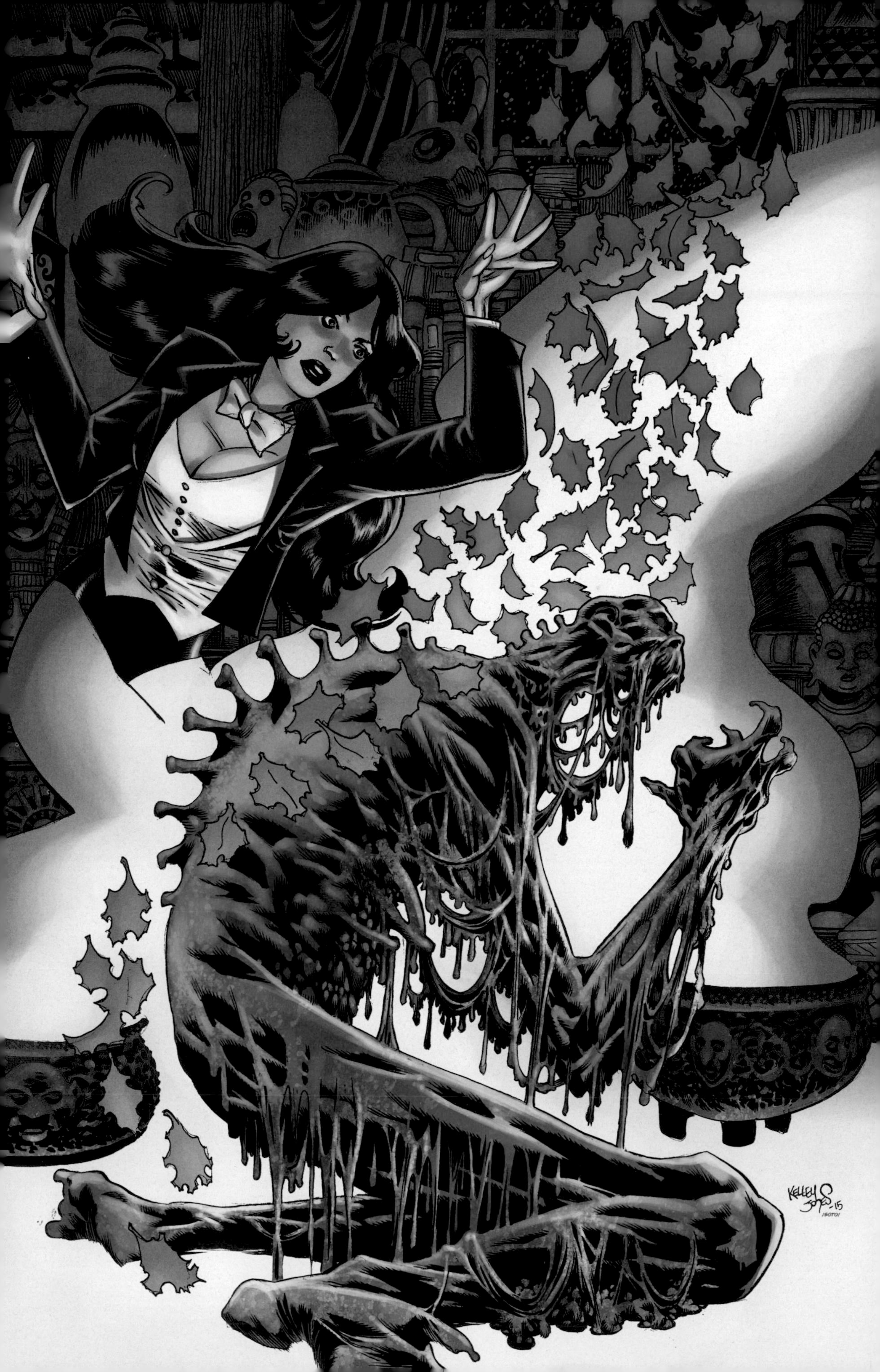

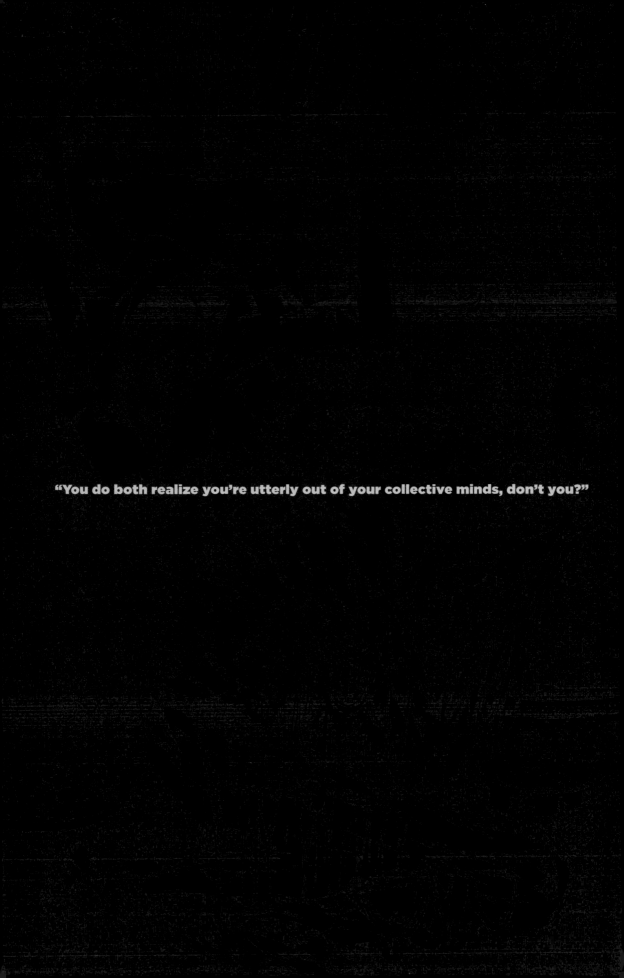

"You do both realize you're utterly out of your collective minds, don't you?"

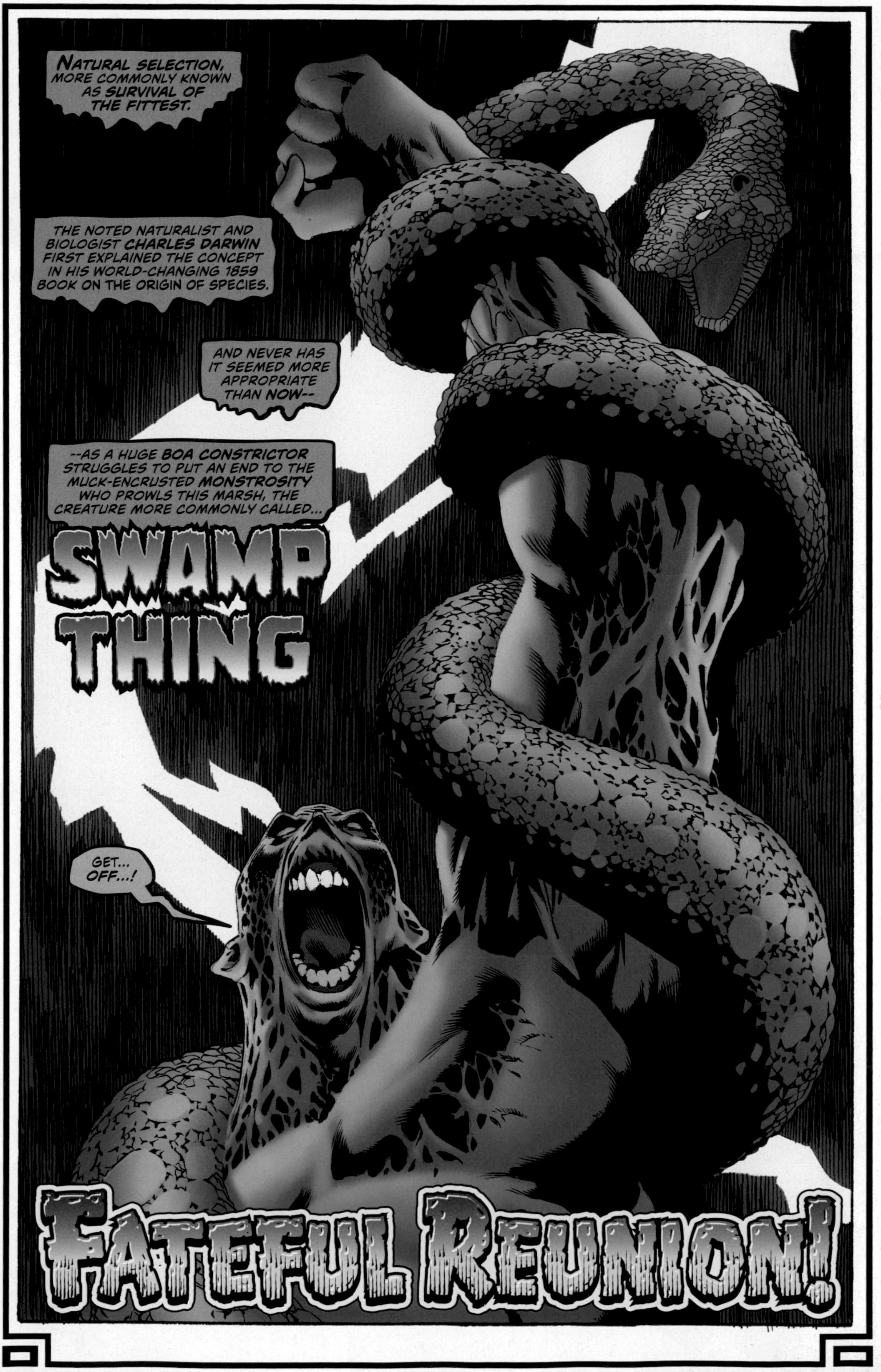
NATURAL SELECTION, MORE COMMONLY KNOWN AS SURVIVAL OF THE FITTEST.
THE NOTED NATURALIST AND BIOLOGIST CHARLES DARWIN FIRST EXPLAINED THE CONCEPT IN HIS WORLD-CHANGING 1859 BOOK ON THE ORIGIN OF SPECIES.
AND NEVER HAS IT SEEMED MORE APPROPRIATE THAN NOW--
--AS A HUGE BOA CONSTRICTOR STRUGGLES TO PUT AN END TO THE MUCK-ENCRUSTED MONSTROSITY WHO PROWLS THIS MARSH, THE CREATURE MORE COMMONLY CALLED...
SWAMP THING
GET... OFF...!
FATEFUL REUNION!

NICE *TRY*, SCALY...

...BUT WE'VE *PLAYED*... THIS GAME *BEFORE*...

...AND YOU *KNOW*... NO MATTER HOW HARD YOU *TRY*...

...IN THE *END*... I ALWAYS--

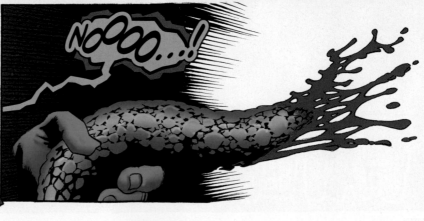

NOOOOO...!

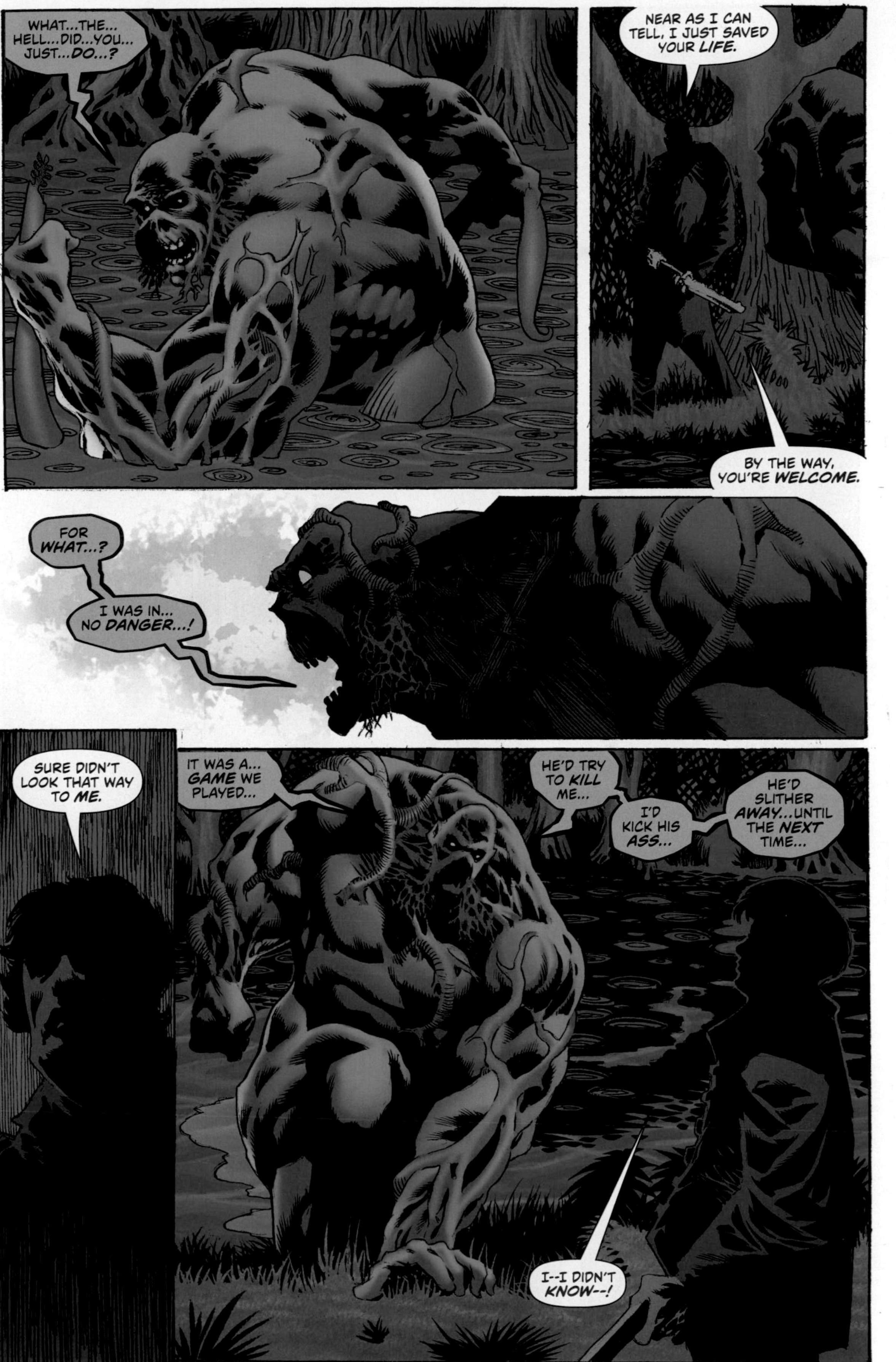
WHAT...THE... HELL...DID...YOU... JUST...DO...?
NEAR AS I CAN TELL, I JUST SAVED YOUR LIFE.
BY THE WAY, YOU'RE WELCOME.
FOR WHAT...?
I WAS IN... NO DANGER...!
SURE DIDN'T LOOK THAT WAY TO ME.
IT WAS A... GAME WE PLAYED...
HE'D TRY TO KILL ME...
I'D KICK HIS ASS...
HE'D SLITHER AWAY...UNTIL THE NEXT TIME...
I--I DIDN'T KNOW--!

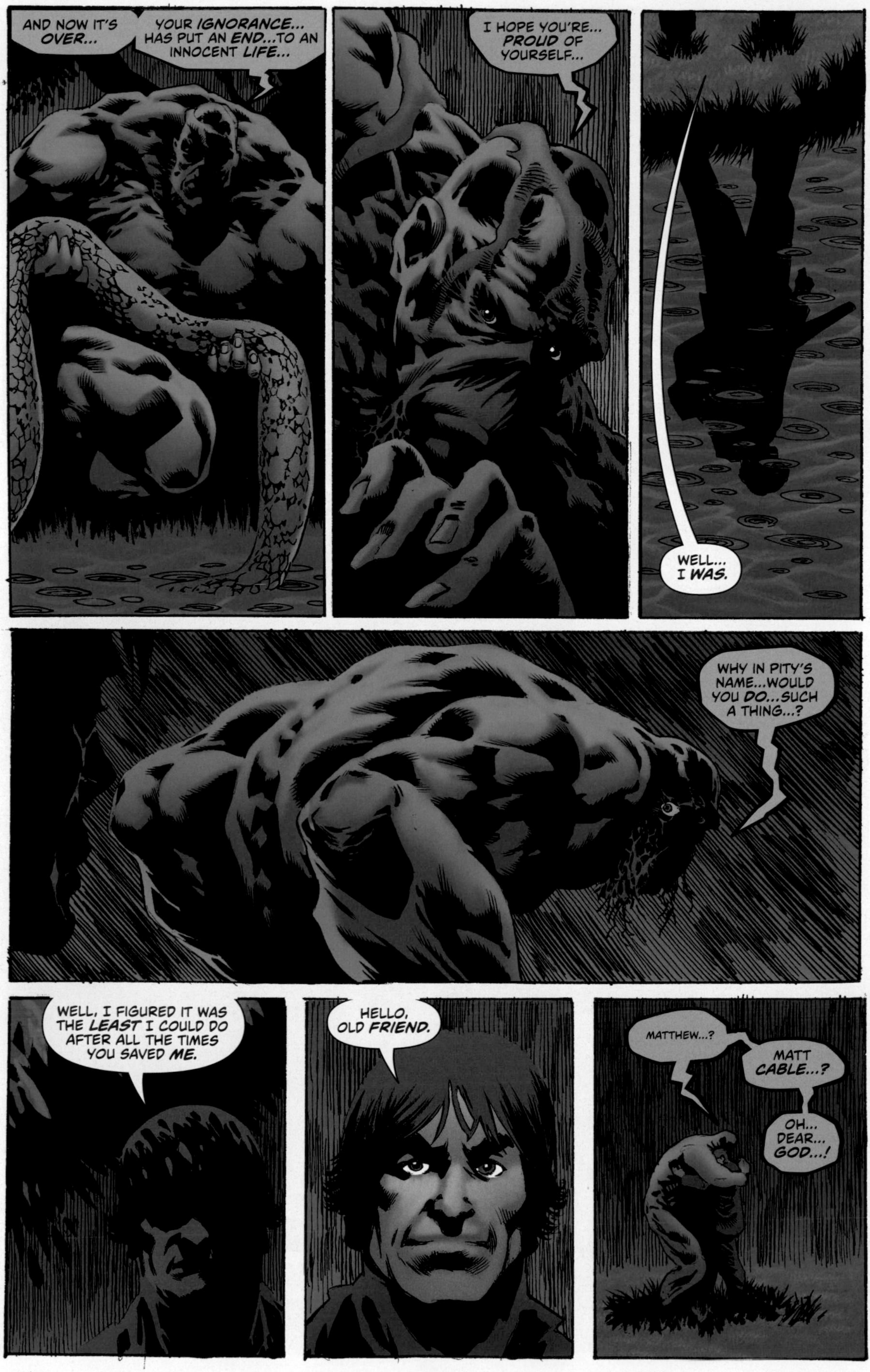
AND NOW IT'S OVER...
YOUR IGNORANCE... HAS PUT AN END...TO AN INNOCENT LIFE...
I HOPE YOU'RE... PROUD OF YOURSELF...
WELL... I WAS.
WHY IN PITY'S NAME...WOULD YOU DO...SUCH A THING...?
WELL, I FIGURED IT WAS THE LEAST I COULD DO AFTER ALL THE TIMES YOU SAVED ME.
HELLO, OLD FRIEND.
MATTHEW...?
MATT CABLE...?
OH... DEAR... GOD...!

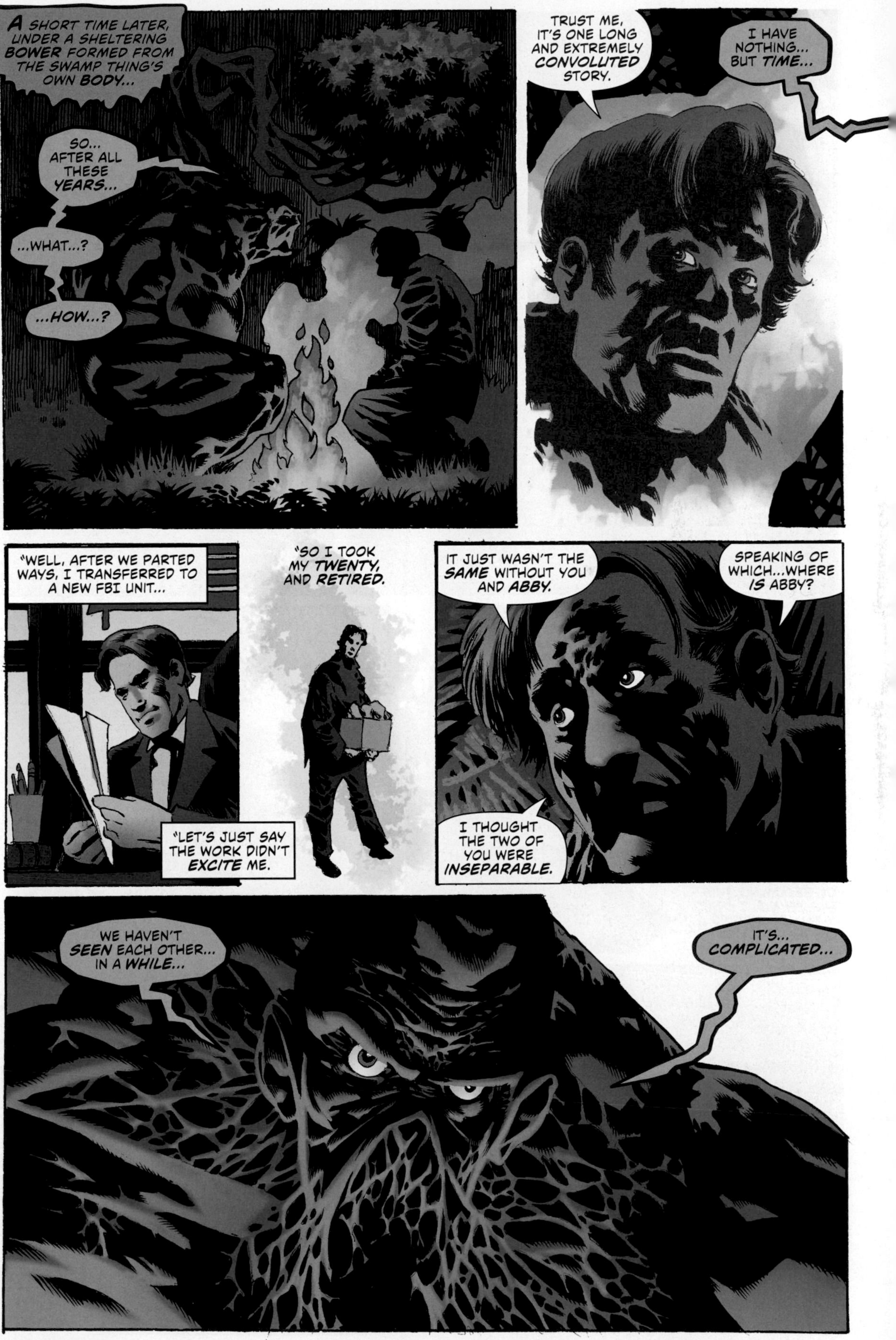
A SHORT TIME LATER, UNDER A SHELTERING BOWER FORMED FROM THE SWAMP THING'S OWN BODY...
SO... AFTER ALL THESE YEARS...
...WHAT...?
...HOW...?
TRUST ME, IT'S ONE LONG AND EXTREMELY CONVOLUTED STORY.
I HAVE NOTHING... BUT TIME...
"WELL, AFTER WE PARTED WAYS, I TRANSFERRED TO A NEW FBI UNIT...
"LET'S JUST SAY THE WORK DIDN'T EXCITE ME.
"SO I TOOK MY TWENTY, AND RETIRED.
IT JUST WASN'T THE SAME WITHOUT YOU AND ABBY.
SPEAKING OF WHICH...WHERE IS ABBY?
I THOUGHT THE TWO OF YOU WERE INSEPARABLE.
WE HAVEN'T SEEN EACH OTHER... IN A WHILE...
IT'S... COMPLICATED...

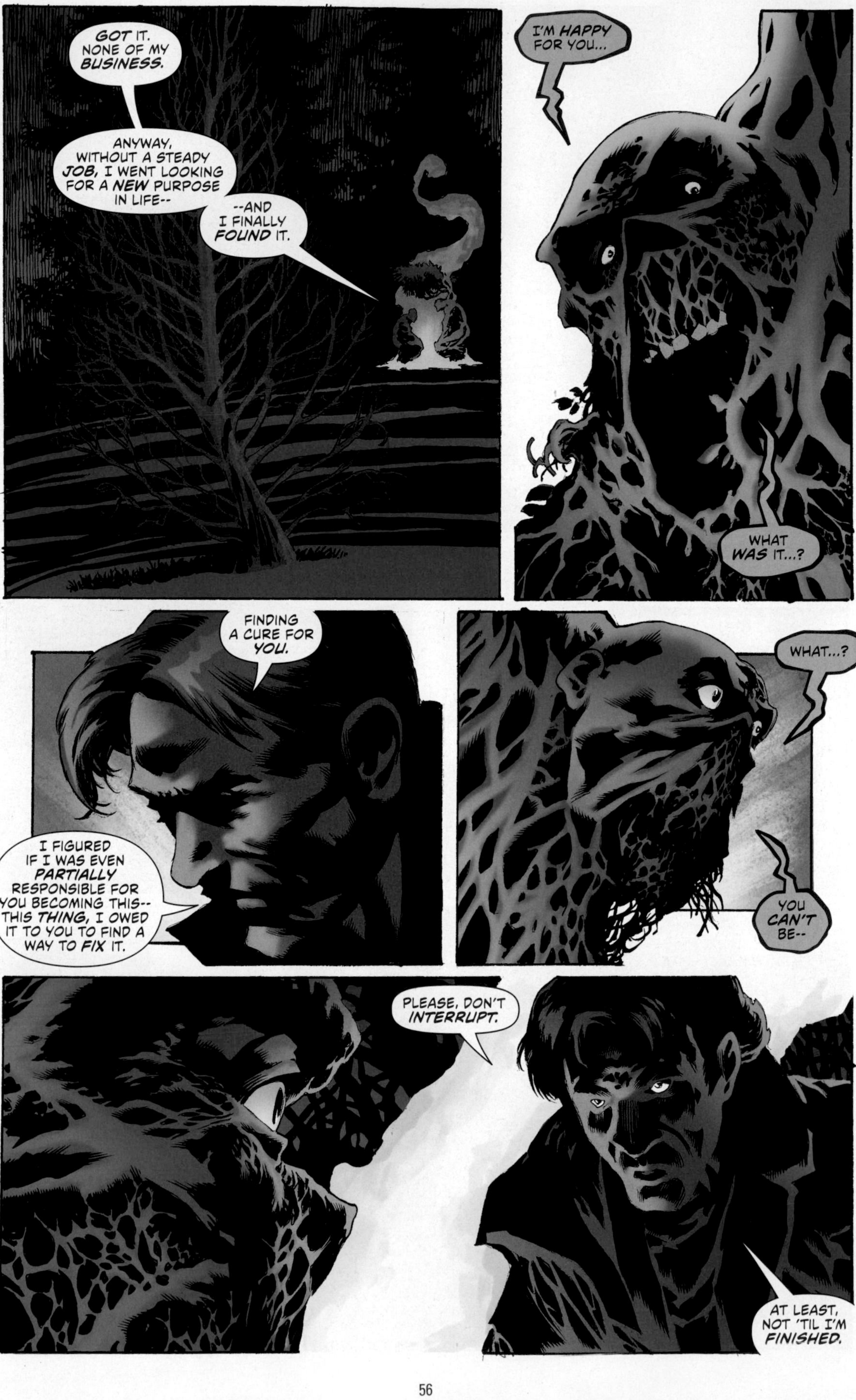
GOT IT. NONE OF MY BUSINESS.
ANYWAY, WITHOUT A STEADY JOB, I WENT LOOKING FOR A NEW PURPOSE IN LIFE--
--AND I FINALLY FOUND IT.
I'M HAPPY FOR YOU...
WHAT WAS IT...?
FINDING A CURE FOR YOU.
I FIGURED IF I WAS EVEN PARTIALLY RESPONSIBLE FOR YOU BECOMING THIS-- THIS THING, I OWED IT TO YOU TO FIND A WAY TO FIX IT.
WHAT...?
YOU CAN'T BE--
PLEASE, DON'T INTERRUPT.
AT LEAST, NOT 'TIL I'M FINISHED.

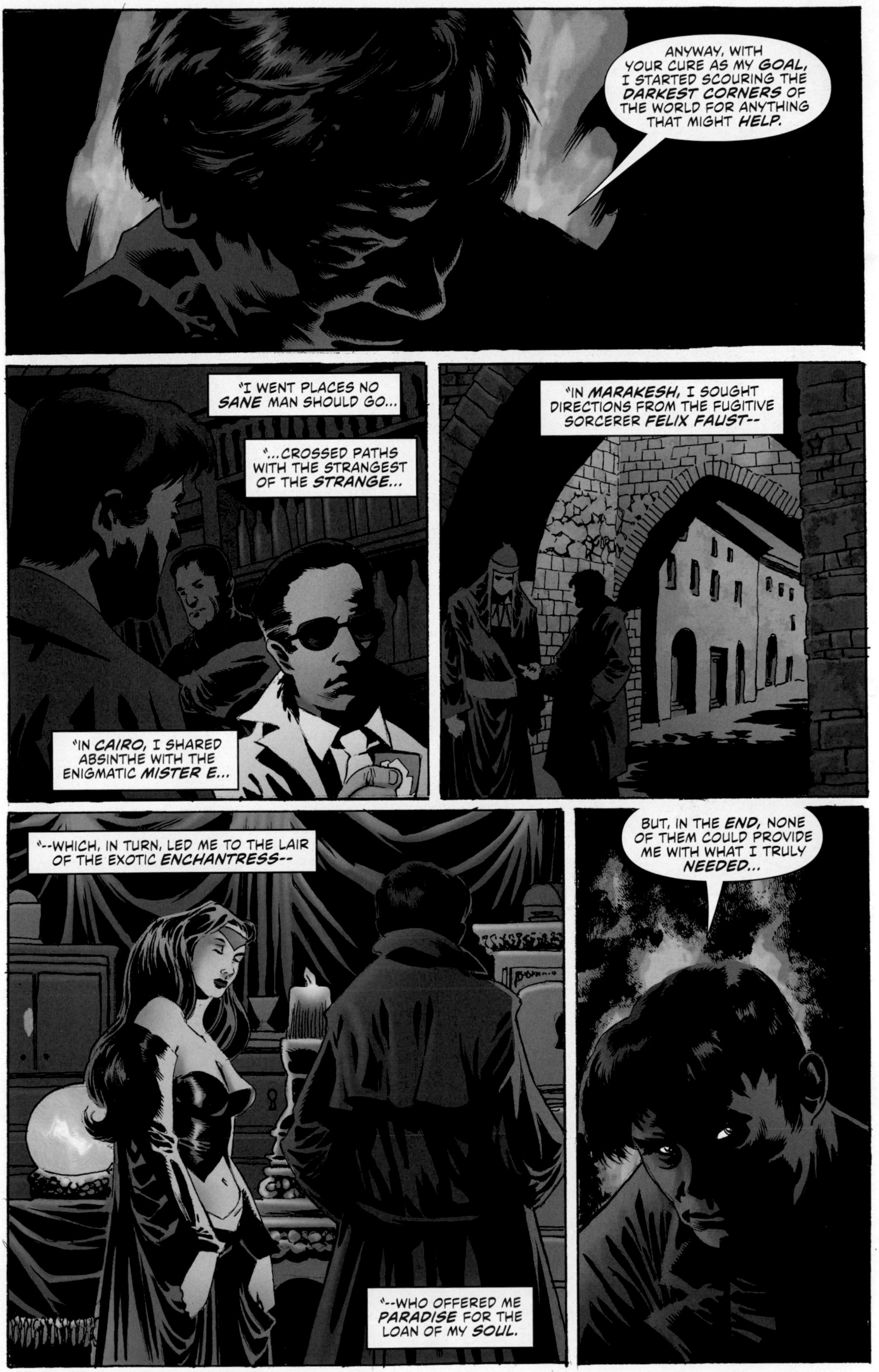
ANYWAY, WITH YOUR CURE AS MY GOAL, I STARTED SCOURING THE DARKEST CORNERS OF THE WORLD FOR ANYTHING THAT MIGHT HELP.
"I WENT PLACES NO SANE MAN SHOULD GO...
"...CROSSED PATHS WITH THE STRANGEST OF THE STRANGE...
"IN CAIRO, I SHARED ABSINTHE WITH THE ENIGMATIC MISTER E...
"IN MARAKESH, I SOUGHT DIRECTIONS FROM THE FUGITIVE SORCERER FELIX FAUST--
"--WHICH, IN TURN, LED ME TO THE LAIR OF THE EXOTIC ENCHANTRESS--
"--WHO OFFERED ME PARADISE FOR THE LOAN OF MY SOUL.
BUT, IN THE END, NONE OF THEM COULD PROVIDE ME WITH WHAT I TRULY NEEDED...

"EVENTUALLY, USING AN ANCIENT MAP THAT COST ME ALMOST ALL MY *LIFE SAVINGS,* I FINALLY *FOUND* WHAT I WAS SEARCHING FOR--"

"--THE MYTHICAL CITY OF *NANDA PARBAT,* NESTLED DEEP IN A SECLUDED VALLEY IN THE *HIMALAYAN MOUNTAINS...*"

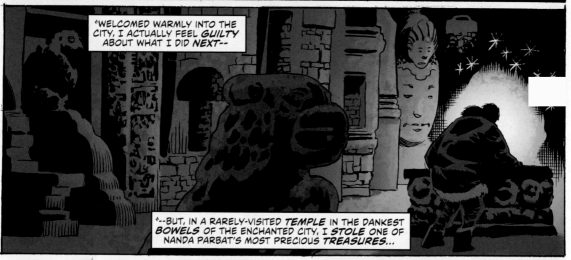

"WELCOMED WARMLY INTO THE CITY, I ACTUALLY FEEL *GUILTY* ABOUT WHAT I DID *NEXT--*"

"--BUT, IN A RARELY-VISITED *TEMPLE* IN THE DANKEST *BOWELS* OF THE ENCHANTED CITY, I *STOLE* ONE OF NANDA PARBAT'S MOST PRECIOUS *TREASURES...*"

...PERHAPS THE *ONLY OCCULT OBJECT* THAT MIGHT MAKE YOU *HUMAN* AGAIN...

TRUST ME, ALEC...

YOU CAN *FEEL* THE OBJECT'S *POWER,* EVEN THROUGH ALL THESE LAYERS OF PROTECTIVE *FABRIC.*

THEY *CALL* IT...

...THE *HAND OF FATIMA!*

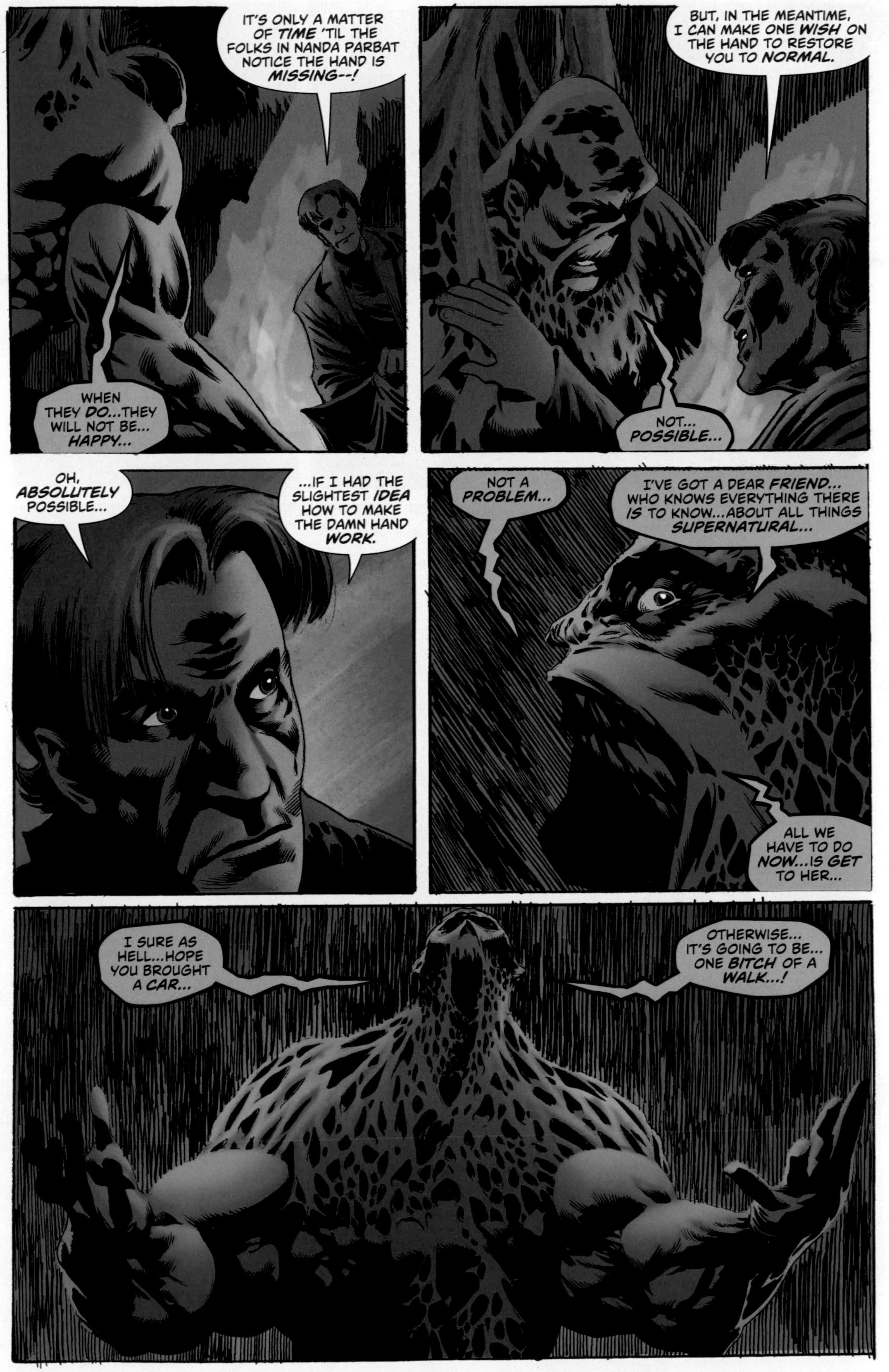
IT'S ONLY A MATTER OF TIME 'TIL THE FOLKS IN NANDA PARBAT NOTICE THE HAND IS MISSING--!
WHEN THEY DO...THEY WILL NOT BE... HAPPY...
BUT, IN THE MEANTIME, I CAN MAKE ONE WISH ON THE HAND TO RESTORE YOU TO NORMAL.
NOT... POSSIBLE...
OH, ABSOLUTELY POSSIBLE...
...IF I HAD THE SLIGHTEST IDEA HOW TO MAKE THE DAMN HAND WORK.
NOT A PROBLEM...
I'VE GOT A DEAR FRIEND... WHO KNOWS EVERYTHING THERE IS TO KNOW...ABOUT ALL THINGS SUPERNATURAL...
ALL WE HAVE TO DO NOW...IS GET TO HER...
I SURE AS HELL...HOPE YOU BROUGHT A CAR...
OTHERWISE... IT'S GOING TO BE... ONE BITCH OF A WALK...!

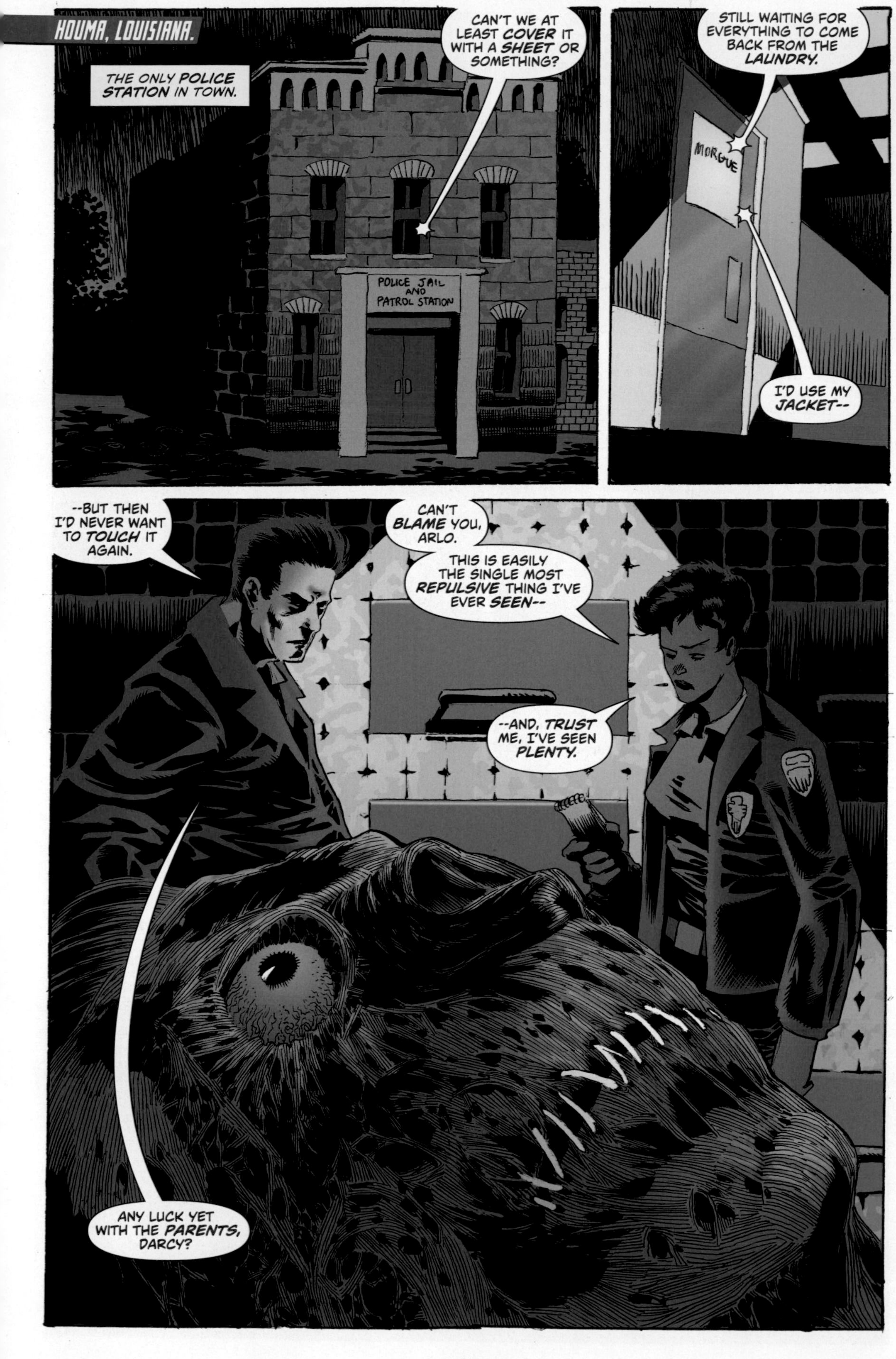
HOUMA, LOUISIANA.
THE ONLY POLICE STATION IN TOWN.
CAN'T WE AT LEAST COVER IT WITH A SHEET OR SOMETHING?
POLICE JAIL AND PATROL STATION
STILL WAITING FOR EVERYTHING TO COME BACK FROM THE LAUNDRY.
MORGUE
I'D USE MY JACKET--
--BUT THEN I'D NEVER WANT TO TOUCH IT AGAIN.
CAN'T BLAME YOU, ARLO.
THIS IS EASILY THE SINGLE MOST REPULSIVE THING I'VE EVER SEEN--
--AND, TRUST ME, I'VE SEEN PLENTY.
ANY LUCK YET WITH THE PARENTS, DARCY?

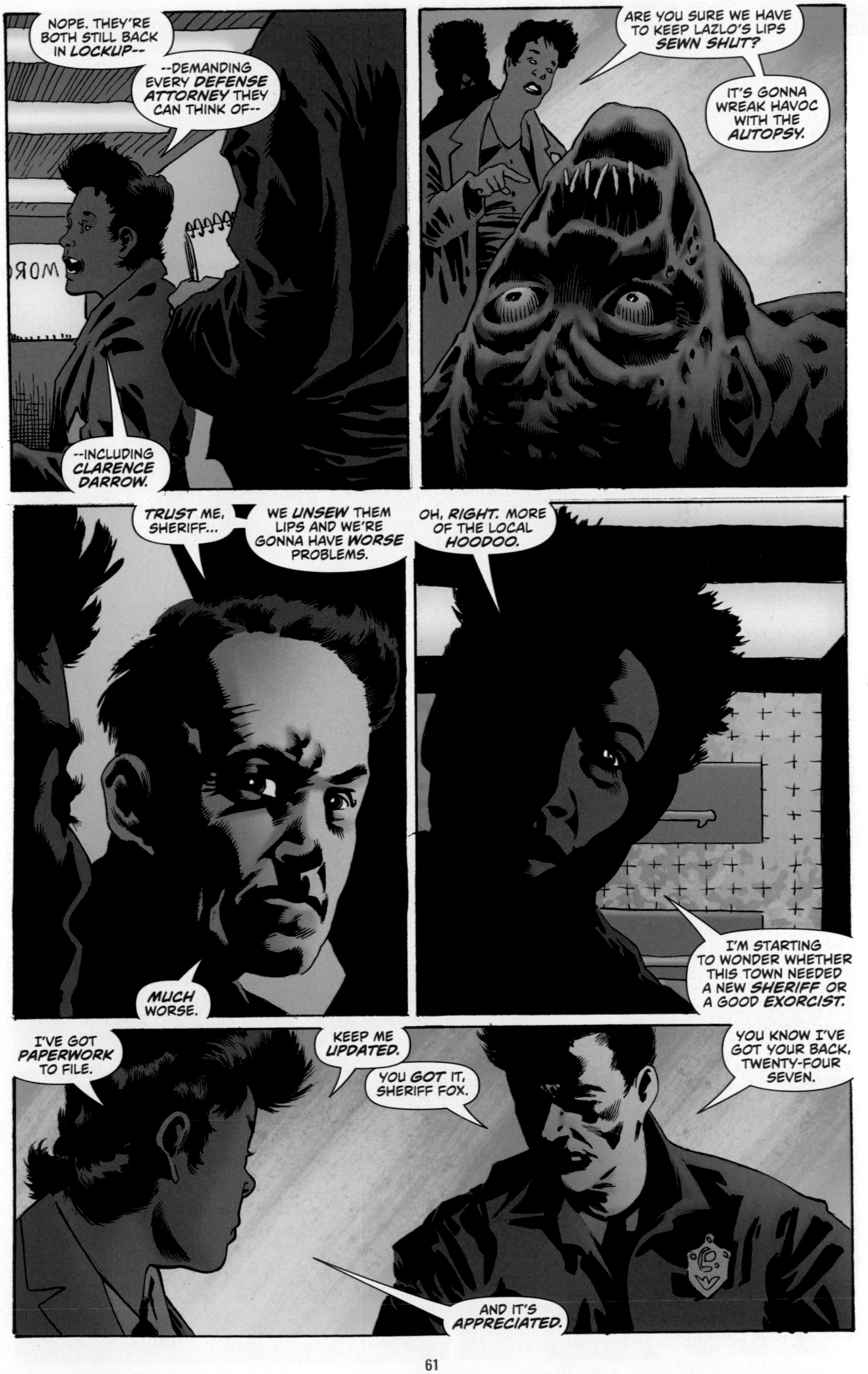
NOPE. THEY'RE BOTH STILL BACK IN LOCKUP--
--DEMANDING EVERY DEFENSE ATTORNEY THEY CAN THINK OF--
--INCLUDING CLARENCE DARROW.
ARE YOU SURE WE HAVE TO KEEP LAZLO'S LIPS SEWN SHUT?
IT'S GONNA WREAK HAVOC WITH THE AUTOPSY.
TRUST ME, SHERIFF...
WE UNSEW THEM LIPS AND WE'RE GONNA HAVE WORSE PROBLEMS.
MUCH WORSE.
OH, RIGHT. MORE OF THE LOCAL HOODOO.
I'M STARTING TO WONDER WHETHER THIS TOWN NEEDED A NEW SHERIFF OR A GOOD EXORCIST.
I'VE GOT PAPERWORK TO FILE.
KEEP ME UPDATED.
YOU GOT IT, SHERIFF FOX.
YOU KNOW I'VE GOT YOUR BACK, TWENTY-FOUR SEVEN.
AND IT'S APPRECIATED.

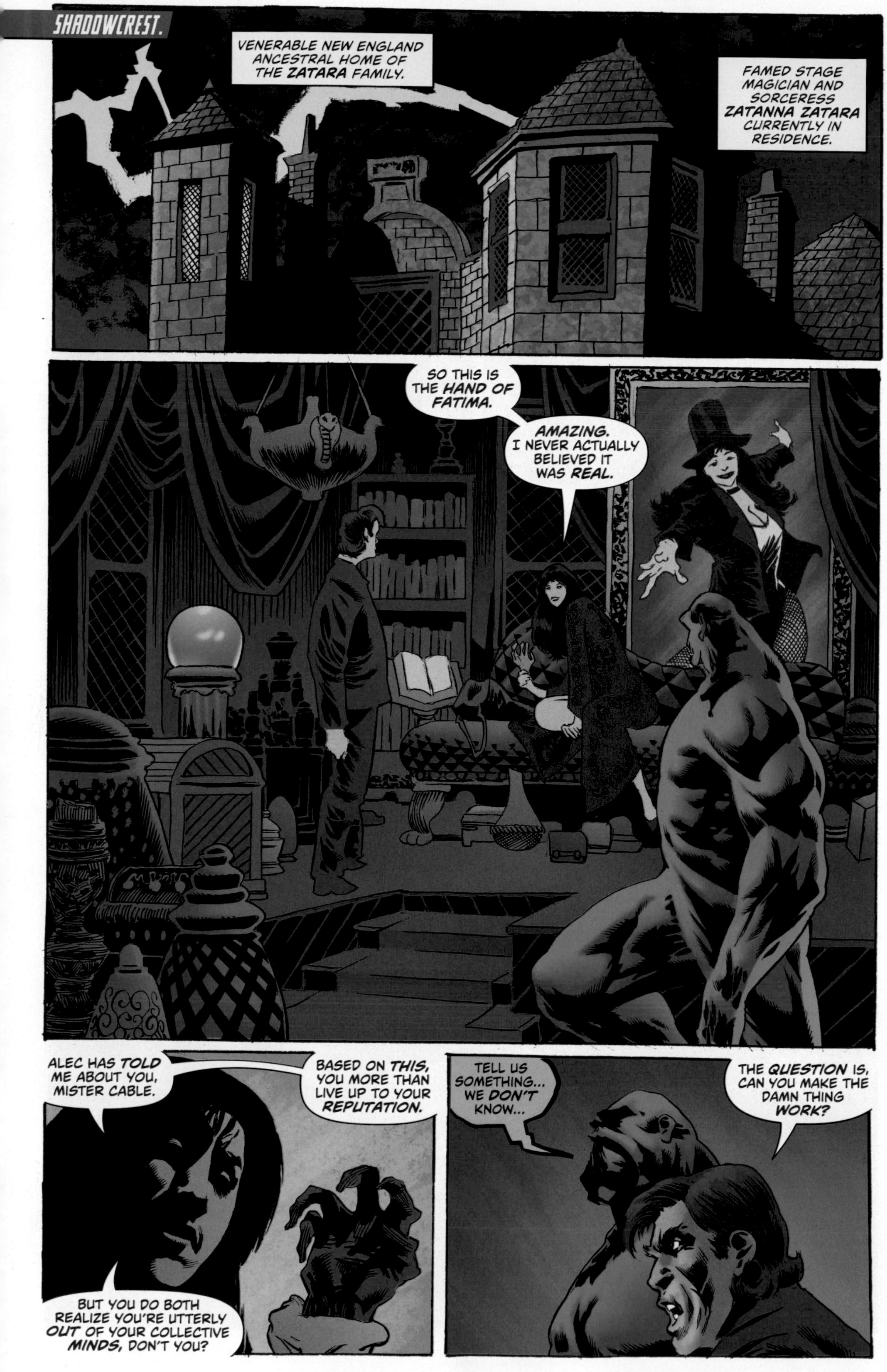
SHADOWCREST.
VENERABLE NEW ENGLAND ANCESTRAL HOME OF THE ZATARA FAMILY.
FAMED STAGE MAGICIAN AND SORCERESS ZATANNA ZATARA CURRENTLY IN RESIDENCE.
SO THIS IS THE HAND OF FATIMA.
AMAZING. I NEVER ACTUALLY BELIEVED IT WAS REAL.
ALEC HAS TOLD ME ABOUT YOU, MISTER CABLE.
BASED ON THIS, YOU MORE THAN LIVE UP TO YOUR REPUTATION.
BUT YOU DO BOTH REALIZE YOU'RE UTTERLY OUT OF YOUR COLLECTIVE MINDS, DON'T YOU?
TELL US SOMETHING... WE DON'T KNOW...
THE QUESTION IS, CAN YOU MAKE THE DAMN THING WORK?

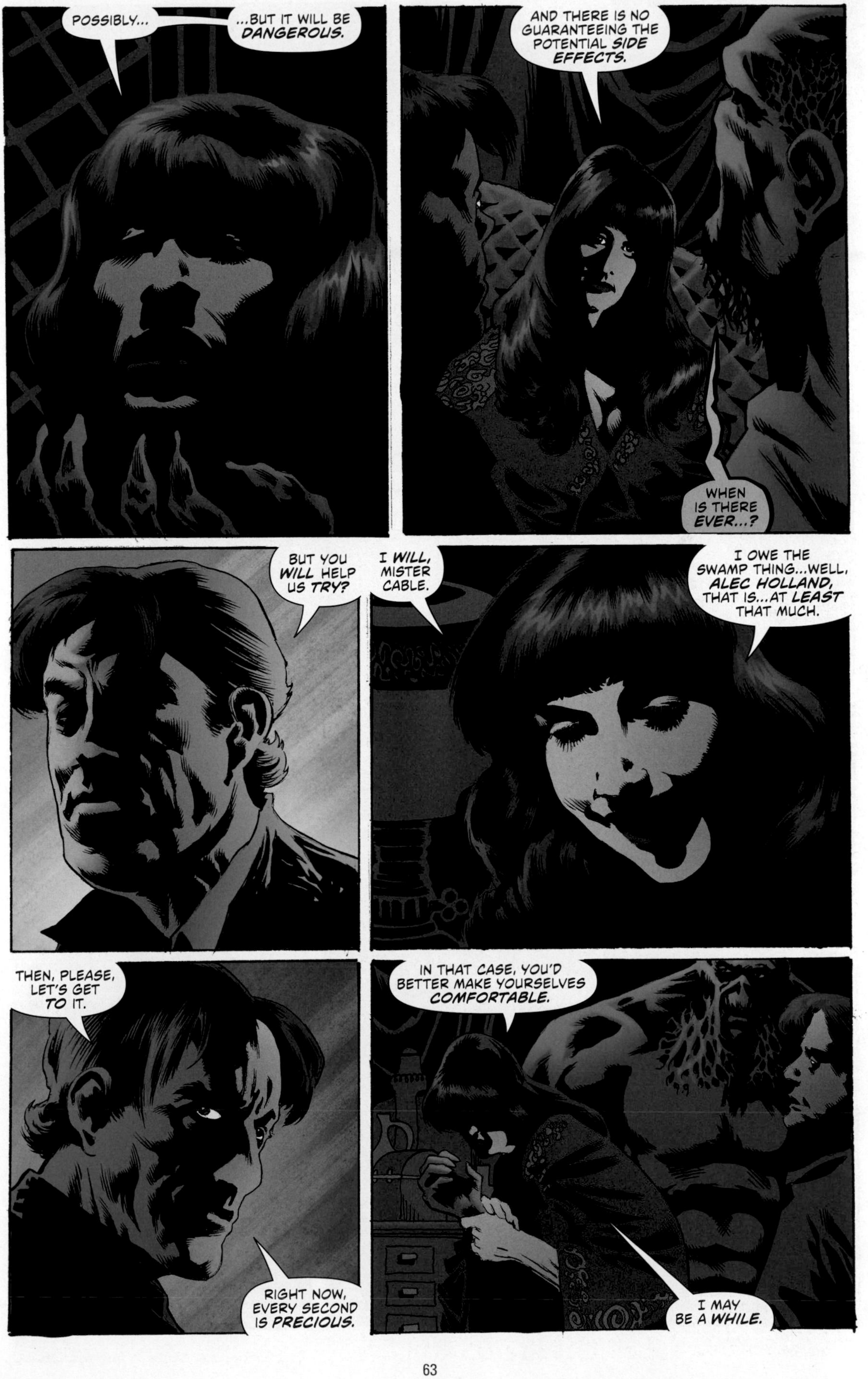
POSSIBLY...
...BUT IT WILL BE *DANGEROUS.*
AND THERE IS NO GUARANTEEING THE POTENTIAL *SIDE EFFECTS.*
WHEN IS THERE *EVER...?*
BUT YOU *WILL* HELP US *TRY?*
I *WILL,* MISTER CABLE.
I OWE THE SWAMP THING...WELL, *ALEC HOLLAND,* THAT IS...AT *LEAST* THAT MUCH.
THEN, PLEASE, LET'S GET *TO* IT.
RIGHT NOW, EVERY SECOND IS *PRECIOUS.*
IN THAT CASE, YOU'D BETTER MAKE YOURSELVES *COMFORTABLE.*
I MAY BE A *WHILE.*

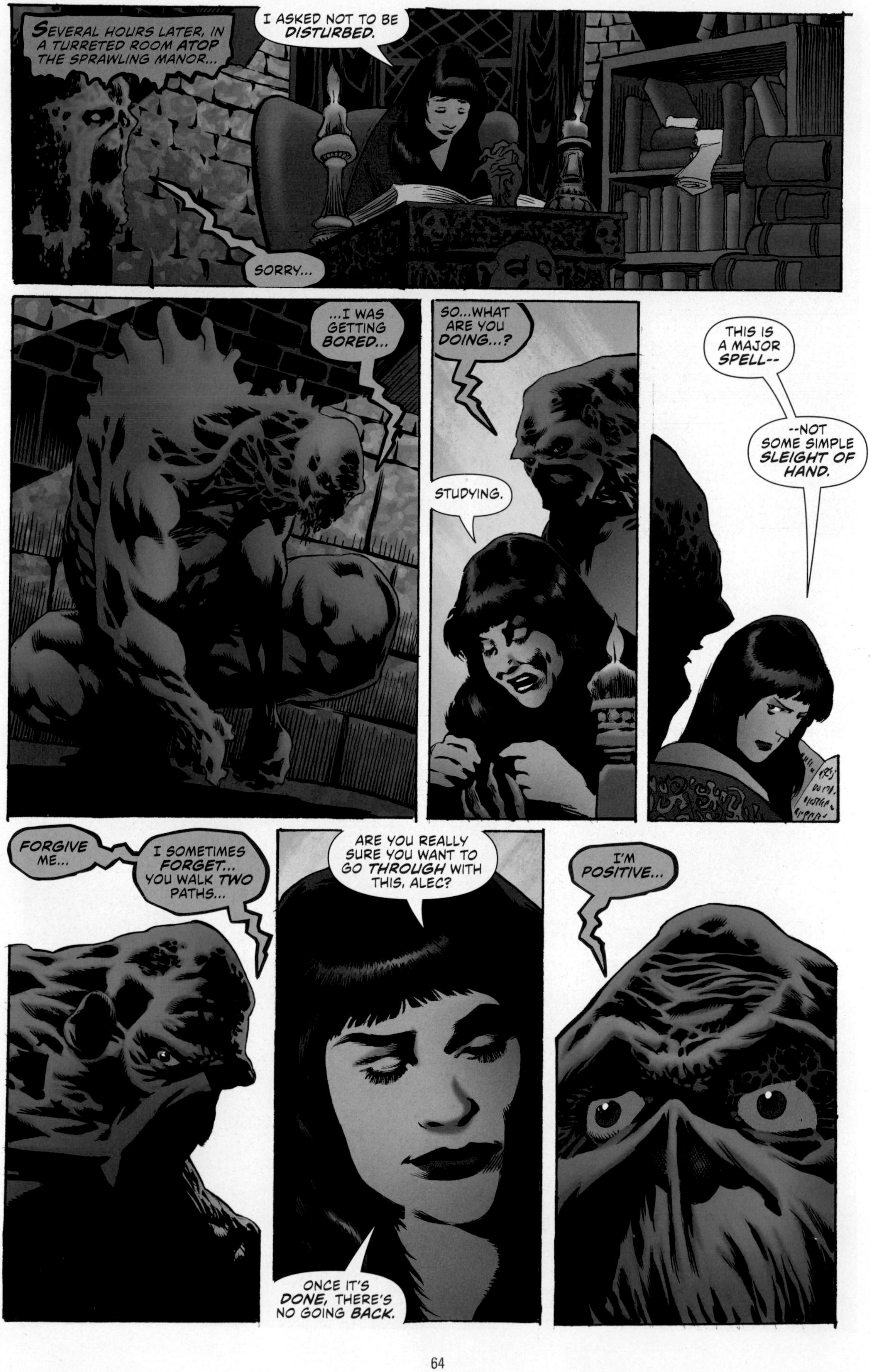
SEVERAL HOURS LATER, IN A TURRETED ROOM ATOP THE SPRAWLING MANOR...
I ASKED NOT TO BE DISTURBED.
SORRY...
...I WAS GETTING BORED...
SO...WHAT ARE YOU DOING...?
STUDYING.
THIS IS A MAJOR SPELL--
--NOT SOME SIMPLE SLEIGHT OF HAND.
FORGIVE ME...
I SOMETIMES FORGET... YOU WALK TWO PATHS...
ARE YOU REALLY SURE YOU WANT TO GO THROUGH WITH THIS, ALEC?
ONCE IT'S DONE, THERE'S NO GOING BACK.
I'M POSITIVE...

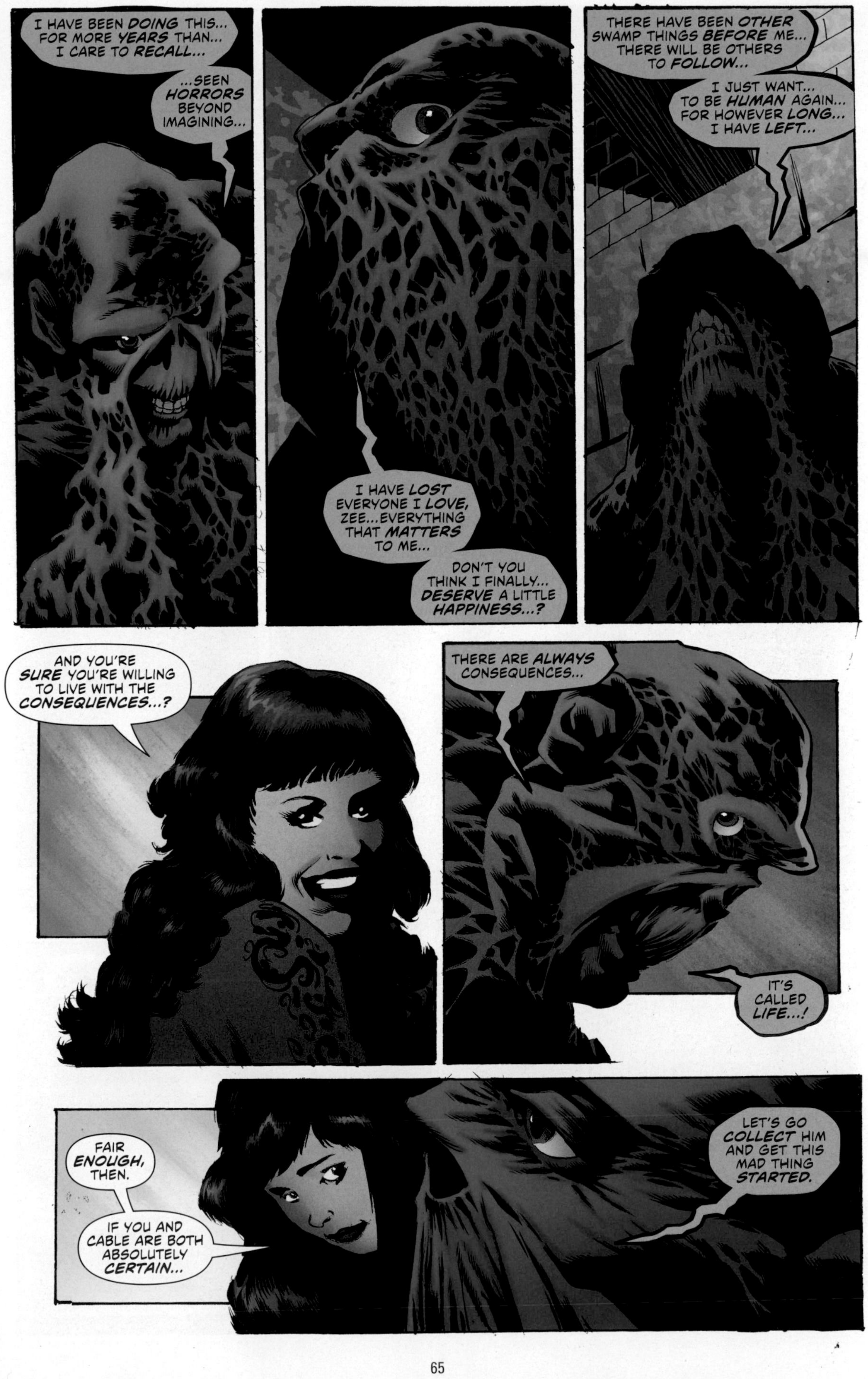

I HAVE BEEN DOING THIS... FOR MORE YEARS THAN... I CARE TO RECALL...
...SEEN HORRORS BEYOND IMAGINING...
I HAVE LOST EVERYONE I LOVE, ZEE...EVERYTHING THAT MATTERS TO ME...
DON'T YOU THINK I FINALLY... DESERVE A LITTLE HAPPINESS...?
THERE HAVE BEEN OTHER SWAMP THINGS BEFORE ME... THERE WILL BE OTHERS TO FOLLOW...
I JUST WANT... TO BE HUMAN AGAIN... FOR HOWEVER LONG... I HAVE LEFT...
AND YOU'RE SURE YOU'RE WILLING TO LIVE WITH THE CONSEQUENCES...?
THERE ARE ALWAYS CONSEQUENCES...
IT'S CALLED LIFE...!
FAIR ENOUGH, THEN.
IF YOU AND CABLE ARE BOTH ABSOLUTELY CERTAIN...
LET'S GO COLLECT HIM AND GET THIS MAD THING STARTED.

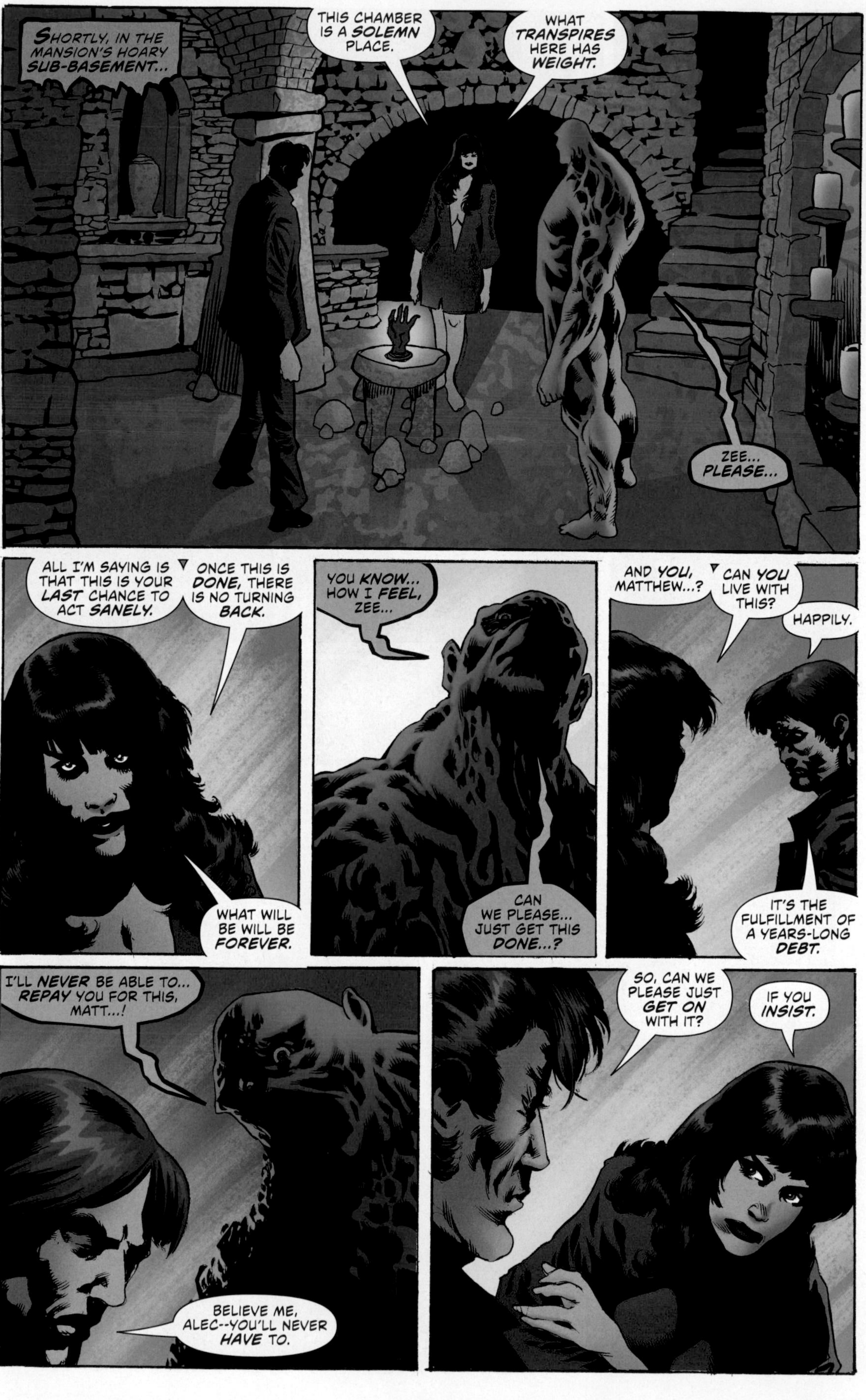
SHORTLY, IN THE MANSION'S HOARY SUB-BASEMENT...
THIS CHAMBER IS A SOLEMN PLACE.
WHAT TRANSPIRES HERE HAS WEIGHT.
ZEE... PLEASE...
ALL I'M SAYING IS THAT THIS IS YOUR LAST CHANCE TO ACT SANELY.
ONCE THIS IS DONE, THERE IS NO TURNING BACK.
WHAT WILL BE WILL BE FOREVER.
YOU KNOW... HOW I FEEL, ZEE...
CAN WE PLEASE... JUST GET THIS DONE...?
AND YOU, MATTHEW...?
CAN YOU LIVE WITH THIS?
HAPPILY.
IT'S THE FULFILLMENT OF A YEARS-LONG DEBT.
I'LL NEVER BE ABLE TO... REPAY YOU FOR THIS, MATT...!
BELIEVE ME, ALEC--YOU'LL NEVER HAVE TO.
SO, CAN WE PLEASE JUST GET ON WITH IT?
IF YOU INSIST.

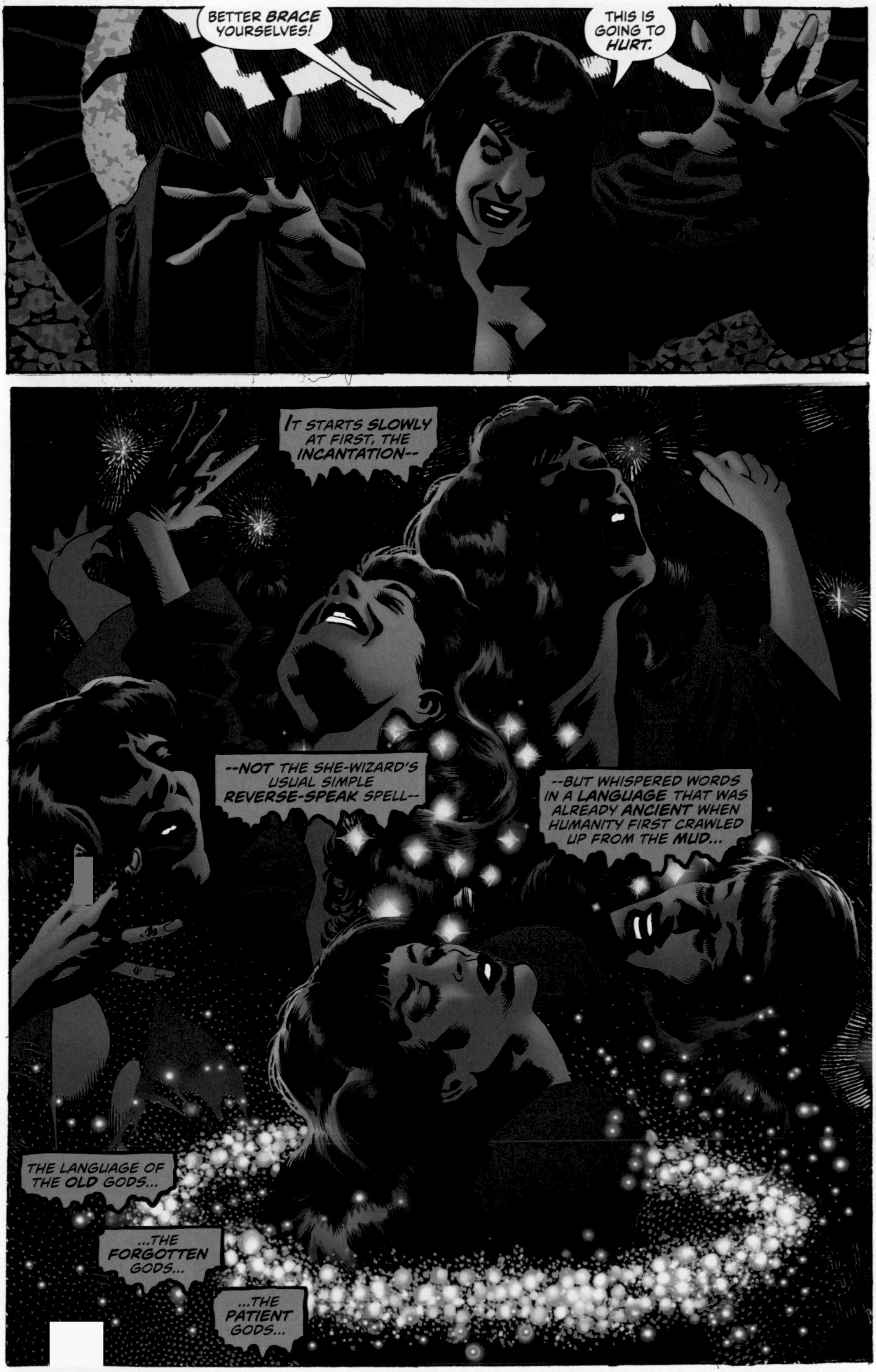
BETTER BRACE YOURSELVES!
THIS IS GOING TO HURT.
IT STARTS SLOWLY AT FIRST, THE INCANTATION--
--NOT THE SHE-WIZARD'S USUAL SIMPLE REVERSE-SPEAK SPELL--
--BUT WHISPERED WORDS IN A LANGUAGE THAT WAS ALREADY ANCIENT WHEN HUMANITY FIRST CRAWLED UP FROM THE MUD...
THE LANGUAGE OF THE OLD GODS...
...THE FORGOTTEN GODS...
...THE PATIENT GODS...

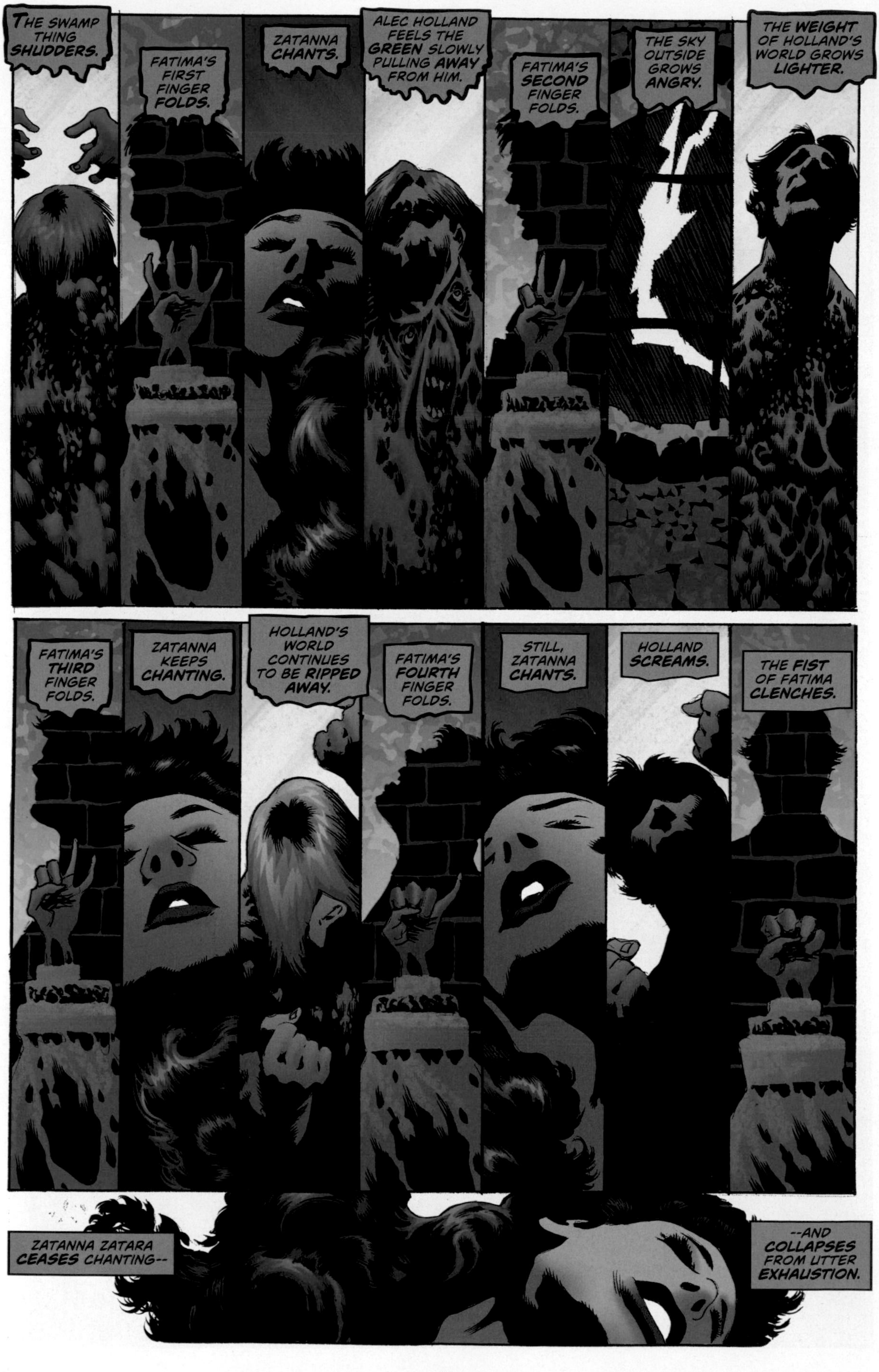
The swamp thing shudders.
Fatima's first finger folds.
Zatanna chants.
Alec Holland feels the green slowly pulling away from him.
Fatima's second finger folds.
The sky outside grows angry.
The weight of Holland's world grows lighter.
Fatima's third finger folds.
Zatanna keeps chanting.
Holland's world continues to be ripped away.
Fatima's fourth finger folds.
Still, Zatanna chants.
Holland screams.
The fist of Fatima clenches.
Zatanna Zatara ceases chanting--
--and collapses from utter exhaustion.

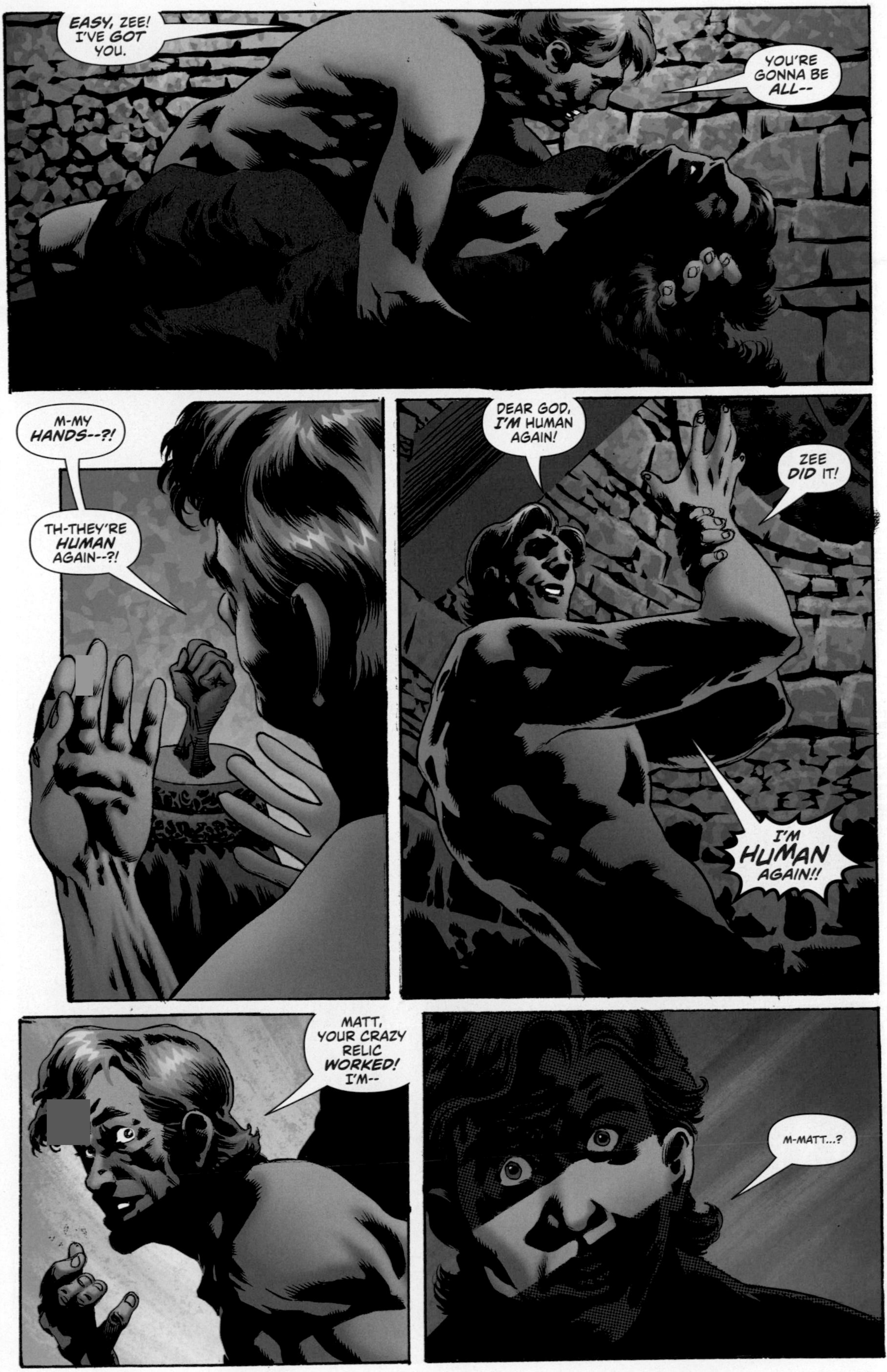
EASY, ZEE! I'VE GOT YOU.
YOU'RE GONNA BE ALL--
M-MY HANDS--?!
TH-THEY'RE HUMAN AGAIN--?!
DEAR GOD, I'M HUMAN AGAIN!
ZEE DID IT!
I'M HUMAN AGAIN!!
MATT, YOUR CRAZY RELIC WORKED! I'M--
M-MATT...?

WHY LOOK SO SURPRISED, ALEC?
WHAT DID YOU THINK WAS GOING TO HAPPEN?
NEXT ISSUE:
BE CAREFUL WHAT YOU WISH FOR!

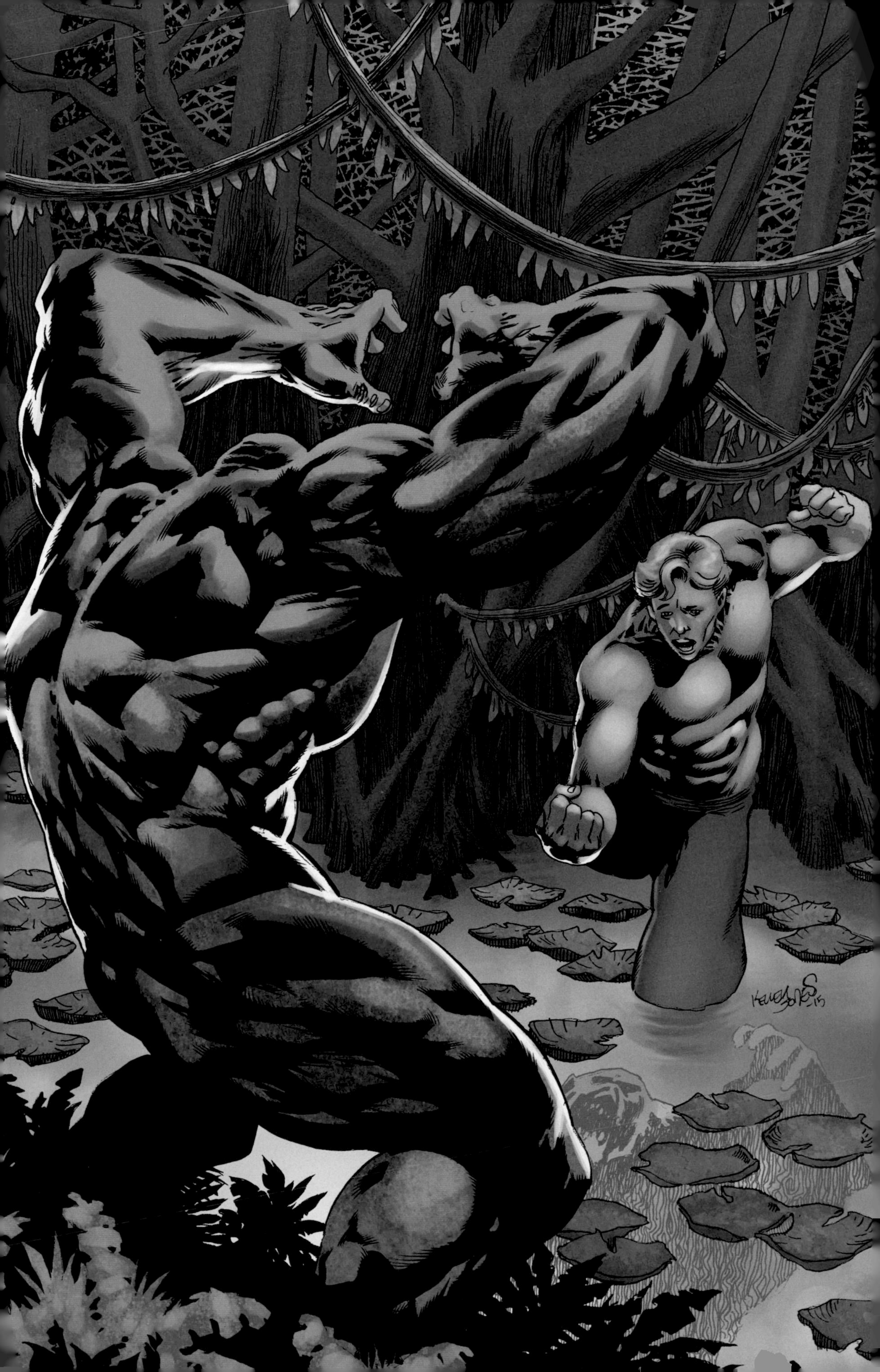

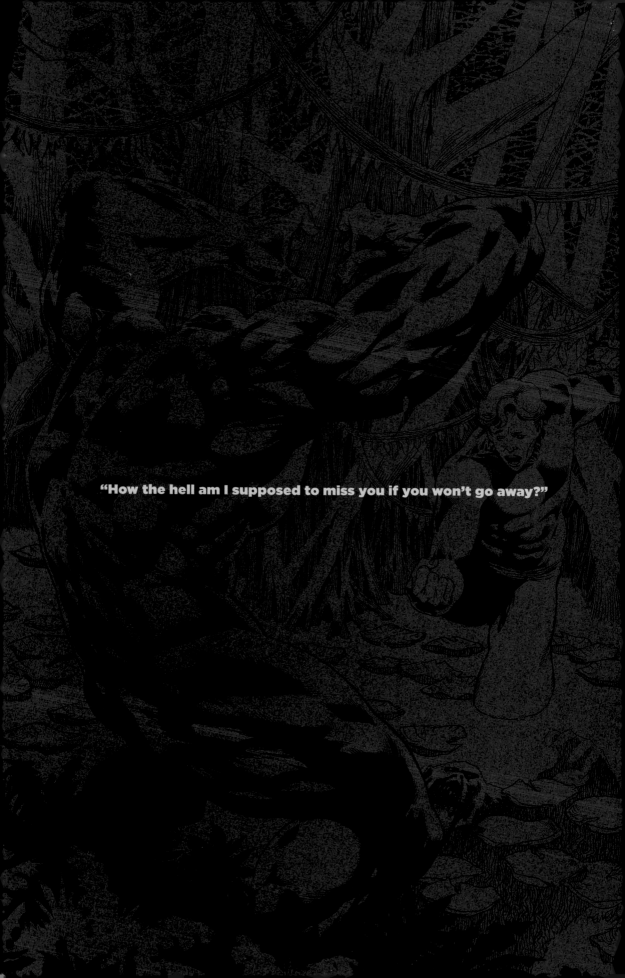

"How the hell am I supposed to miss you if you won't go away?"

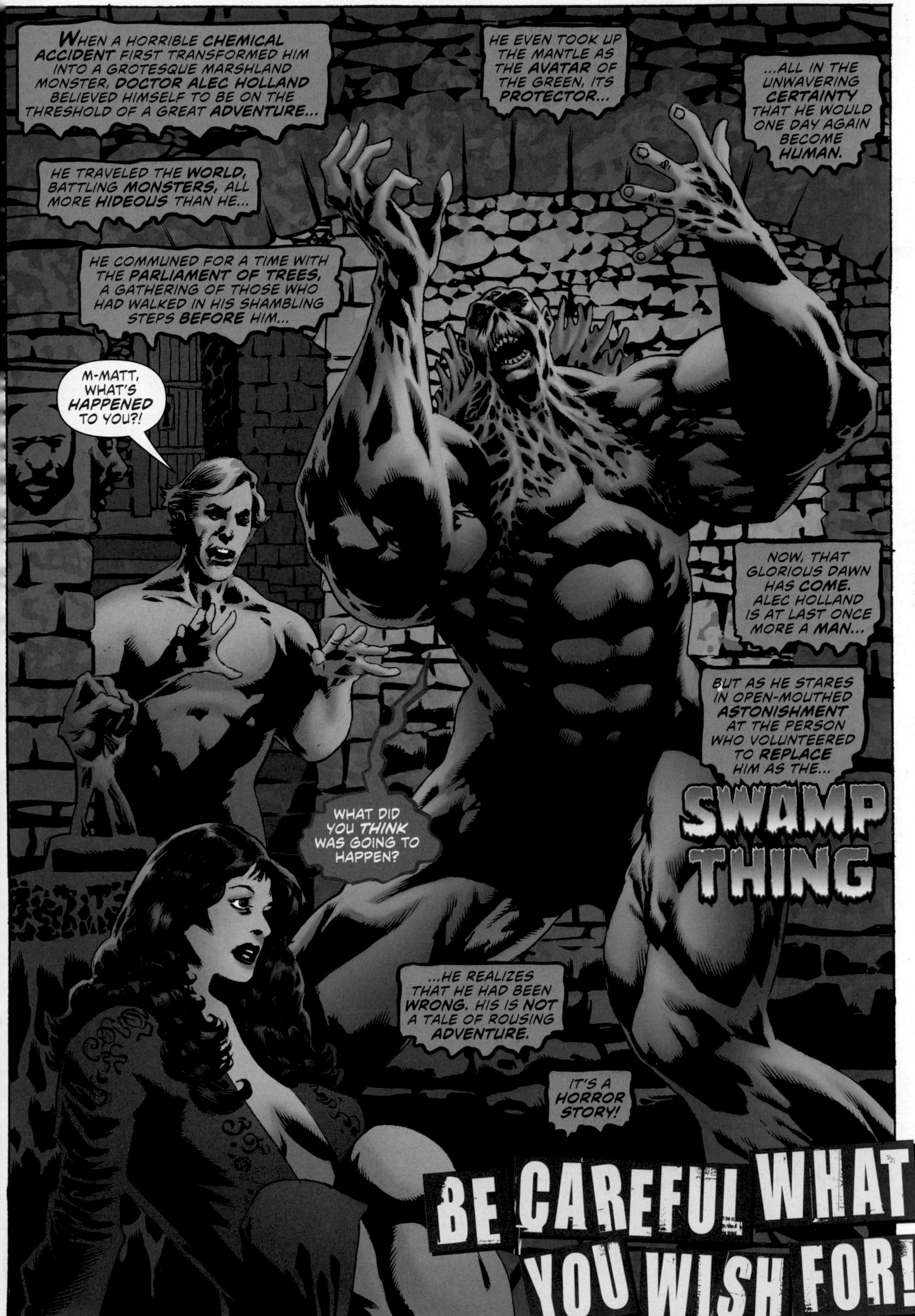
WHEN A HORRIBLE CHEMICAL ACCIDENT FIRST TRANSFORMED HIM INTO A GROTESQUE MARSHLAND MONSTER, DOCTOR ALEC HOLLAND BELIEVED HIMSELF TO BE ON THE THRESHOLD OF A GREAT ADVENTURE...
HE TRAVELED THE WORLD, BATTLING MONSTERS, ALL MORE HIDEOUS THAN HE...
HE COMMUNED FOR A TIME WITH THE PARLIAMENT OF TREES, A GATHERING OF THOSE WHO HAD WALKED IN HIS SHAMBLING STEPS BEFORE HIM...
HE EVEN TOOK UP THE MANTLE AS THE AVATAR OF THE GREEN, ITS PROTECTOR...
...ALL IN THE UNWAVERING CERTAINTY THAT HE WOULD ONE DAY AGAIN BECOME HUMAN.
M-MATT, WHAT'S HAPPENED TO YOU?!
NOW, THAT GLORIOUS DAWN HAS COME. ALEC HOLLAND IS AT LAST ONCE MORE A MAN...
BUT AS HE STARES IN OPEN-MOUTHED ASTONISHMENT AT THE PERSON WHO VOLUNTEERED TO REPLACE HIM AS THE...
SWAMP THING
WHAT DID YOU THINK WAS GOING TO HAPPEN?
...HE REALIZES THAT HE HAD BEEN WRONG. HIS IS NOT A TALE OF ROUSING ADVENTURE.
IT'S A HORROR STORY!
BE CAREFUL WHAT YOU WISH FOR!

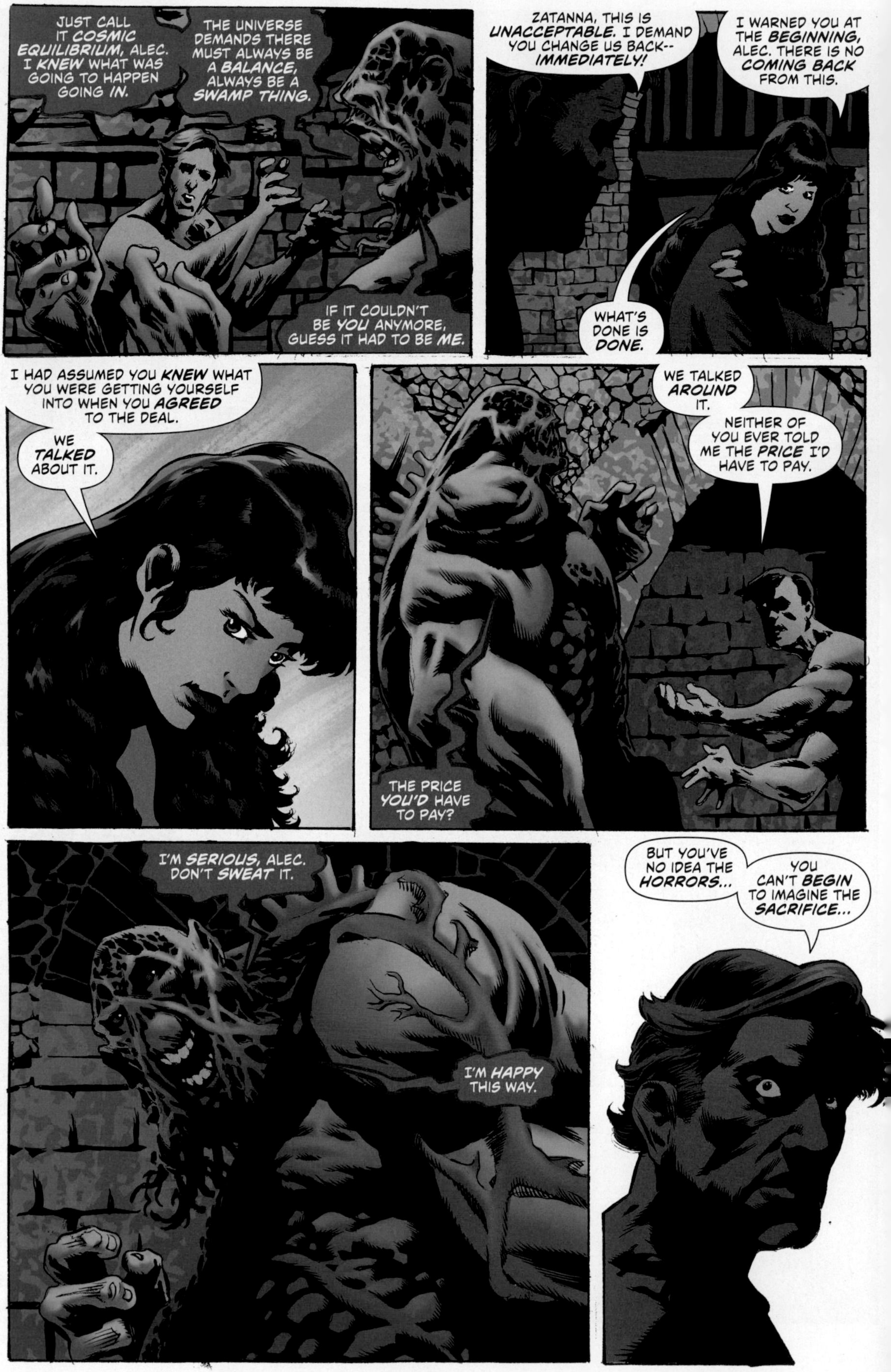
JUST CALL IT COSMIC EQUILIBRIUM, ALEC. I KNEW WHAT WAS GOING TO HAPPEN GOING IN.
THE UNIVERSE DEMANDS THERE MUST ALWAYS BE A BALANCE, ALWAYS BE A SWAMP THING.
IF IT COULDN'T BE YOU ANYMORE, GUESS IT HAD TO BE ME.
ZATANNA, THIS IS UNACCEPTABLE. I DEMAND YOU CHANGE US BACK-- IMMEDIATELY!
I WARNED YOU AT THE BEGINNING, ALEC. THERE IS NO COMING BACK FROM THIS.
WHAT'S DONE IS DONE.
I HAD ASSUMED YOU KNEW WHAT YOU WERE GETTING YOURSELF INTO WHEN YOU AGREED TO THE DEAL.
WE TALKED ABOUT IT.
WE TALKED AROUND IT.
NEITHER OF YOU EVER TOLD ME THE PRICE I'D HAVE TO PAY.
THE PRICE YOU'D HAVE TO PAY?
I'M SERIOUS, ALEC. DON'T SWEAT IT.
I'M HAPPY THIS WAY.
BUT YOU'VE NO IDEA THE HORRORS...
YOU CAN'T BEGIN TO IMAGINE THE SACRIFICE...

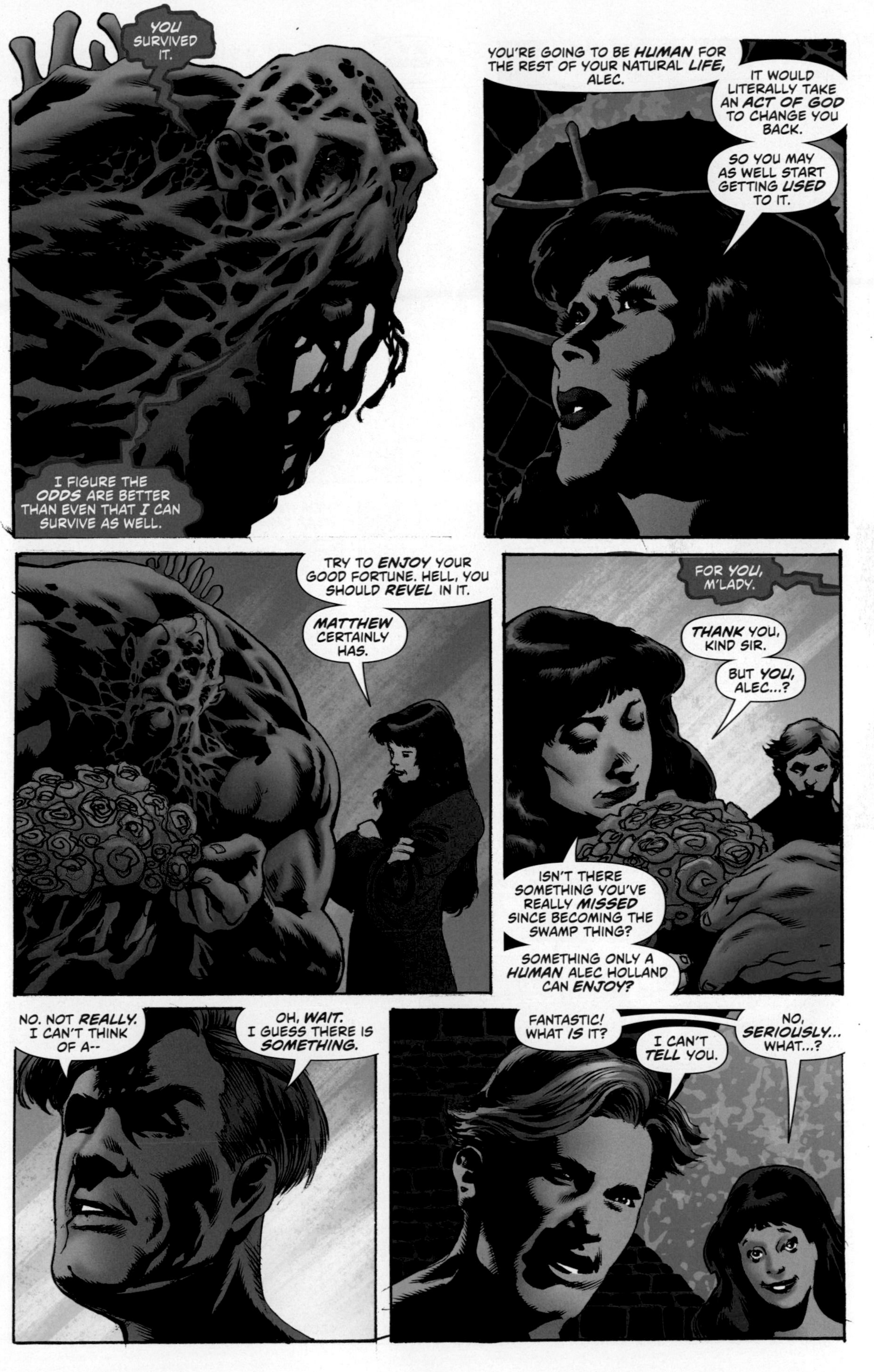
YOU SURVIVED IT.
I FIGURE THE ODDS ARE BETTER THAN EVEN THAT I CAN SURVIVE AS WELL.
YOU'RE GOING TO BE HUMAN FOR THE REST OF YOUR NATURAL LIFE, ALEC.
IT WOULD LITERALLY TAKE AN ACT OF GOD TO CHANGE YOU BACK.
SO YOU MAY AS WELL START GETTING USED TO IT.
TRY TO ENJOY YOUR GOOD FORTUNE. HELL, YOU SHOULD REVEL IN IT.
MATTHEW CERTAINLY HAS.
FOR YOU, M'LADY.
THANK YOU, KIND SIR.
BUT YOU, ALEC...?
ISN'T THERE SOMETHING YOU'VE REALLY MISSED SINCE BECOMING THE SWAMP THING?
SOMETHING ONLY A HUMAN ALEC HOLLAND CAN ENJOY?
NO. NOT REALLY. I CAN'T THINK OF A--
OH, WAIT. I GUESS THERE IS SOMETHING.
FANTASTIC! WHAT IS IT?
I CAN'T TELL YOU.
NO, SERIOUSLY... WHAT...?

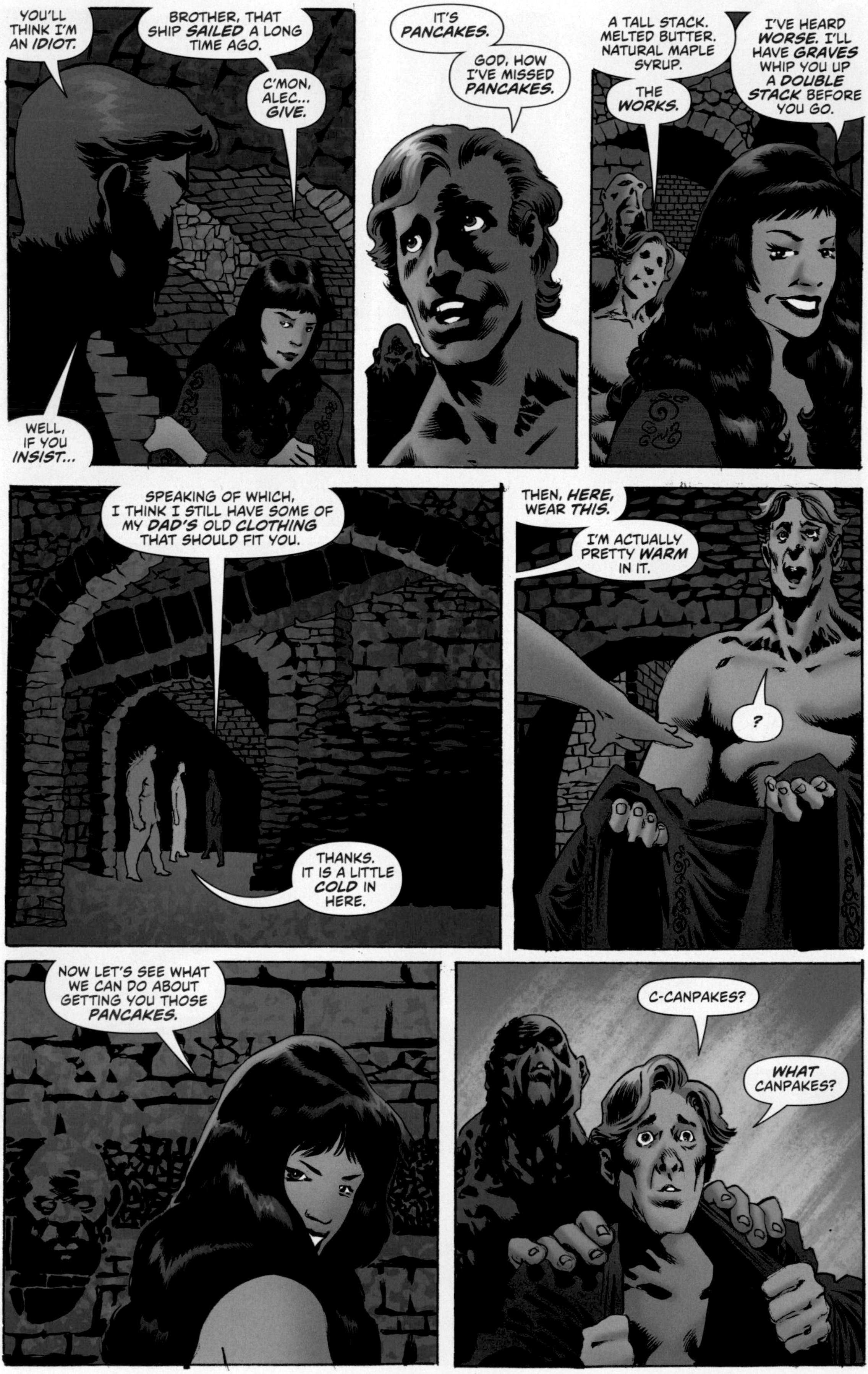

YOU'LL THINK I'M AN IDIOT.
BROTHER, THAT SHIP SAILED A LONG TIME AGO.
C'MON, ALEC... GIVE.
WELL, IF YOU INSIST...
IT'S PANCAKES.
GOD, HOW I'VE MISSED PANCAKES.
A TALL STACK. MELTED BUTTER. NATURAL MAPLE SYRUP.
THE WORKS.
I'VE HEARD WORSE. I'LL HAVE GRAVES WHIP YOU UP A DOUBLE STACK BEFORE YOU GO.
SPEAKING OF WHICH, I THINK I STILL HAVE SOME OF MY DAD'S OLD CLOTHING THAT SHOULD FIT YOU.
THANKS. IT IS A LITTLE COLD IN HERE.
THEN, HERE, WEAR THIS.
I'M ACTUALLY PRETTY WARM IN IT.
?
NOW LET'S SEE WHAT WE CAN DO ABOUT GETTING YOU THOSE PANCAKES.
C-CANPAKES?
WHAT CANPAKES?

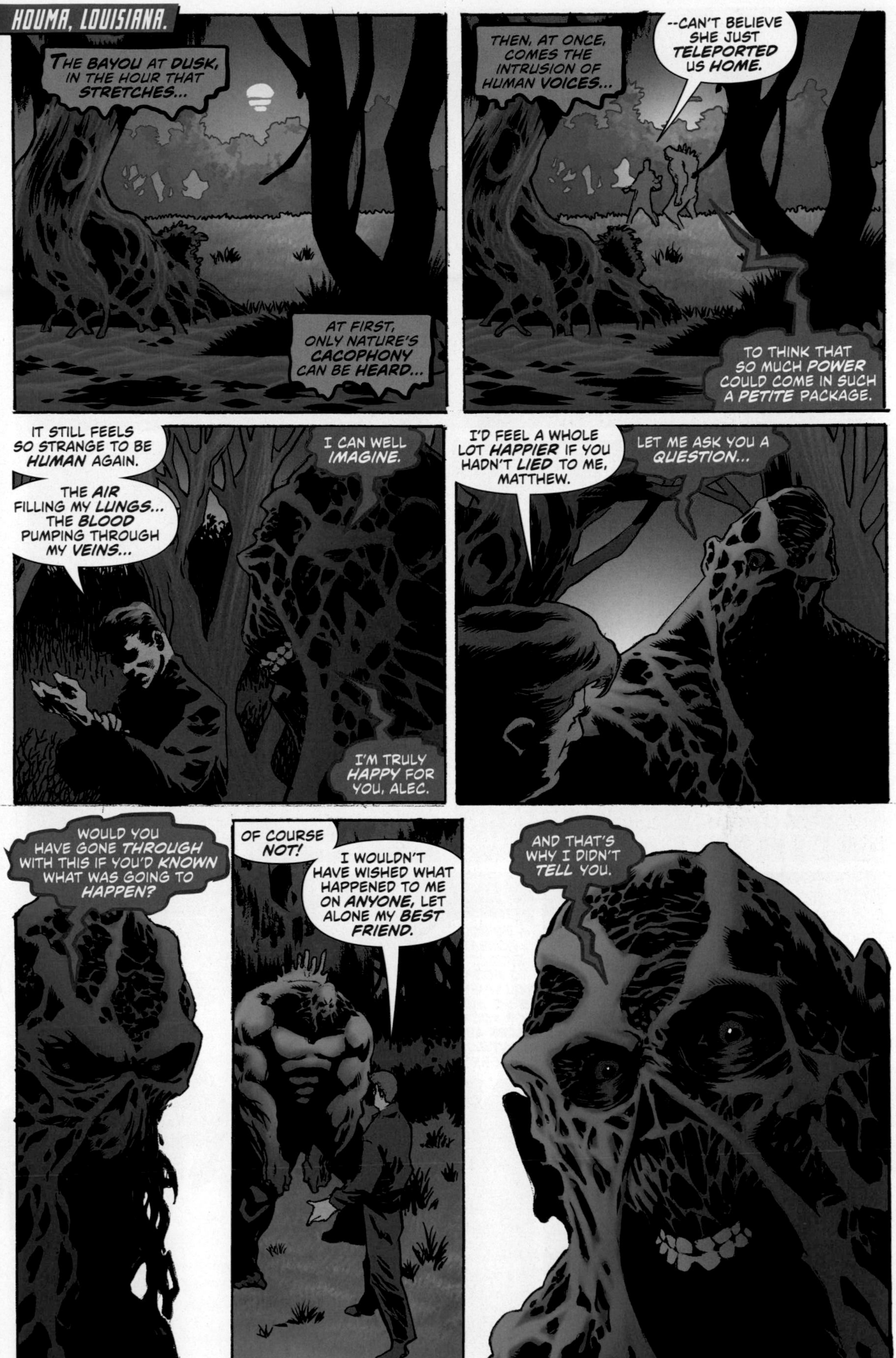
HOUMA, LOUISIANA.
THE BAYOU AT DUSK, IN THE HOUR THAT STRETCHES...
AT FIRST, ONLY NATURE'S CACOPHONY CAN BE HEARD...
THEN, AT ONCE, COMES THE INTRUSION OF HUMAN VOICES...
--CAN'T BELIEVE SHE JUST TELEPORTED US HOME.
TO THINK THAT SO MUCH POWER COULD COME IN SUCH A PETITE PACKAGE.
IT STILL FEELS SO STRANGE TO BE HUMAN AGAIN.
THE AIR FILLING MY LUNGS... THE BLOOD PUMPING THROUGH MY VEINS...
I CAN WELL IMAGINE.
I'M TRULY HAPPY FOR YOU, ALEC.
I'D FEEL A WHOLE LOT HAPPIER IF YOU HADN'T LIED TO ME, MATTHEW.
LET ME ASK YOU A QUESTION...
WOULD YOU HAVE GONE THROUGH WITH THIS IF YOU'D KNOWN WHAT WAS GOING TO HAPPEN?
OF COURSE NOT!
I WOULDN'T HAVE WISHED WHAT HAPPENED TO ME ON ANYONE, LET ALONE MY BEST FRIEND.
AND THAT'S WHY I DIDN'T TELL YOU.

LOOK, PAL, I'M AT *PEACE* WITH MY DECISION. I REALLY *AM.*

I DID WHAT I DID OUT OF *LOVE* AND *SACRIFICE*, AND I WOULD DO IT *AGAIN.*

BESIDES, THERE'S NOTHING YOU CAN *DO* ABOUT IT NOW, ANYWAY.

LOOK, I LEFT MY *JEEP* NEAR HERE. THE *KEYS* SHOULD BE UNDER THE *VISOR.*

YOU CAN USE IT TO GO WHEREVER YOU *WANT.*

HELL, YOU CAN GO SEARCH FOR *ABBY* IF YOU'D LIKE.

YOU'RE *KIDDING*, RIGHT?

THERE'S NO WAY IN HELL I'M LEAVING YOU *HIGH* AND *DRY* LIKE THIS.

BUT...

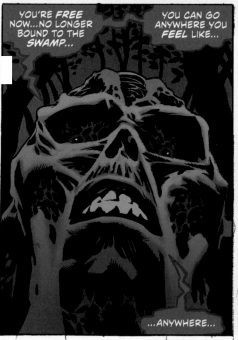

YOU'RE *FREE* NOW...NO LONGER BOUND TO THE *SWAMP...*

YOU CAN GO ANYWHERE YOU *FEEL* LIKE...

...ANYWHERE...

DO YOU HONESTLY EXPECT ME TO *ABANDON* YOU WHEN THERE IS *SO MUCH* FOR YOU TO LEARN ABOUT *CONTROLLING* THE *GREEN*--

--AND I'M THE *ONLY* ONE WHO CAN *TEACH* YOU?

ALL RIGHT. *FINE.*

IF YOU WON'T *LEAVE*, WE MIGHT AS WELL *GET ON* WITH IT.

TRUST ME, PAL-- YOU WON'T *REGRET* IT.

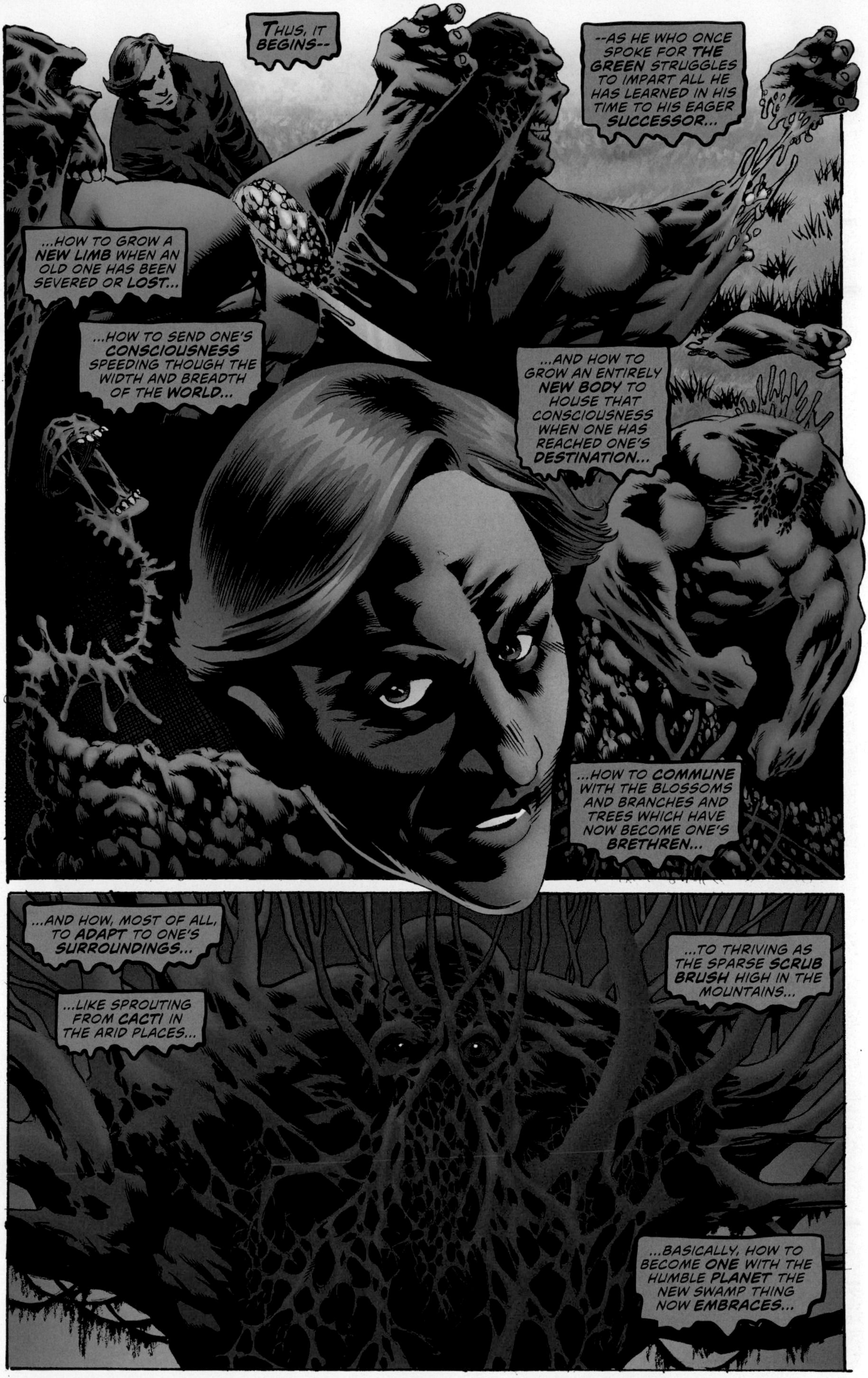
THUS, IT BEGINS--
--AS HE WHO ONCE SPOKE FOR THE GREEN STRUGGLES TO IMPART ALL HE HAS LEARNED IN HIS TIME TO HIS EAGER SUCCESSOR...
...HOW TO GROW A NEW LIMB WHEN AN OLD ONE HAS BEEN SEVERED OR LOST...
...HOW TO SEND ONE'S CONSCIOUSNESS SPEEDING THOUGH THE WIDTH AND BREADTH OF THE WORLD...
...AND HOW TO GROW AN ENTIRELY NEW BODY TO HOUSE THAT CONSCIOUSNESS WHEN ONE HAS REACHED ONE'S DESTINATION...
...HOW TO COMMUNE WITH THE BLOSSOMS AND BRANCHES AND TREES WHICH HAVE NOW BECOME ONE'S BRETHREN...
...AND HOW, MOST OF ALL, TO ADAPT TO ONE'S SURROUNDINGS...
...LIKE SPROUTING FROM CACTI IN THE ARID PLACES...
...TO THRIVING AS THE SPARSE SCRUB BRUSH HIGH IN THE MOUNTAINS...
...BASICALLY, HOW TO BECOME ONE WITH THE HUMBLE PLANET THE NEW SWAMP THING NOW EMBRACES...

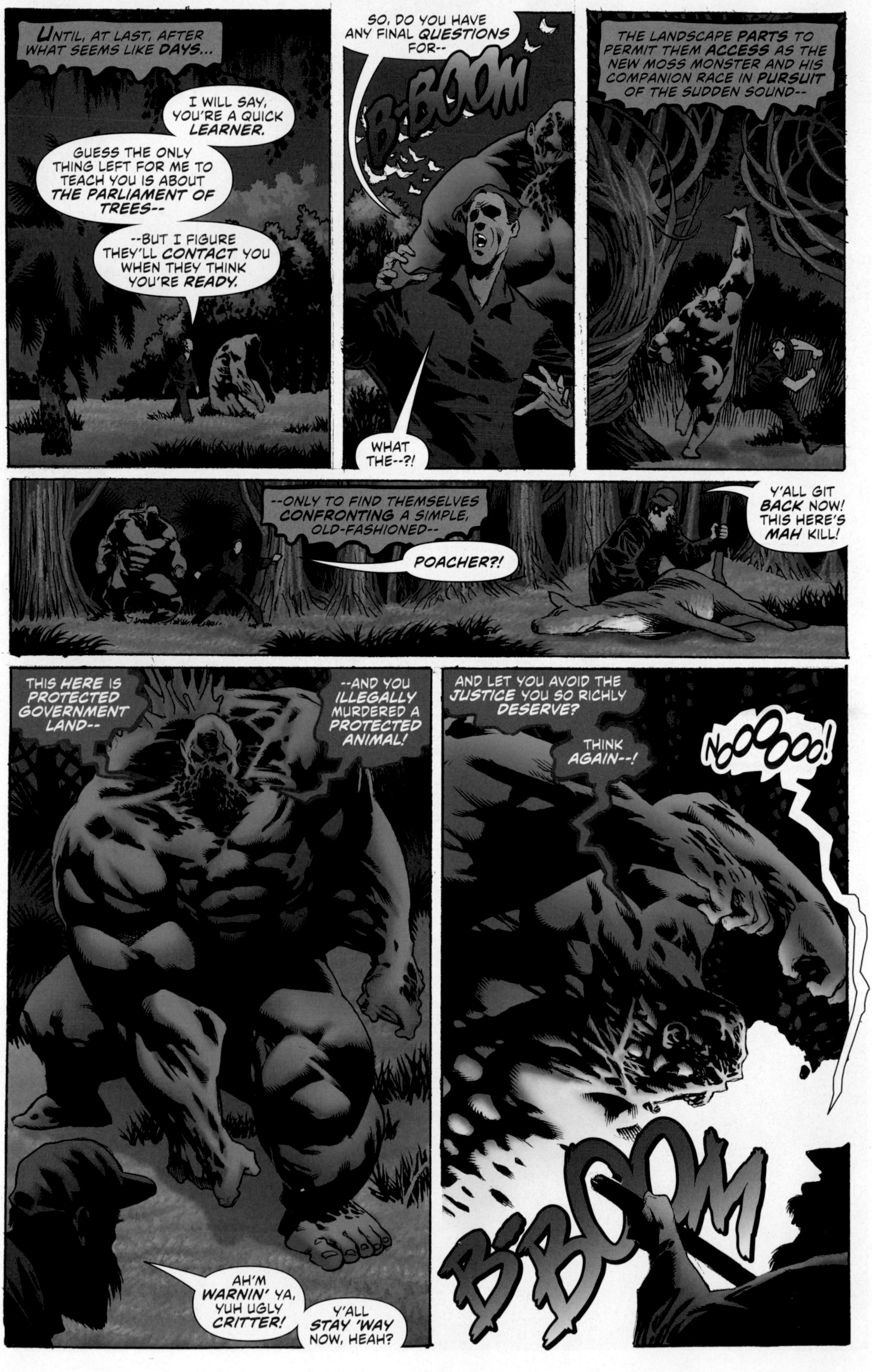
UNTIL, AT LAST, AFTER WHAT SEEMS LIKE DAYS...
I WILL SAY, YOU'RE A QUICK LEARNER.
GUESS THE ONLY THING LEFT FOR ME TO TEACH YOU IS ABOUT THE PARLIAMENT OF TREES--
--BUT I FIGURE THEY'LL CONTACT YOU WHEN THEY THINK YOU'RE READY.
SO, DO YOU HAVE ANY FINAL QUESTIONS FOR--
B-BOOM
WHAT THE--?!
THE LANDSCAPE PARTS TO PERMIT THEM ACCESS AS THE NEW MOSS MONSTER AND HIS COMPANION RACE IN PURSUIT OF THE SUDDEN SOUND--
--ONLY TO FIND THEMSELVES CONFRONTING A SIMPLE, OLD-FASHIONED--
POACHER?!
Y'ALL GIT BACK NOW! THIS HERE'S MAH KILL!
THIS HERE IS PROTECTED GOVERNMENT LAND--
--AND YOU ILLEGALLY MURDERED A PROTECTED ANIMAL!
AH'M WARNIN' YA, YUH UGLY CRITTER!
Y'ALL STAY 'WAY NOW, HEAH?
AND LET YOU AVOID THE JUSTICE YOU SO RICHLY DESERVE?
THINK AGAIN--!
NOOOOOO!
B-BOOM

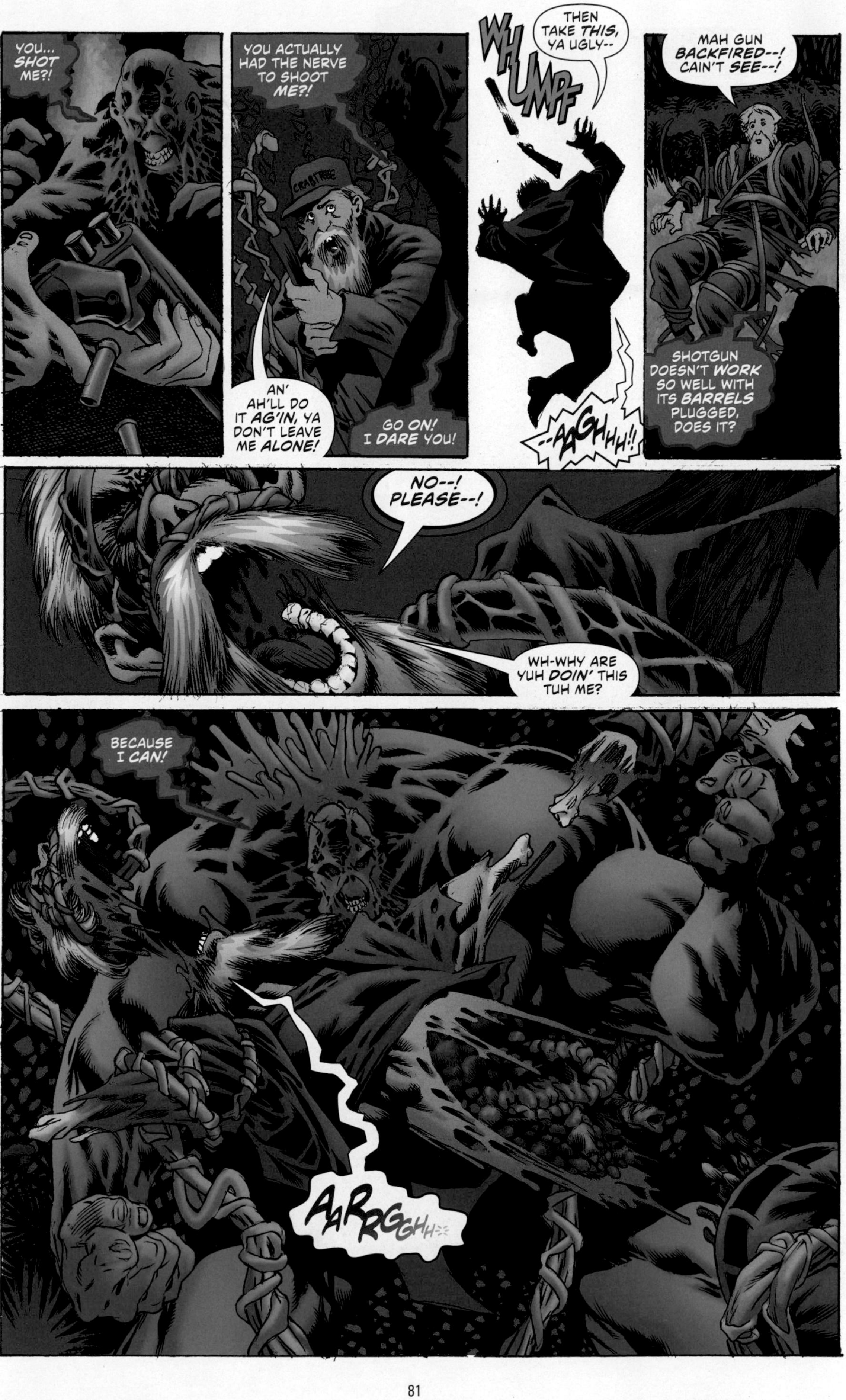
YOU... SHOT ME?!
YOU ACTUALLY HAD THE NERVE TO SHOOT ME?!
CRABTREE
AN' AH'LL DO IT AG'IN, YA DON'T LEAVE ME ALONE!
GO ON! I DARE YOU!
THEN TAKE THIS, YA UGLY--
WHUMPF
--AAGHHH!!
MAH GUN BACKFIRED--! CAIN'T SEE--!
SHOTGUN DOESN'T WORK SO WELL WITH ITS BARRELS PLUGGED, DOES IT?
NO--! PLEASE--!
WH-WHY ARE YUH DOIN' THIS TUH ME?
BECAUSE I CAN!
AARRGGHH

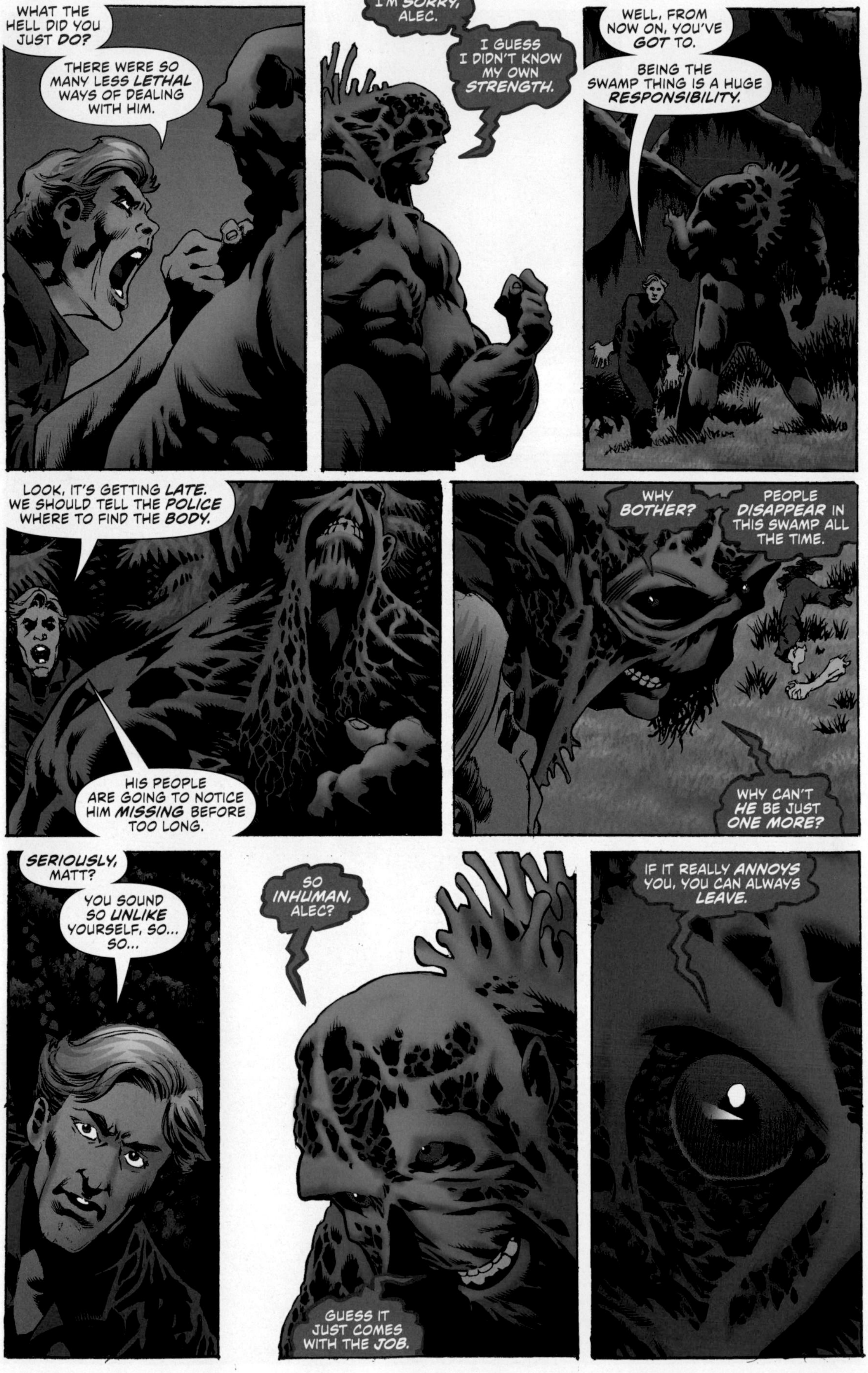
WHAT THE HELL DID YOU JUST DO?
THERE WERE SO MANY LESS LETHAL WAYS OF DEALING WITH HIM.
I... I'M SORRY, ALEC.
I GUESS I DIDN'T KNOW MY OWN STRENGTH.
WELL, FROM NOW ON, YOU'VE GOT TO.
BEING THE SWAMP THING IS A HUGE RESPONSIBILITY.
LOOK, IT'S GETTING LATE. WE SHOULD TELL THE POLICE WHERE TO FIND THE BODY.
HIS PEOPLE ARE GOING TO NOTICE HIM MISSING BEFORE TOO LONG.
WHY BOTHER?
PEOPLE DISAPPEAR IN THIS SWAMP ALL THE TIME.
WHY CAN'T HE BE JUST ONE MORE?
SERIOUSLY, MATT?
YOU SOUND SO UNLIKE YOURSELF, SO... SO...
SO INHUMAN, ALEC?
GUESS IT JUST COMES WITH THE JOB.
IF IT REALLY ANNOYS YOU, YOU CAN ALWAYS LEAVE.

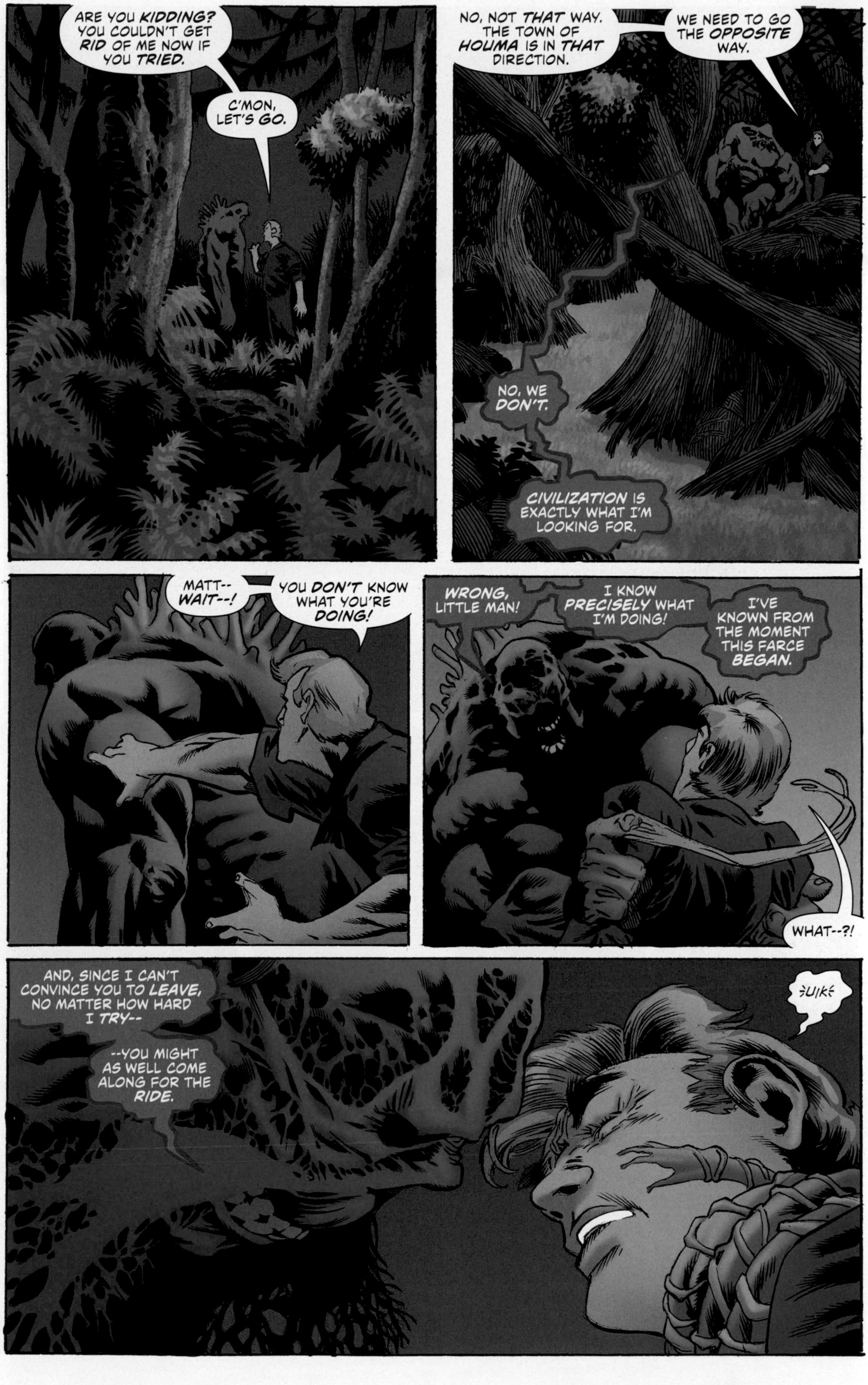
ARE YOU KIDDING? YOU COULDN'T GET RID OF ME NOW IF YOU TRIED.
C'MON, LET'S GO.
NO, NOT THAT WAY. THE TOWN OF HOUMA IS IN THAT DIRECTION.
WE NEED TO GO THE OPPOSITE WAY.
NO, WE DON'T.
CIVILIZATION IS EXACTLY WHAT I'M LOOKING FOR.
MATT-- WAIT--!
YOU DON'T KNOW WHAT YOU'RE DOING!
WRONG, LITTLE MAN!
I KNOW PRECISELY WHAT I'M DOING!
I'VE KNOWN FROM THE MOMENT THIS FARCE BEGAN.
WHAT--?!
AND, SINCE I CAN'T CONVINCE YOU TO LEAVE, NO MATTER HOW HARD I TRY--
--YOU MIGHT AS WELL COME ALONG FOR THE RIDE.
UIK

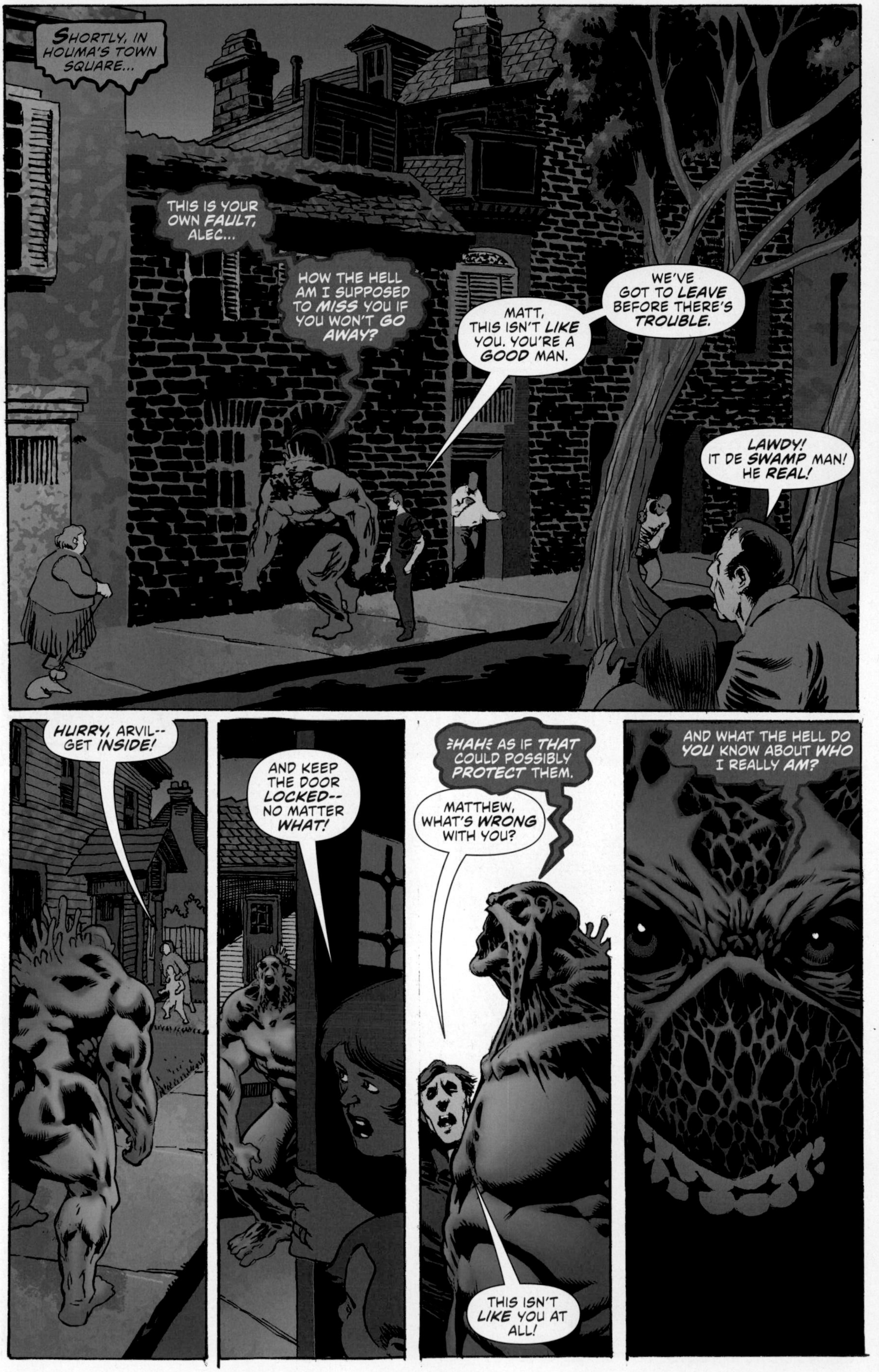
SHORTLY, IN HOUMA'S TOWN SQUARE...
THIS IS YOUR OWN FAULT, ALEC...
HOW THE HELL AM I SUPPOSED TO MISS YOU IF YOU WON'T GO AWAY?
MATT, THIS ISN'T LIKE YOU. YOU'RE A GOOD MAN.
WE'VE GOT TO LEAVE BEFORE THERE'S TROUBLE.
LAWDY! IT DE SWAMP MAN! HE REAL!
HURRY, ARVIL-- GET INSIDE!
AND KEEP THE DOOR LOCKED-- NO MATTER WHAT!
HAH AS IF THAT COULD POSSIBLY PROTECT THEM.
MATTHEW, WHAT'S WRONG WITH YOU?
THIS ISN'T LIKE YOU AT ALL!
AND WHAT THE HELL DO YOU KNOW ABOUT WHO I REALLY AM?

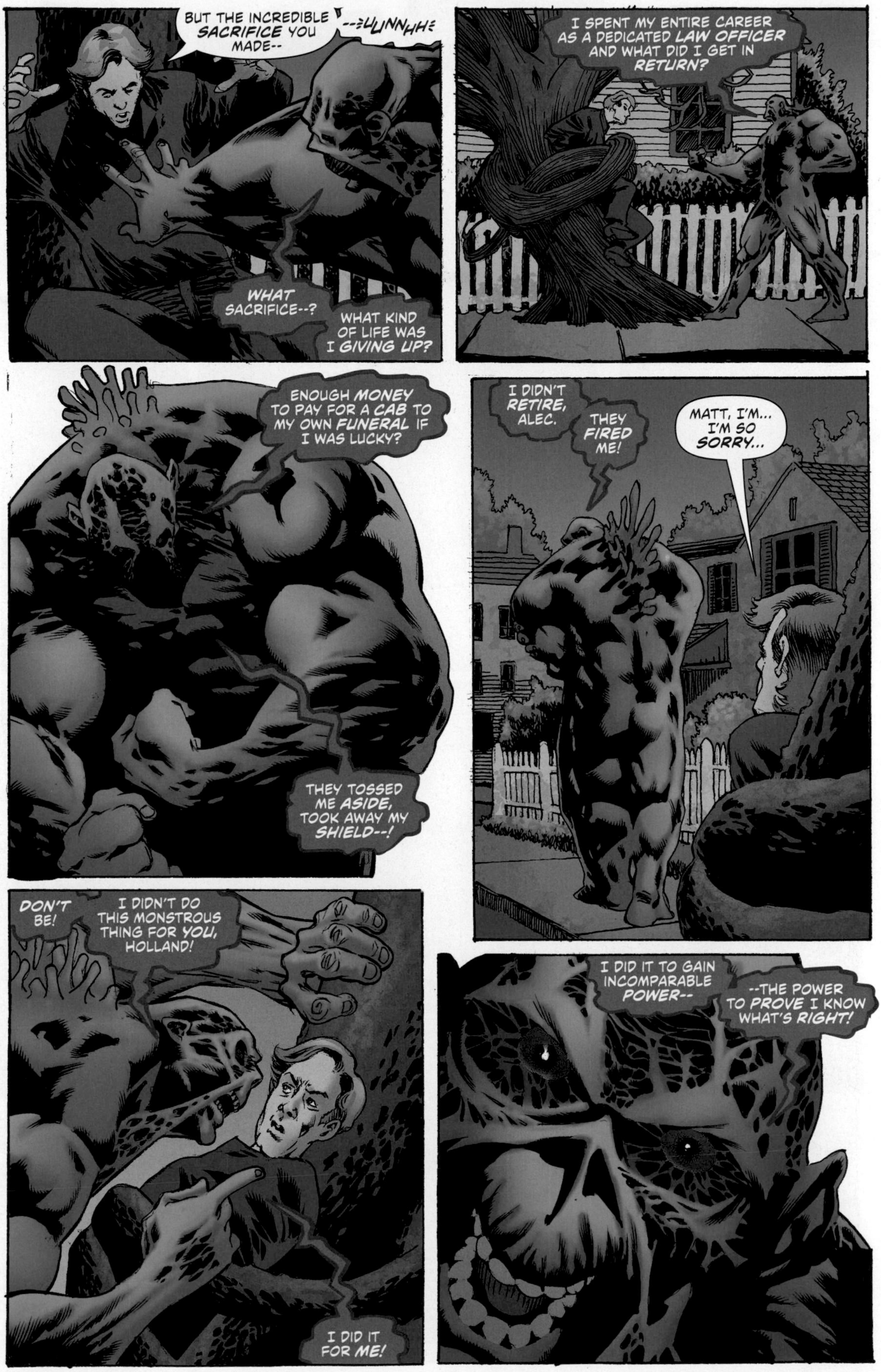
BUT THE INCREDIBLE SACRIFICE YOU MADE--
--UUNNHH!
WHAT SACRIFICE--?
WHAT KIND OF LIFE WAS I GIVING UP?
I SPENT MY ENTIRE CAREER AS A DEDICATED LAW OFFICER AND WHAT DID I GET IN RETURN?
ENOUGH MONEY TO PAY FOR A CAB TO MY OWN FUNERAL IF I WAS LUCKY?
THEY TOSSED ME ASIDE, TOOK AWAY MY SHIELD--!
I DIDN'T RETIRE, ALEC.
THEY FIRED ME!
MATT, I'M... I'M SO SORRY...
DON'T BE!
I DIDN'T DO THIS MONSTROUS THING FOR YOU, HOLLAND!
I DID IT FOR ME!
I DID IT TO GAIN INCOMPARABLE POWER--
--THE POWER TO PROVE I KNOW WHAT'S RIGHT!

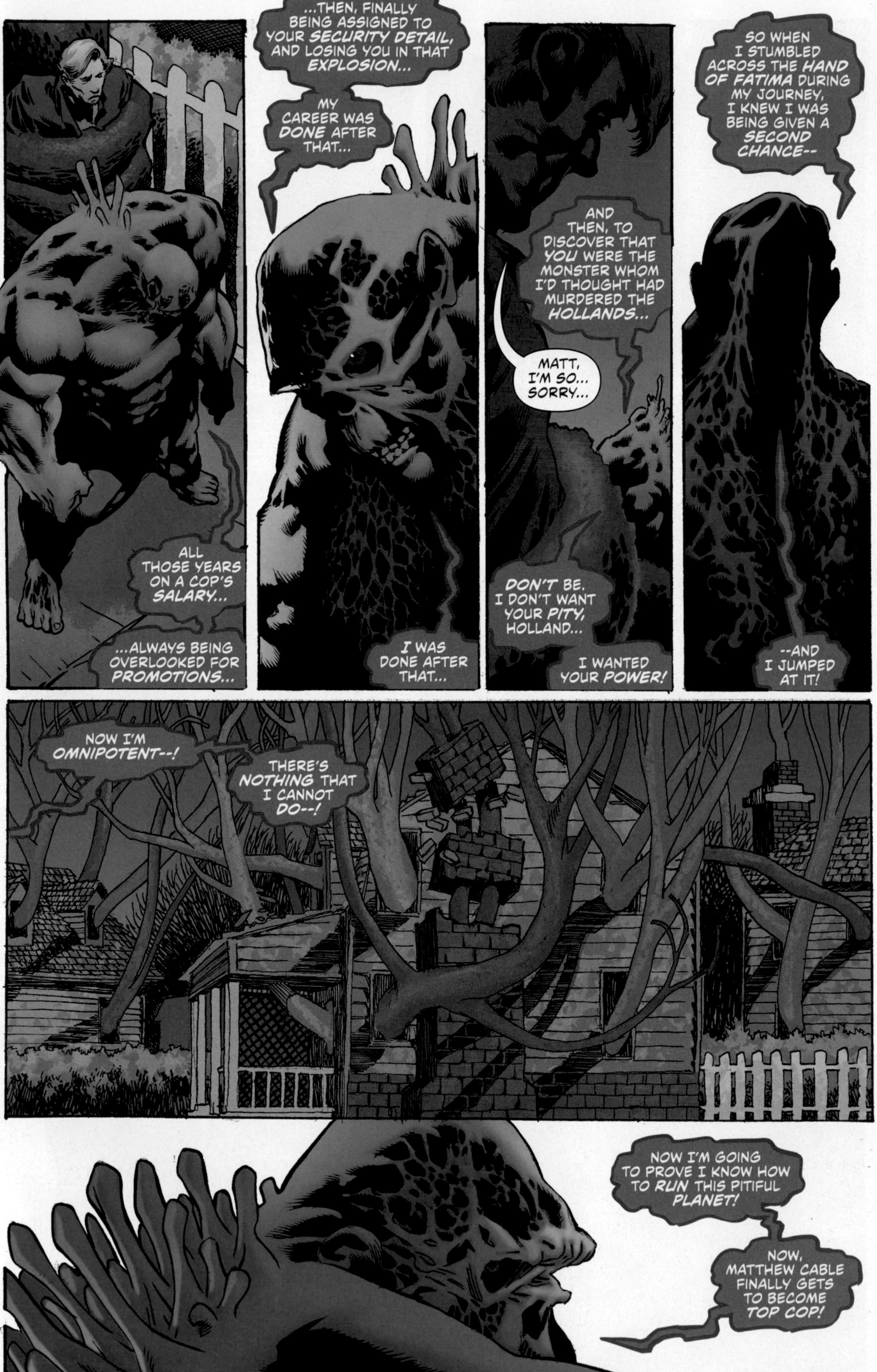
ALL THOSE YEARS ON A COP'S SALARY...
...ALWAYS BEING OVERLOOKED FOR PROMOTIONS...
...THEN, FINALLY BEING ASSIGNED TO YOUR SECURITY DETAIL, AND LOSING YOU IN THAT EXPLOSION...
MY CAREER WAS DONE AFTER THAT...
I WAS DONE AFTER THAT...
AND THEN, TO DISCOVER THAT YOU WERE THE MONSTER WHOM I'D THOUGHT HAD MURDERED THE HOLLANDS...
MATT, I'M SO... SORRY...
DON'T BE. I DON'T WANT YOUR PITY, HOLLAND...
I WANTED YOUR POWER!
SO WHEN I STUMBLED ACROSS THE HAND OF FATIMA DURING MY JOURNEY, I KNEW I WAS BEING GIVEN A SECOND CHANCE--
--AND I JUMPED AT IT!
NOW I'M OMNIPOTENT--!
THERE'S NOTHING THAT I CANNOT DO--!
NOW I'M GOING TO PROVE I KNOW HOW TO RUN THIS PITIFUL PLANET!
NOW, MATTHEW CABLE FINALLY GETS TO BECOME TOP COP!

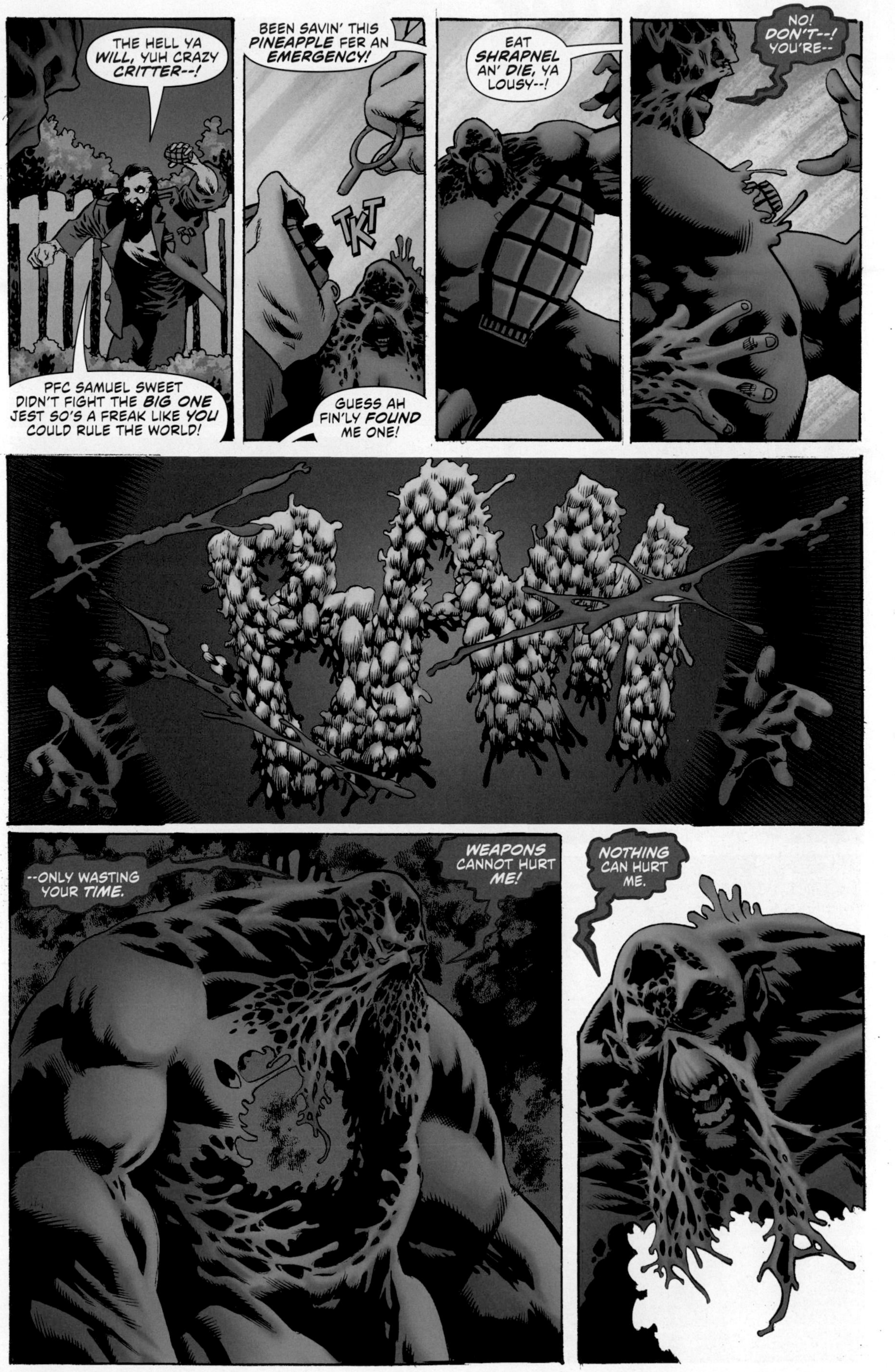
THE HELL YA WILL, YUH CRAZY CRITTER--!
PFC SAMUEL SWEET DIDN'T FIGHT THE BIG ONE JEST SO'S A FREAK LIKE YOU COULD RULE THE WORLD!
BEEN SAVIN' THIS PINEAPPLE FER AN EMERGENCY!
TKT
GUESS AH FIN'LY FOUND ME ONE!
EAT SHRAPNEL AN' DIE, YA LOUSY--!
NO! DON'T--! YOU'RE--
--ONLY WASTING YOUR TIME.
WEAPONS CANNOT HURT ME!
NOTHING CAN HURT ME.

'TAIN'T POSSIBLE--!

EVER'THING GOTTA DIE SOMETIME!

NOT EVERYTHING, PRIVATE.

SOME OF US ARE CURSED TO LIVE FOREVER!

SOME OF US ARE BLESSED TO LIVE FOREVER!

SOMEBODY HELP ME STOP THIS MONSTER--!

YOU ALREADY TRIED. ASSAULTING A SUPERIOR OFFICER IS A SERIOUS OFFENSE--

--AND IT COMES WITH SERIOUS CONSEQUENCES!

BRING 'EM ON, YA LO--

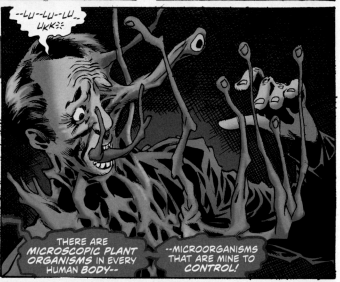

--LU--LU--LU-- UKK※

THERE ARE MICROSCOPIC PLANT ORGANISMS IN EVERY HUMAN BODY--

--MICROORGANISMS THAT ARE MINE TO CONTROL!

SO...

...ANYONE ELSE CARE TO TRY CHALLENGING THE LAW?

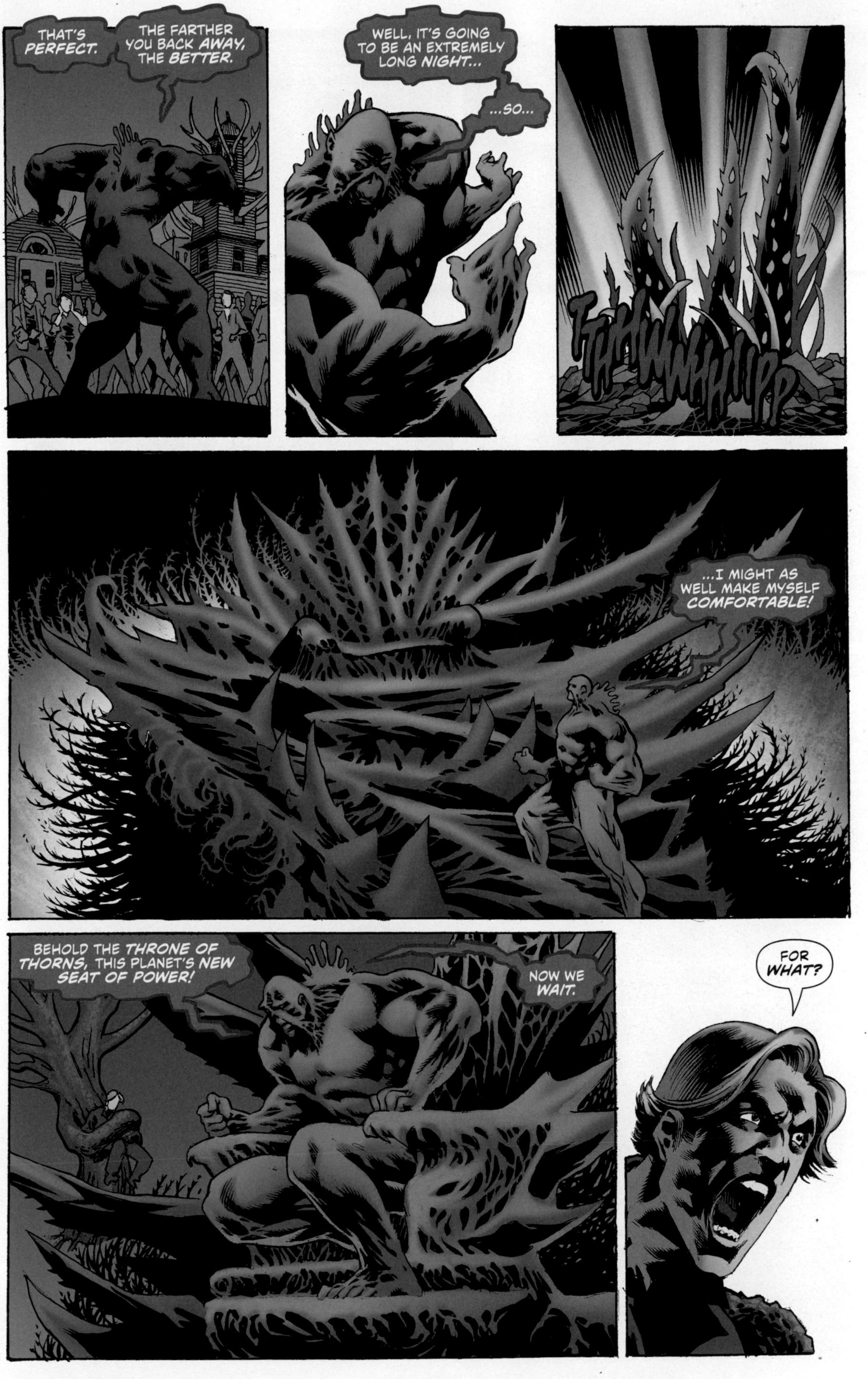
THAT'S PERFECT.
THE FARTHER YOU BACK AWAY, THE BETTER.
WELL, IT'S GOING TO BE AN EXTREMELY LONG NIGHT...
...SO...
TTHHWWHHUPP
...I MIGHT AS WELL MAKE MYSELF COMFORTABLE!
BEHOLD THE THRONE OF THORNS, THIS PLANET'S NEW SEAT OF POWER!
NOW WE WAIT.
FOR WHAT?

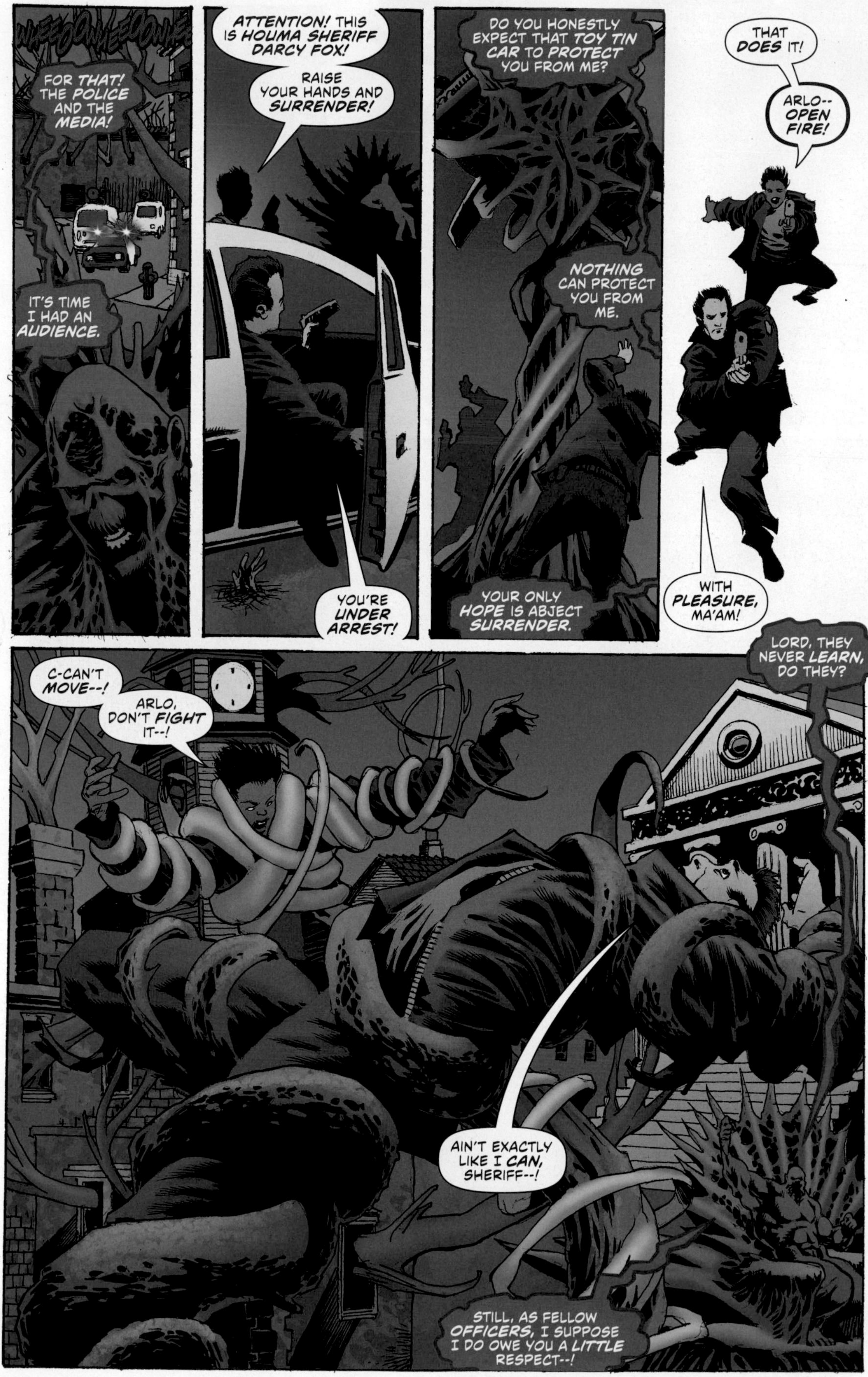
FOR THAT! THE POLICE AND THE MEDIA!
IT'S TIME I HAD AN AUDIENCE.
ATTENTION! THIS IS HOUMA SHERIFF DARCY FOX!
RAISE YOUR HANDS AND SURRENDER!
YOU'RE UNDER ARREST!
DO YOU HONESTLY EXPECT THAT TOY TIN CAR TO PROTECT YOU FROM ME?
NOTHING CAN PROTECT YOU FROM ME.
YOUR ONLY HOPE IS ABJECT SURRENDER.
THAT DOES IT!
ARLO-- OPEN FIRE!
WITH PLEASURE, MA'AM!
C-CAN'T MOVE--!
ARLO, DON'T FIGHT IT--!
LORD, THEY NEVER LEARN, DO THEY?
AIN'T EXACTLY LIKE I CAN, SHERIFF--!
STILL, AS FELLOW OFFICERS, I SUPPOSE I DO OWE YOU A LITTLE RESPECT--!

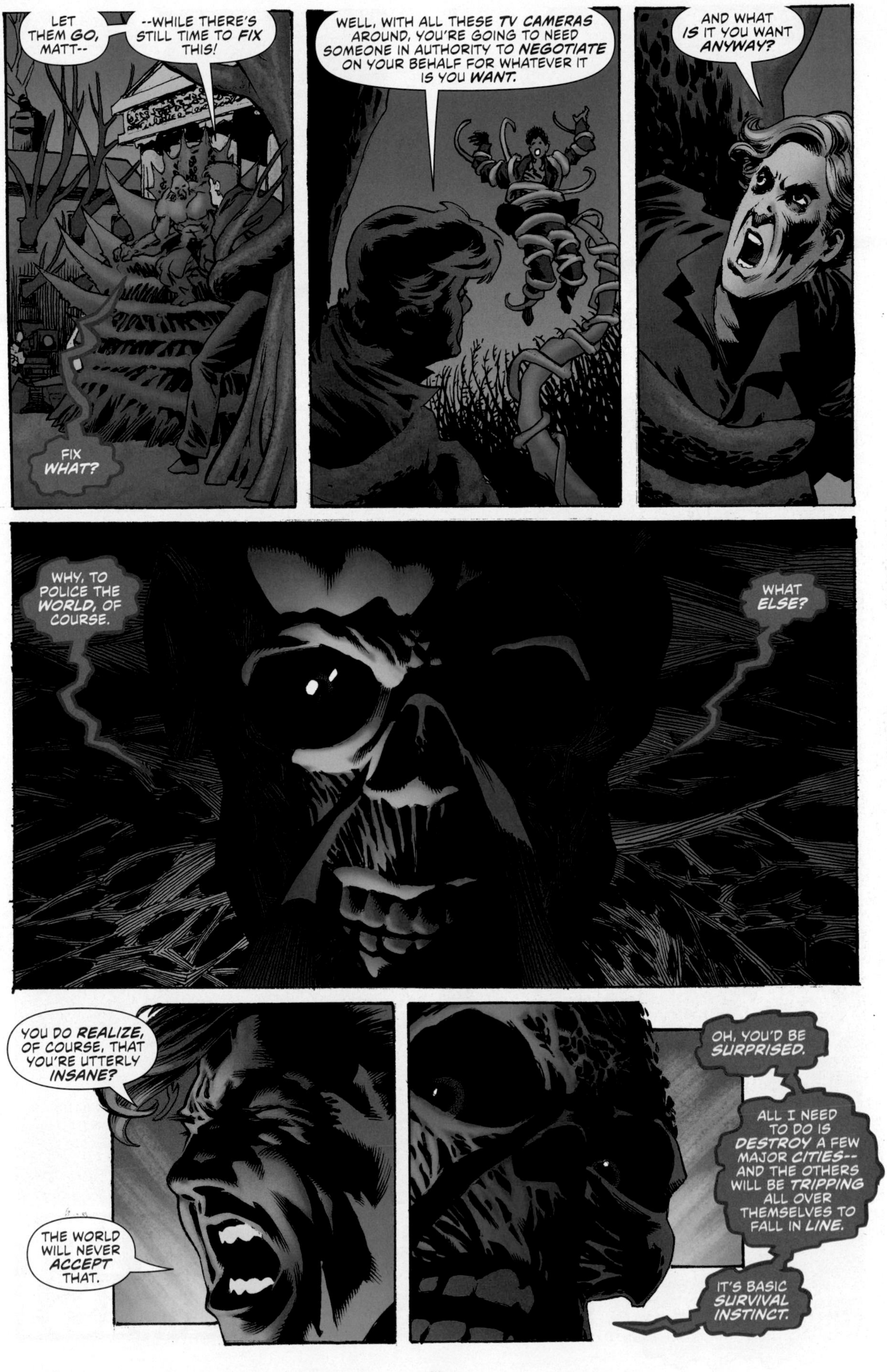

LET THEM GO, MATT--
--WHILE THERE'S STILL TIME TO FIX THIS!
FIX WHAT?
WELL, WITH ALL THESE TV CAMERAS AROUND, YOU'RE GOING TO NEED SOMEONE IN AUTHORITY TO NEGOTIATE ON YOUR BEHALF FOR WHATEVER IT IS YOU WANT.
AND WHAT IS IT YOU WANT ANYWAY?
WHY, TO POLICE THE WORLD, OF COURSE.
WHAT ELSE?
YOU DO REALIZE, OF COURSE, THAT YOU'RE UTTERLY INSANE?
THE WORLD WILL NEVER ACCEPT THAT.
OH, YOU'D BE SURPRISED.
ALL I NEED TO DO IS DESTROY A FEW MAJOR CITIES-- AND THE OTHERS WILL BE TRIPPING ALL OVER THEMSELVES TO FALL IN LINE.
IT'S BASIC SURVIVAL INSTINCT.

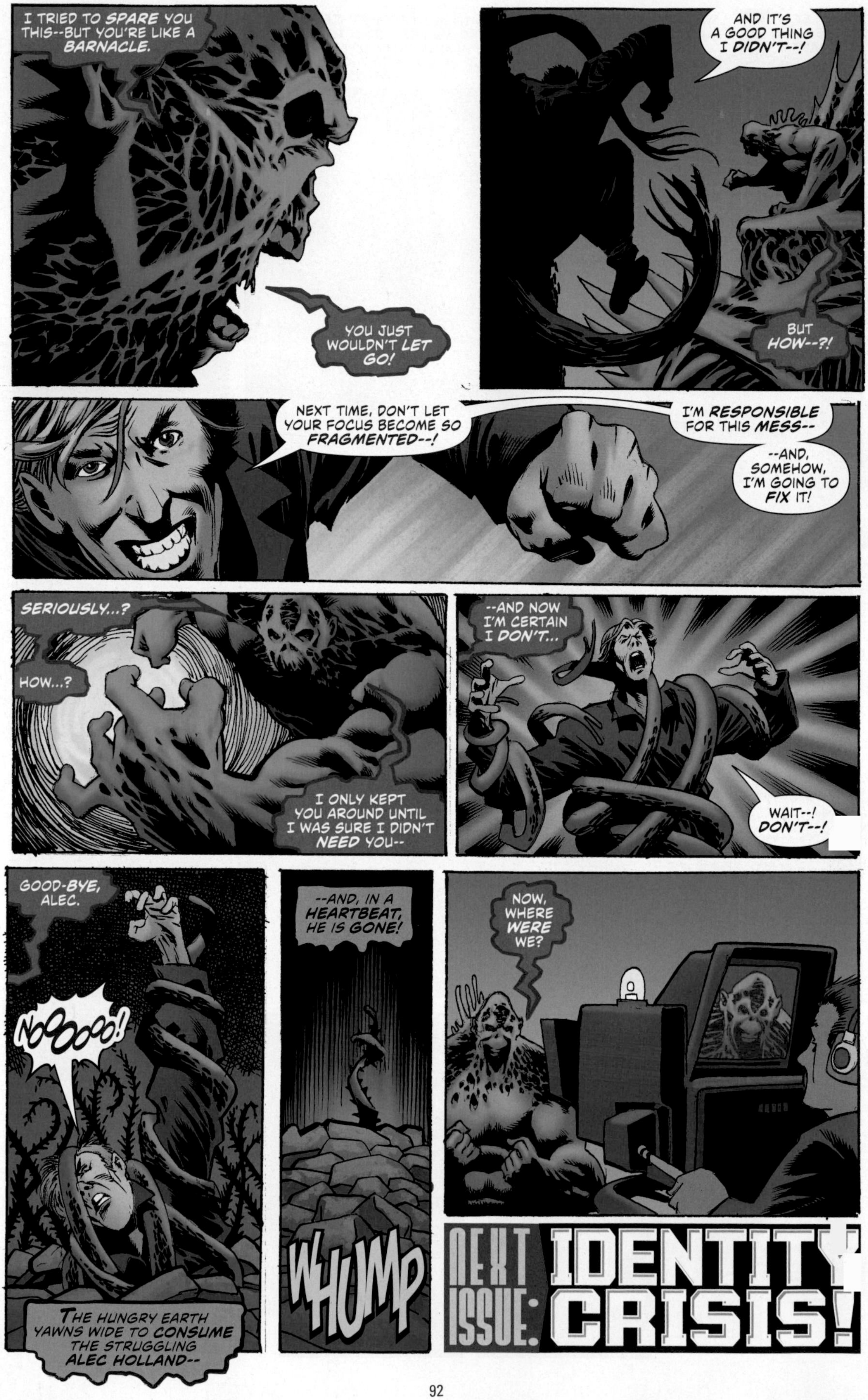
I TRIED TO SPARE YOU THIS--BUT YOU'RE LIKE A BARNACLE.
YOU JUST WOULDN'T LET GO!
AND IT'S A GOOD THING I DIDN'T--!
BUT HOW--?!
NEXT TIME, DON'T LET YOUR FOCUS BECOME SO FRAGMENTED--!
I'M RESPONSIBLE FOR THIS MESS--
--AND, SOMEHOW, I'M GOING TO FIX IT!
SERIOUSLY...?
HOW...?
I ONLY KEPT YOU AROUND UNTIL I WAS SURE I DIDN'T NEED YOU--
--AND NOW I'M CERTAIN I DON'T...
WAIT--! DON'T--!
GOOD-BYE, ALEC.
NOOOOOO!
THE HUNGRY EARTH YAWNS WIDE TO CONSUME THE STRUGGLING ALEC HOLLAND--
--AND, IN A HEARTBEAT, HE IS GONE!
WHUMP
NOW, WHERE WERE WE?
NEXT ISSUE: IDENTITY CRISIS!

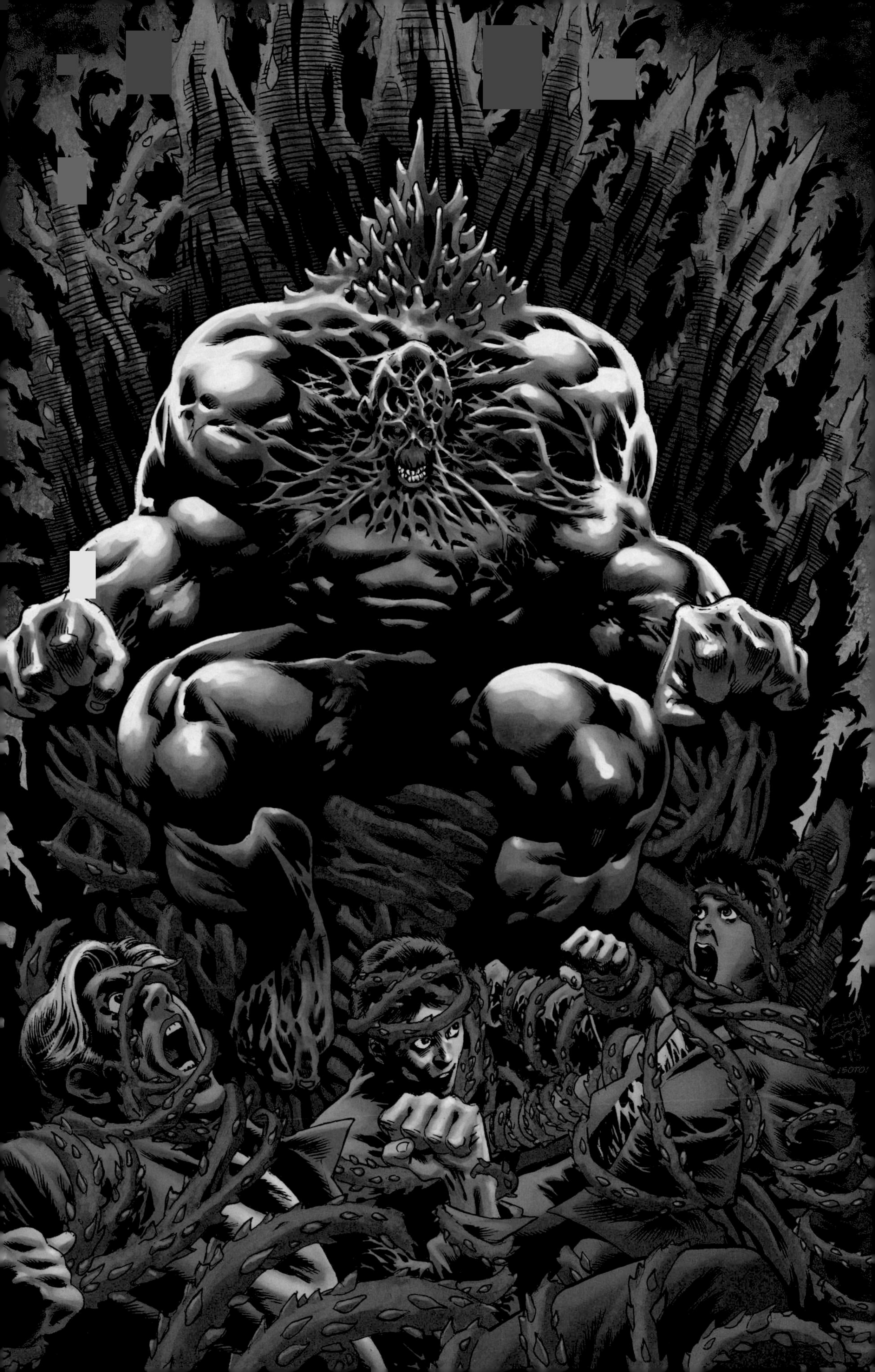

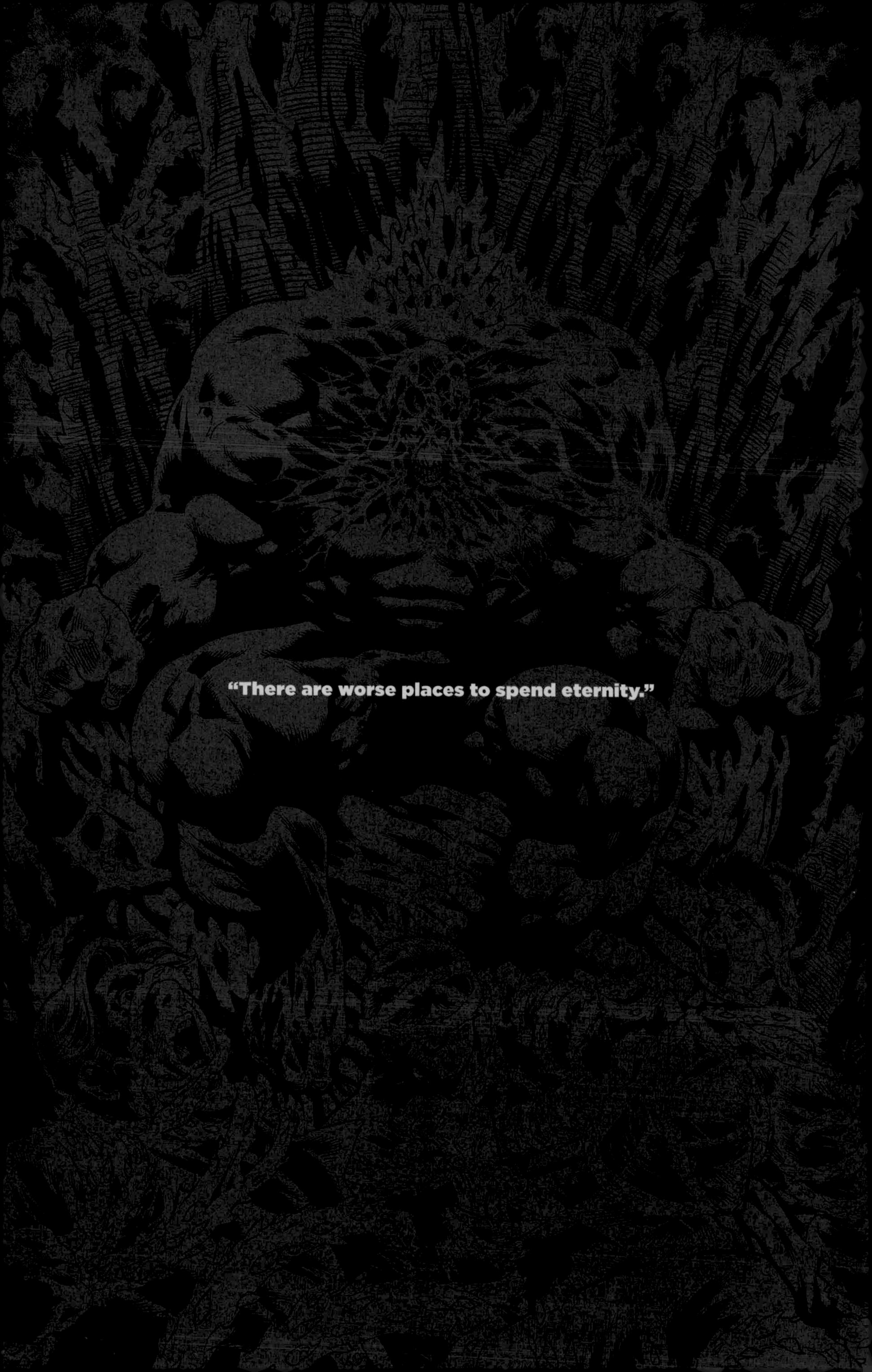
"There are worse places to spend eternity."

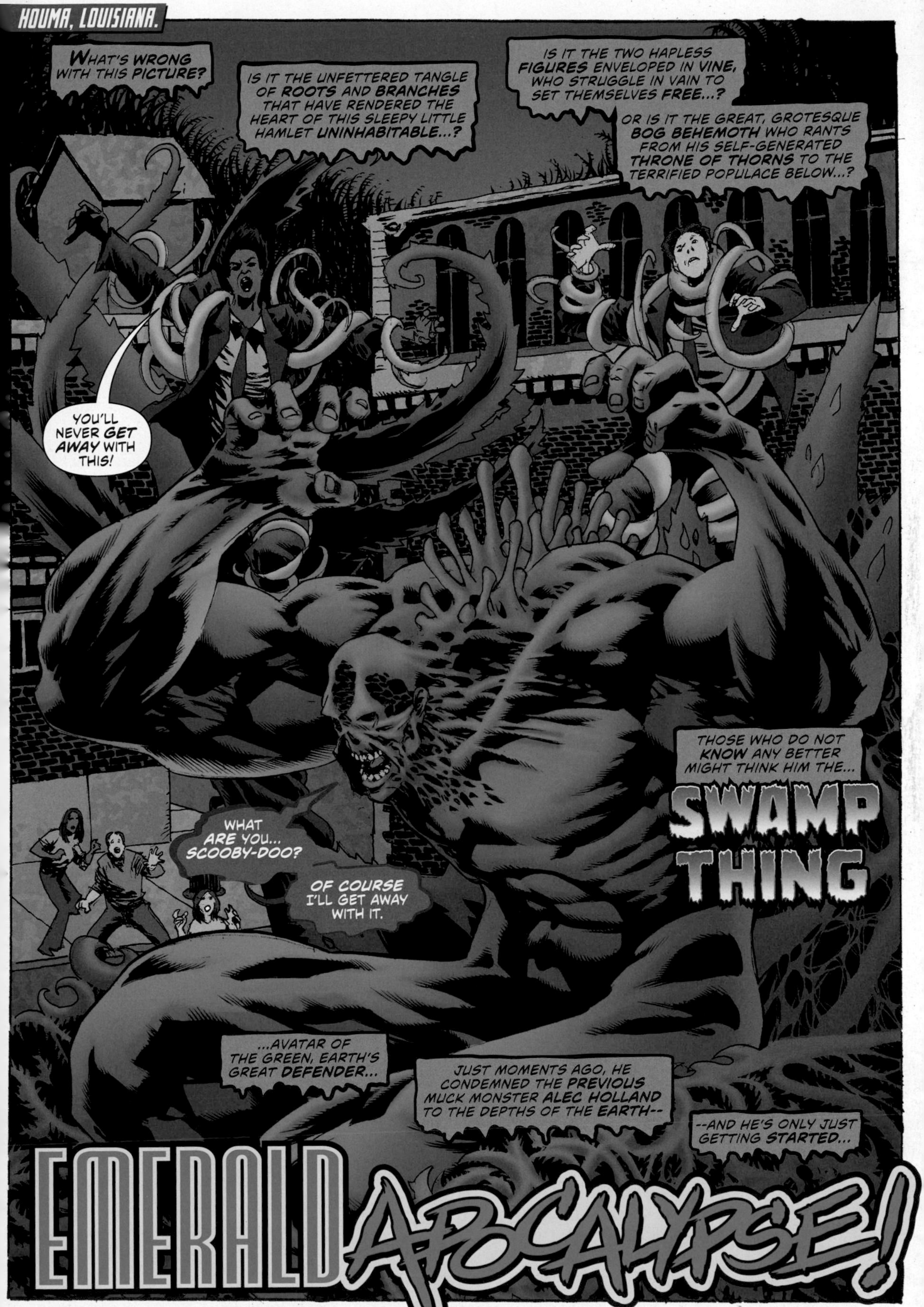
HOUMA, LOUISIANA.
WHAT'S WRONG WITH THIS PICTURE?
IS IT THE UNFETTERED TANGLE OF ROOTS AND BRANCHES THAT HAVE RENDERED THE HEART OF THIS SLEEPY LITTLE HAMLET UNINHABITABLE...?
IS IT THE TWO HAPLESS FIGURES ENVELOPED IN VINE, WHO STRUGGLE IN VAIN TO SET THEMSELVES FREE...?
OR IS IT THE GREAT, GROTESQUE BOG BEHEMOTH WHO RANTS FROM HIS SELF-GENERATED THRONE OF THORNS TO THE TERRIFIED POPULACE BELOW...?
YOU'LL NEVER GET AWAY WITH THIS!
THOSE WHO DO NOT KNOW ANY BETTER MIGHT THINK HIM THE...
SWAMP THING
WHAT ARE YOU... SCOOBY-DOO?
OF COURSE I'LL GET AWAY WITH IT.
...AVATAR OF THE GREEN, EARTH'S GREAT DEFENDER...
JUST MOMENTS AGO, HE CONDEMNED THE PREVIOUS MUCK MONSTER ALEC HOLLAND TO THE DEPTHS OF THE EARTH--
--AND HE'S ONLY JUST GETTING STARTED...
EMERALD APOCALYPSE!

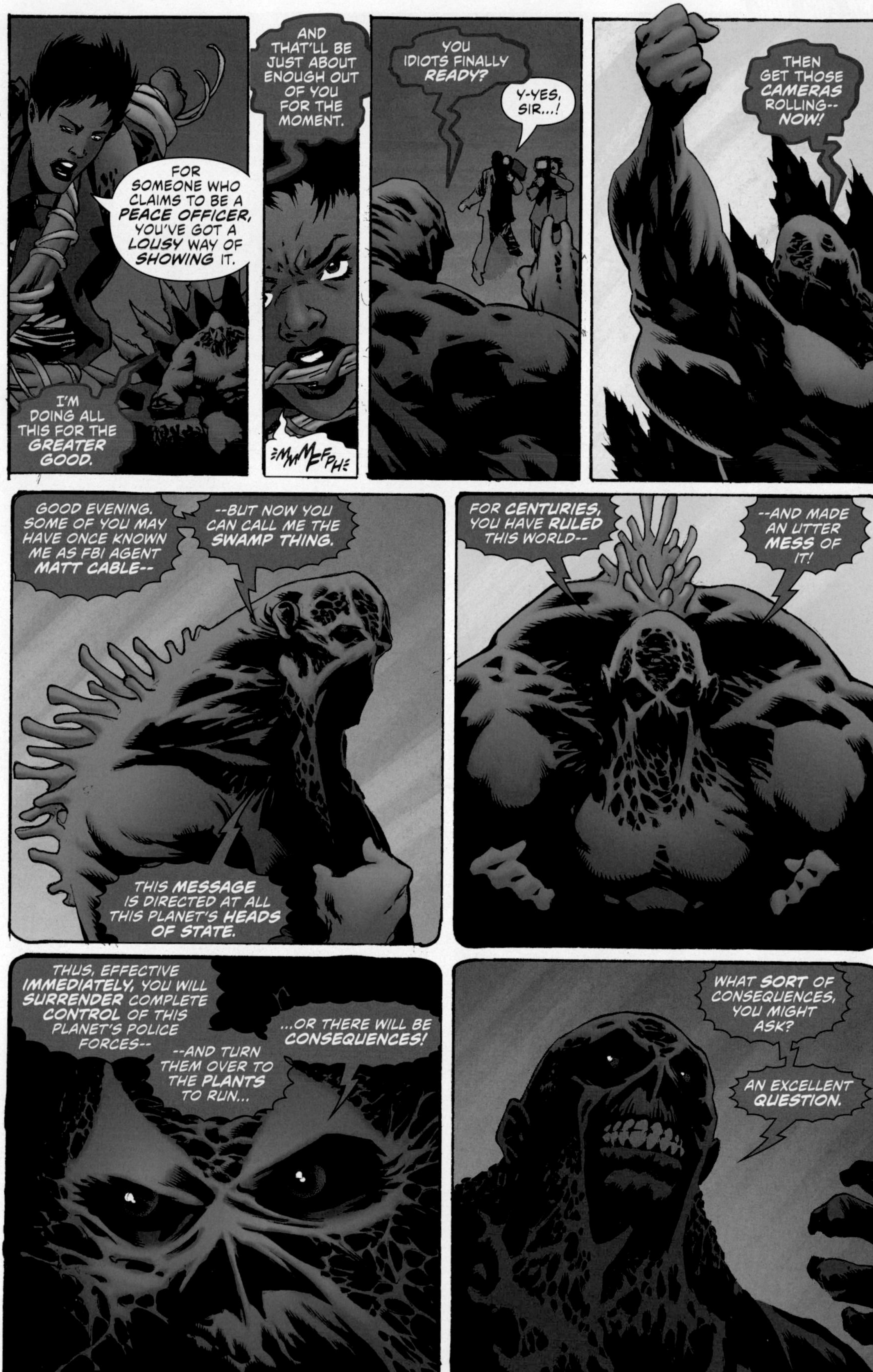
FOR SOMEONE WHO CLAIMS TO BE A PEACE OFFICER, YOU'VE GOT A LOUSY WAY OF SHOWING IT.
I'M DOING ALL THIS FOR THE GREATER GOOD.
AND THAT'LL BE JUST ABOUT ENOUGH OUT OF YOU FOR THE MOMENT.
MMMFFPH
YOU IDIOTS FINALLY READY?
Y-YES, SIR...!
THEN GET THOSE CAMERAS ROLLING-- NOW!
GOOD EVENING. SOME OF YOU MAY HAVE ONCE KNOWN ME AS FBI AGENT MATT CABLE--
--BUT NOW YOU CAN CALL ME THE SWAMP THING.
THIS MESSAGE IS DIRECTED AT ALL THIS PLANET'S HEADS OF STATE.
FOR CENTURIES, YOU HAVE RULED THIS WORLD--
--AND MADE AN UTTER MESS OF IT!
THUS, EFFECTIVE IMMEDIATELY, YOU WILL SURRENDER COMPLETE CONTROL OF THIS PLANET'S POLICE FORCES--
--AND TURN THEM OVER TO THE PLANTS TO RUN...
...OR THERE WILL BE CONSEQUENCES!
WHAT SORT OF CONSEQUENCES, YOU MIGHT ASK?
AN EXCELLENT QUESTION.

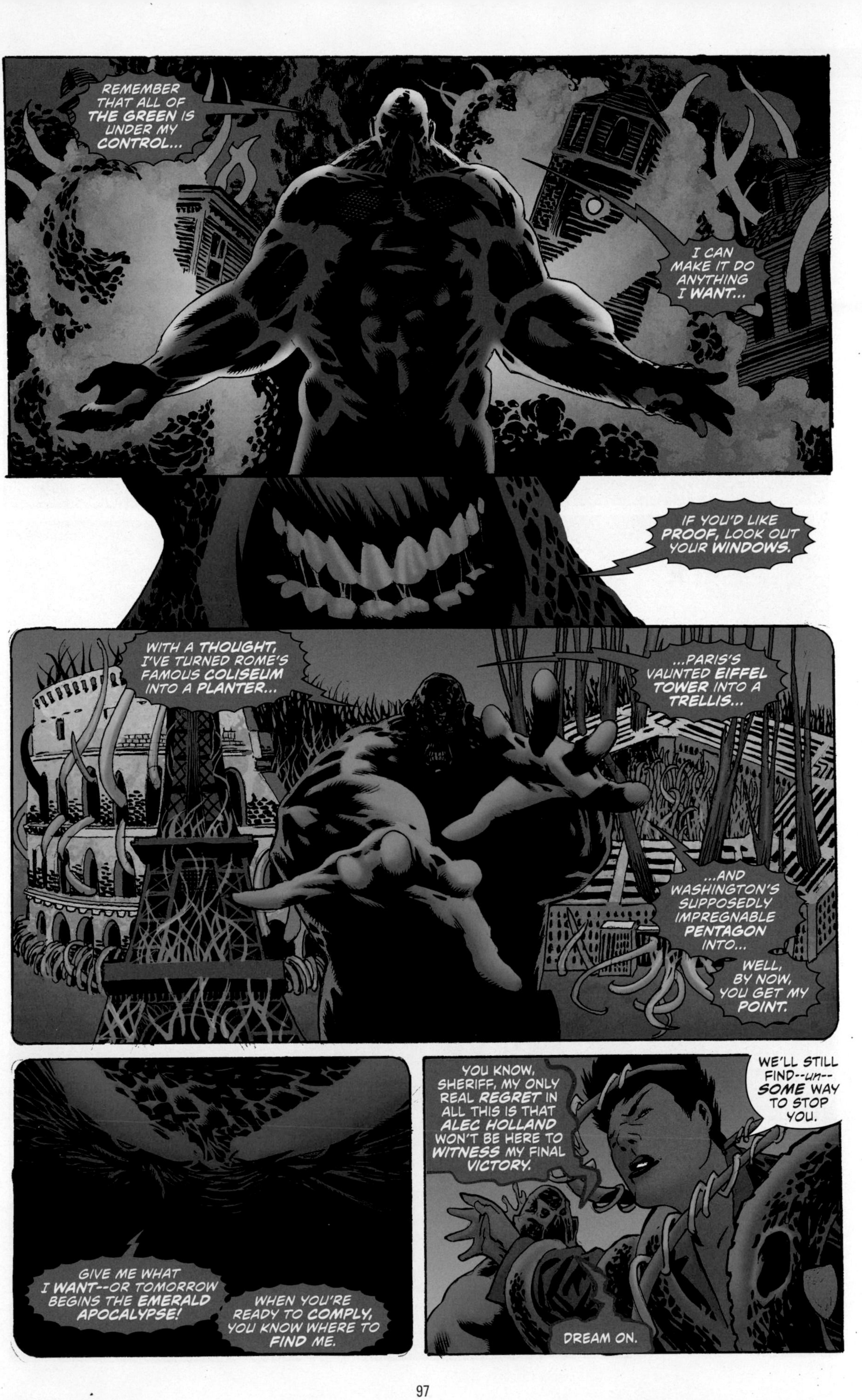
REMEMBER THAT ALL OF THE GREEN IS UNDER MY CONTROL...
I CAN MAKE IT DO ANYTHING I WANT...
IF YOU'D LIKE PROOF, LOOK OUT YOUR WINDOWS.
WITH A THOUGHT, I'VE TURNED ROME'S FAMOUS COLISEUM INTO A PLANTER...
...PARIS'S VAUNTED EIFFEL TOWER INTO A TRELLIS...
...AND WASHINGTON'S SUPPOSEDLY IMPREGNABLE PENTAGON INTO...
WELL, BY NOW, YOU GET MY POINT.
GIVE ME WHAT I WANT--OR TOMORROW BEGINS THE EMERALD APOCALYPSE!
WHEN YOU'RE READY TO COMPLY, YOU KNOW WHERE TO FIND ME.
WE'LL STILL FIND--un-- SOME WAY TO STOP YOU.
YOU KNOW, SHERIFF, MY ONLY REAL REGRET IN ALL THIS IS THAT ALEC HOLLAND WON'T BE HERE TO WITNESS MY FINAL VICTORY.
DREAM ON.

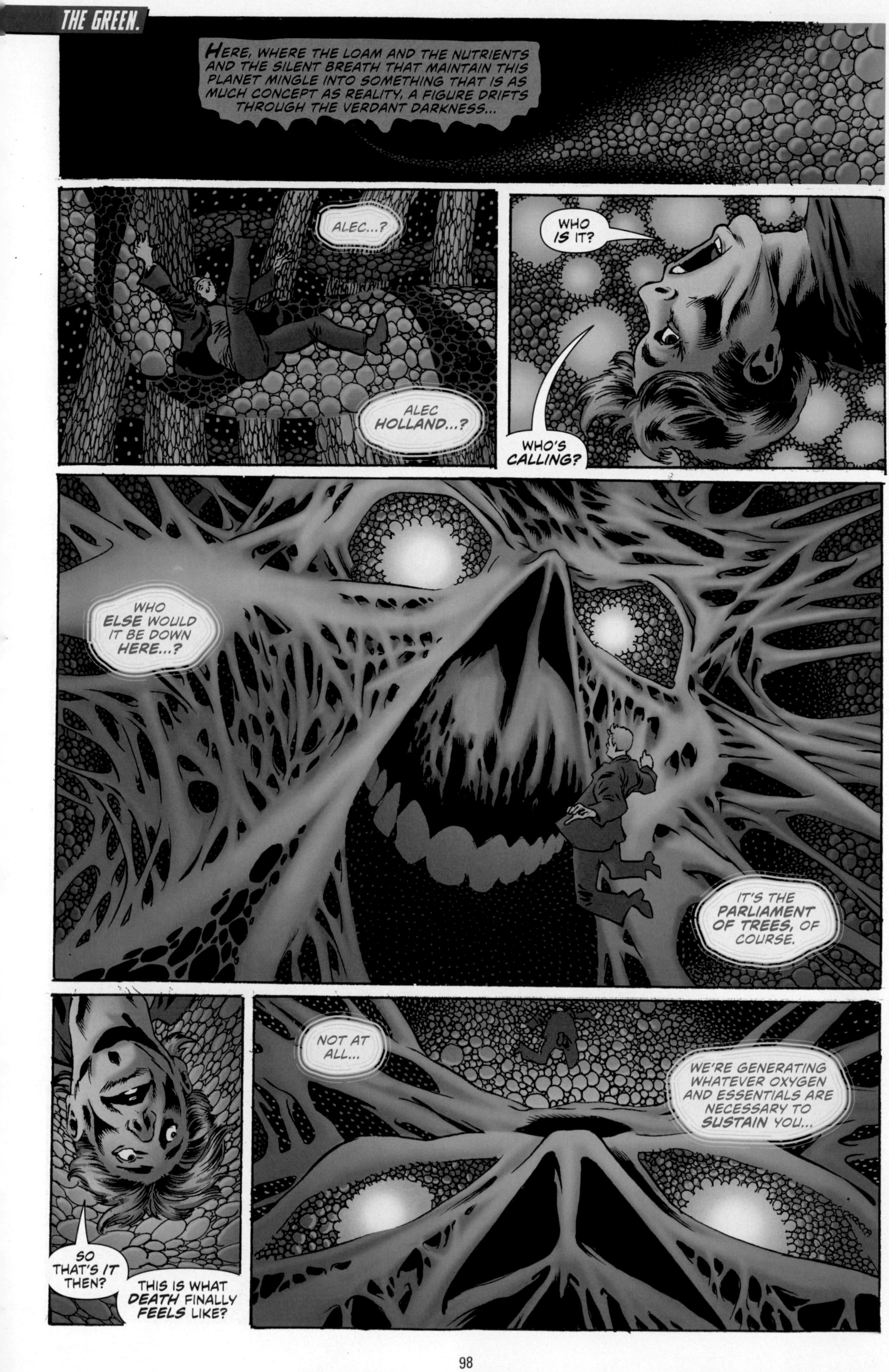
THE GREEN.
HERE, WHERE THE LOAM AND THE NUTRIENTS AND THE SILENT BREATH THAT MAINTAIN THIS PLANET MINGLE INTO SOMETHING THAT IS AS MUCH CONCEPT AS REALITY, A FIGURE DRIFTS THROUGH THE VERDANT DARKNESS...
ALEC...?
ALEC HOLLAND...?
WHO IS IT?
WHO'S CALLING?
WHO ELSE WOULD IT BE DOWN HERE...?
IT'S THE PARLIAMENT OF TREES, OF COURSE.
SO THAT'S IT THEN?
THIS IS WHAT DEATH FINALLY FEELS LIKE?
NOT AT ALL...
WE'RE GENERATING WHATEVER OXYGEN AND ESSENTIALS ARE NECESSARY TO SUSTAIN YOU...

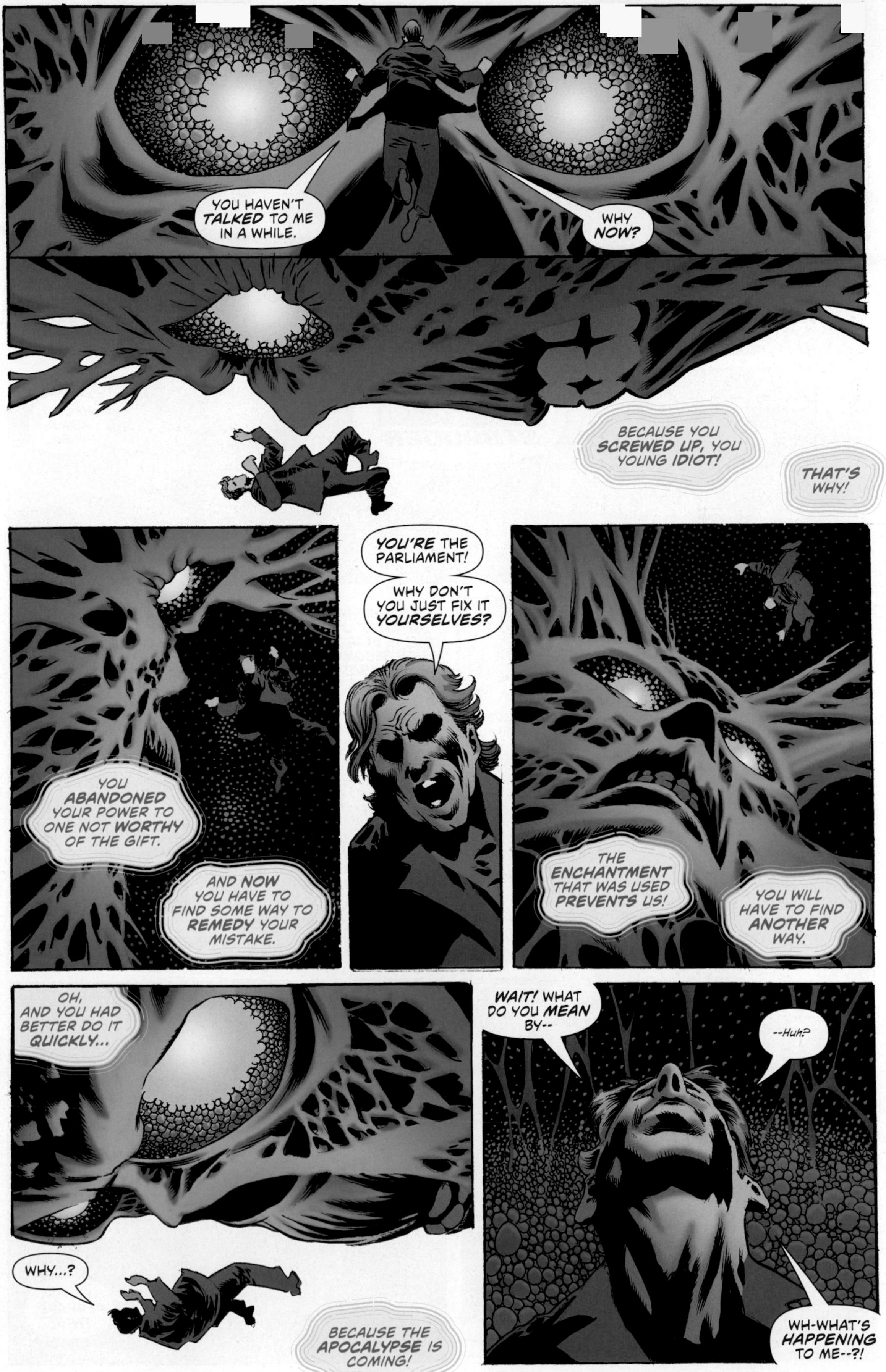
YOU HAVEN'T TALKED TO ME IN A WHILE.
WHY NOW?
BECAUSE YOU SCREWED UP, YOU YOUNG IDIOT!
THAT'S WHY!
YOU ABANDONED YOUR POWER TO ONE NOT WORTHY OF THE GIFT.
AND NOW YOU HAVE TO FIND SOME WAY TO REMEDY YOUR MISTAKE.
YOU'RE THE PARLIAMENT!
WHY DON'T YOU JUST FIX IT YOURSELVES?
THE ENCHANTMENT THAT WAS USED PREVENTS US!
YOU WILL HAVE TO FIND ANOTHER WAY.
OH, AND YOU HAD BETTER DO IT QUICKLY...
WHY...?
BECAUSE THE APOCALYPSE IS COMING!
WAIT! WHAT DO YOU MEAN BY--
--Huh?
WH-WHAT'S HAPPENING TO ME--?!

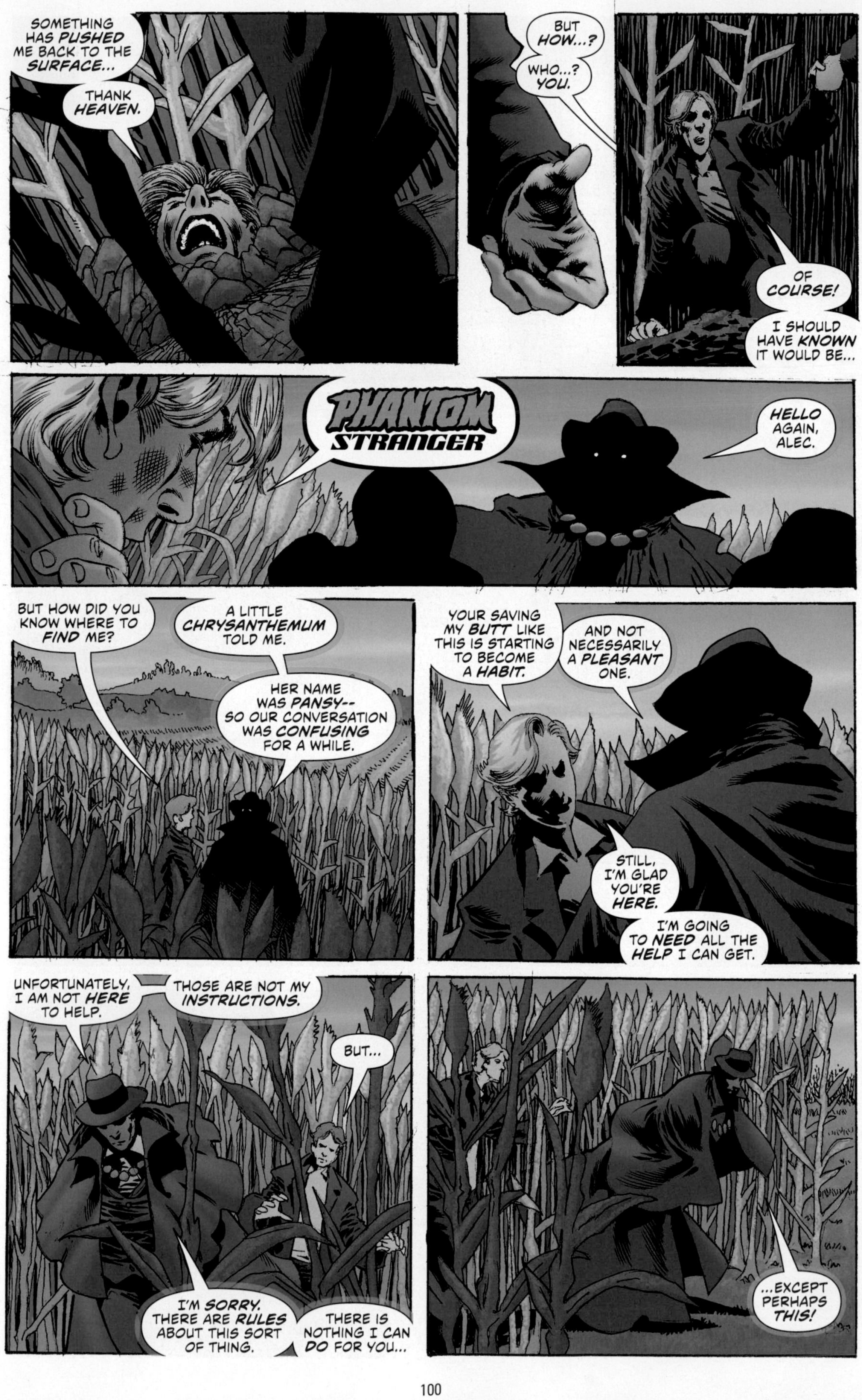
SOMETHING HAS PUSHED ME BACK TO THE SURFACE...
THANK HEAVEN.
BUT HOW...?
WHO...? YOU.
OF COURSE!
I SHOULD HAVE KNOWN IT WOULD BE...
PHANTOM STRANGER
HELLO AGAIN, ALEC.
BUT HOW DID YOU KNOW WHERE TO FIND ME?
A LITTLE CHRYSANTHEMUM TOLD ME.
HER NAME WAS PANSY-- SO OUR CONVERSATION WAS CONFUSING FOR A WHILE.
YOUR SAVING MY BUTT LIKE THIS IS STARTING TO BECOME A HABIT.
AND NOT NECESSARILY A PLEASANT ONE.
STILL, I'M GLAD YOU'RE HERE.
I'M GOING TO NEED ALL THE HELP I CAN GET.
UNFORTUNATELY, I AM NOT HERE TO HELP.
THOSE ARE NOT MY INSTRUCTIONS.
BUT...
I'M SORRY. THERE ARE RULES ABOUT THIS SORT OF THING.
THERE IS NOTHING I CAN DO FOR YOU...
...EXCEPT PERHAPS THIS!

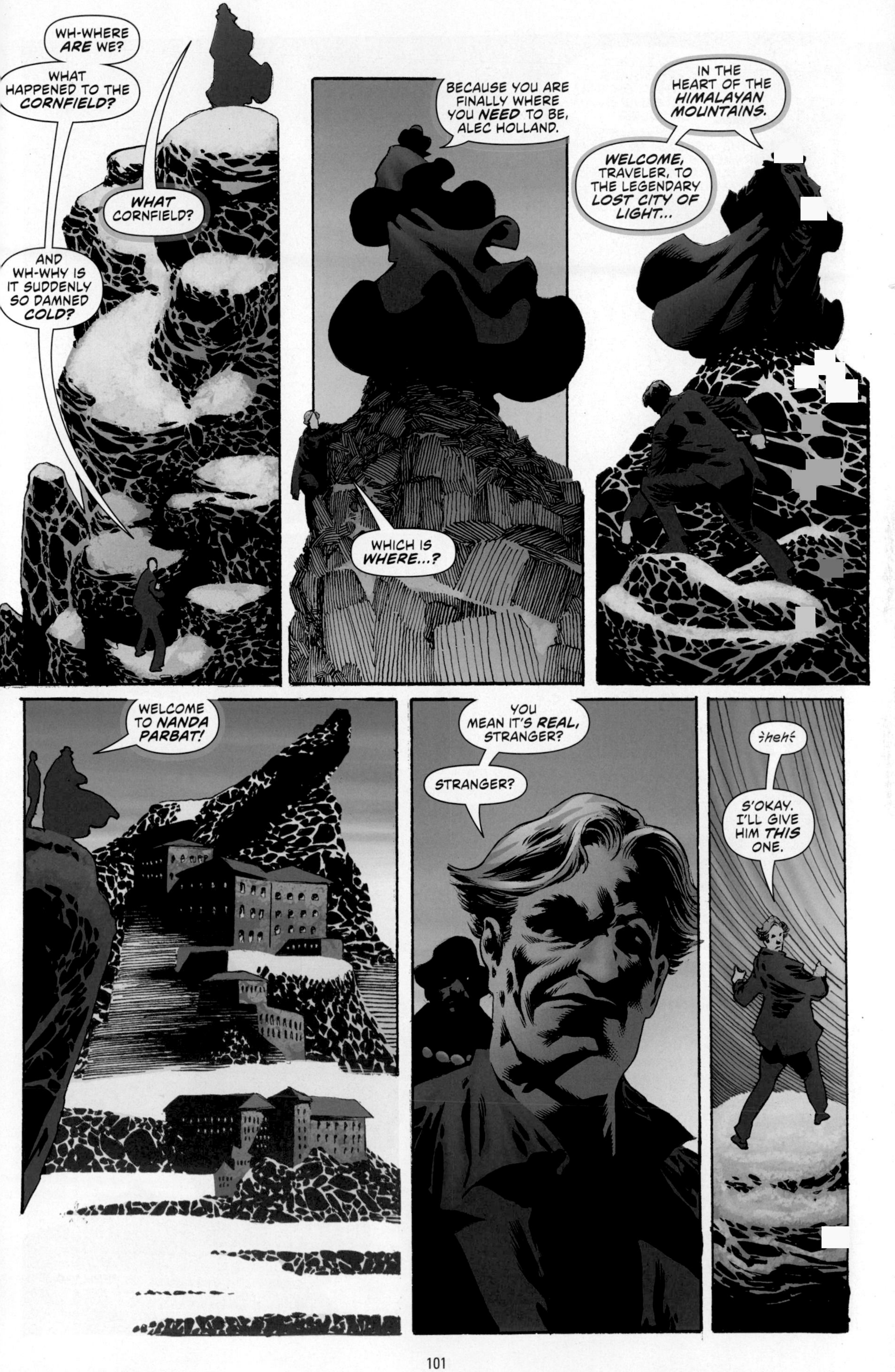
WH-WHERE ARE WE?
WHAT HAPPENED TO THE CORNFIELD?
WHAT CORNFIELD?
AND WH-WHY IS IT SUDDENLY SO DAMNED COLD?
BECAUSE YOU ARE FINALLY WHERE YOU NEED TO BE, ALEC HOLLAND.
WHICH IS WHERE...?
IN THE HEART OF THE HIMALAYAN MOUNTAINS.
WELCOME, TRAVELER, TO THE LEGENDARY LOST CITY OF LIGHT...
WELCOME TO NANDA PARBAT!
YOU MEAN IT'S REAL, STRANGER?
STRANGER?
heh
S'OKAY. I'LL GIVE HIM THIS ONE.

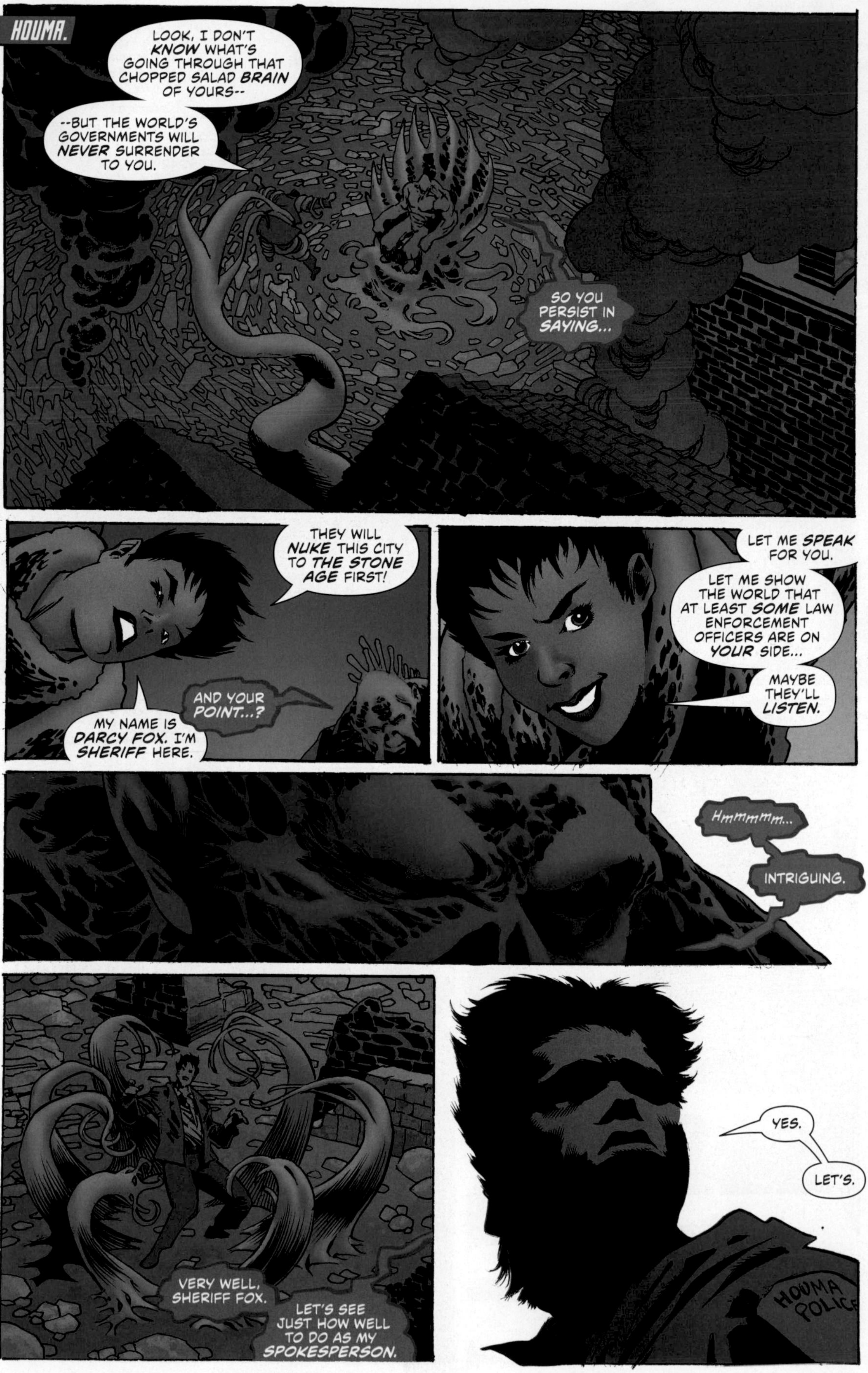
HOUMA.
LOOK, I DON'T KNOW WHAT'S GOING THROUGH THAT CHOPPED SALAD BRAIN OF YOURS--
--BUT THE WORLD'S GOVERNMENTS WILL NEVER SURRENDER TO YOU.
SO YOU PERSIST IN SAYING...
THEY WILL NUKE THIS CITY TO THE STONE AGE FIRST!
AND YOUR POINT...?
MY NAME IS DARCY FOX. I'M SHERIFF HERE.
LET ME SPEAK FOR YOU.
LET ME SHOW THE WORLD THAT AT LEAST SOME LAW ENFORCEMENT OFFICERS ARE ON YOUR SIDE...
MAYBE THEY'LL LISTEN.
Hmmmmm...
INTRIGUING.
VERY WELL, SHERIFF FOX.
LET'S SEE JUST HOW WELL TO DO AS MY SPOKESPERSON.
YES.
LET'S.
HOUMA POLICE

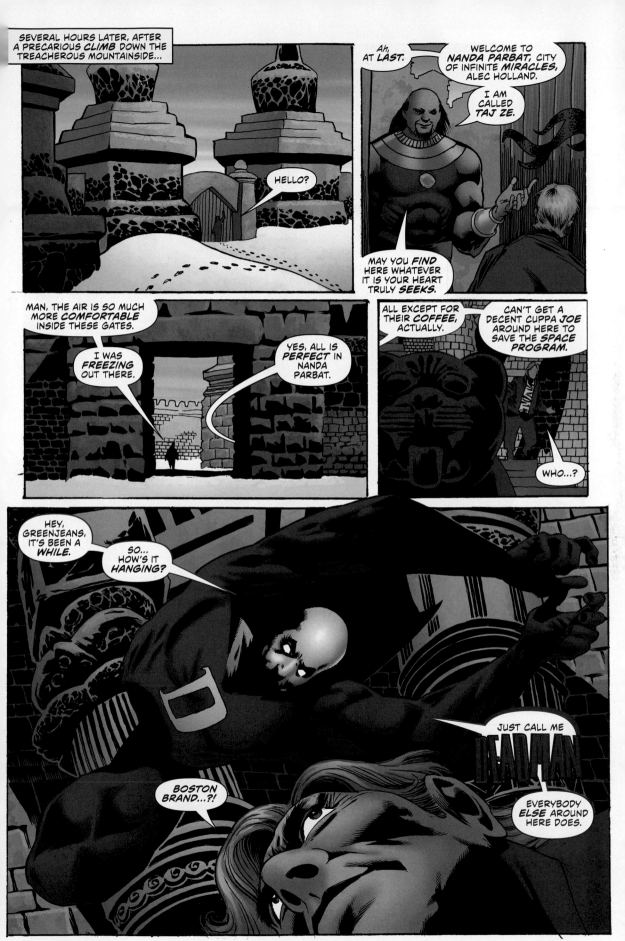

SEVERAL HOURS LATER, AFTER A PRECARIOUS *CLIMB* DOWN THE TREACHEROUS MOUNTAINSIDE...

HELLO?

Ah, AT *LAST.*

WELCOME TO *NANDA PARBAT,* CITY OF INFINITE *MIRACLES,* ALEC HOLLAND.

I AM CALLED *TAJ ZE.*

MAY YOU *FIND* HERE WHATEVER IT IS YOUR HEART TRULY *SEEKS.*

MAN, THE AIR IS SO MUCH MORE *COMFORTABLE* INSIDE THESE GATES.

I WAS *FREEZING* OUT THERE.

YES, ALL IS *PERFECT* IN NANDA PARBAT.

ALL EXCEPT FOR THEIR *COFFEE,* ACTUALLY.

CAN'T GET A DECENT CUPPA JOE AROUND HERE TO SAVE THE *SPACE PROGRAM.*

WHO...?

HEY, GREENJEANS, IT'S BEEN A *WHILE.*

SO... HOW'S IT *HANGING?*

JUST CALL ME

BOSTON BRAND...?!

EVERYBODY *ELSE* AROUND HERE DOES.

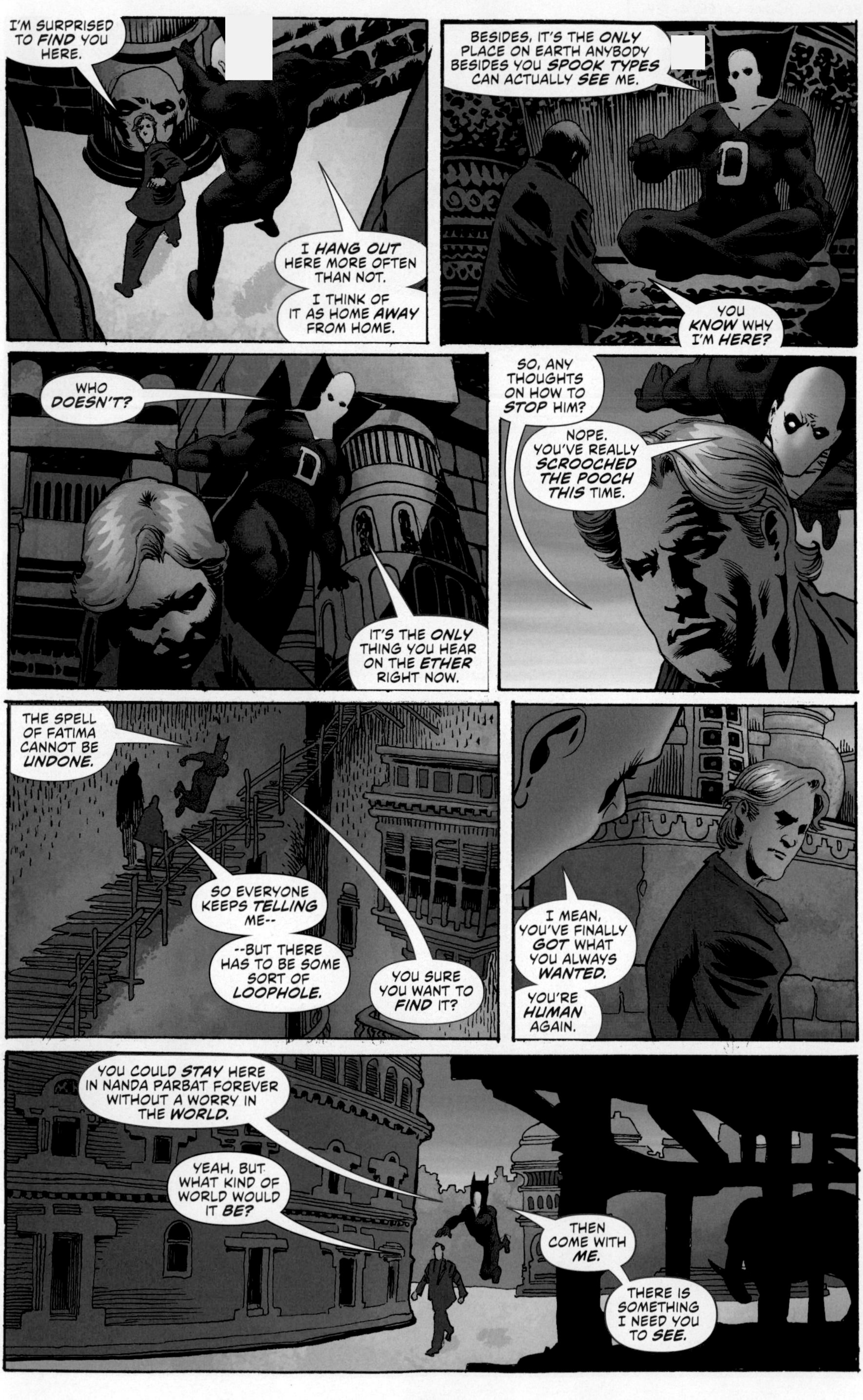
I'M SURPRISED TO FIND YOU HERE.
I HANG OUT HERE MORE OFTEN THAN NOT.
I THINK OF IT AS HOME AWAY FROM HOME.
BESIDES, IT'S THE ONLY PLACE ON EARTH ANYBODY BESIDES YOU SPOOK TYPES CAN ACTUALLY SEE ME.
YOU KNOW WHY I'M HERE?
WHO DOESN'T?
IT'S THE ONLY THING YOU HEAR ON THE ETHER RIGHT NOW.
SO, ANY THOUGHTS ON HOW TO STOP HIM?
NOPE. YOU'VE REALLY SCROOCHED THE POOCH THIS TIME.
THE SPELL OF FATIMA CANNOT BE UNDONE.
SO EVERYONE KEEPS TELLING ME--
--BUT THERE HAS TO BE SOME SORT OF LOOPHOLE.
YOU SURE YOU WANT TO FIND IT?
I MEAN, YOU'VE FINALLY GOT WHAT YOU ALWAYS WANTED.
YOU'RE HUMAN AGAIN.
YOU COULD STAY HERE IN NANDA PARBAT FOREVER WITHOUT A WORRY IN THE WORLD.
YEAH, BUT WHAT KIND OF WORLD WOULD IT BE?
THEN COME WITH ME.
THERE IS SOMETHING I NEED YOU TO SEE.

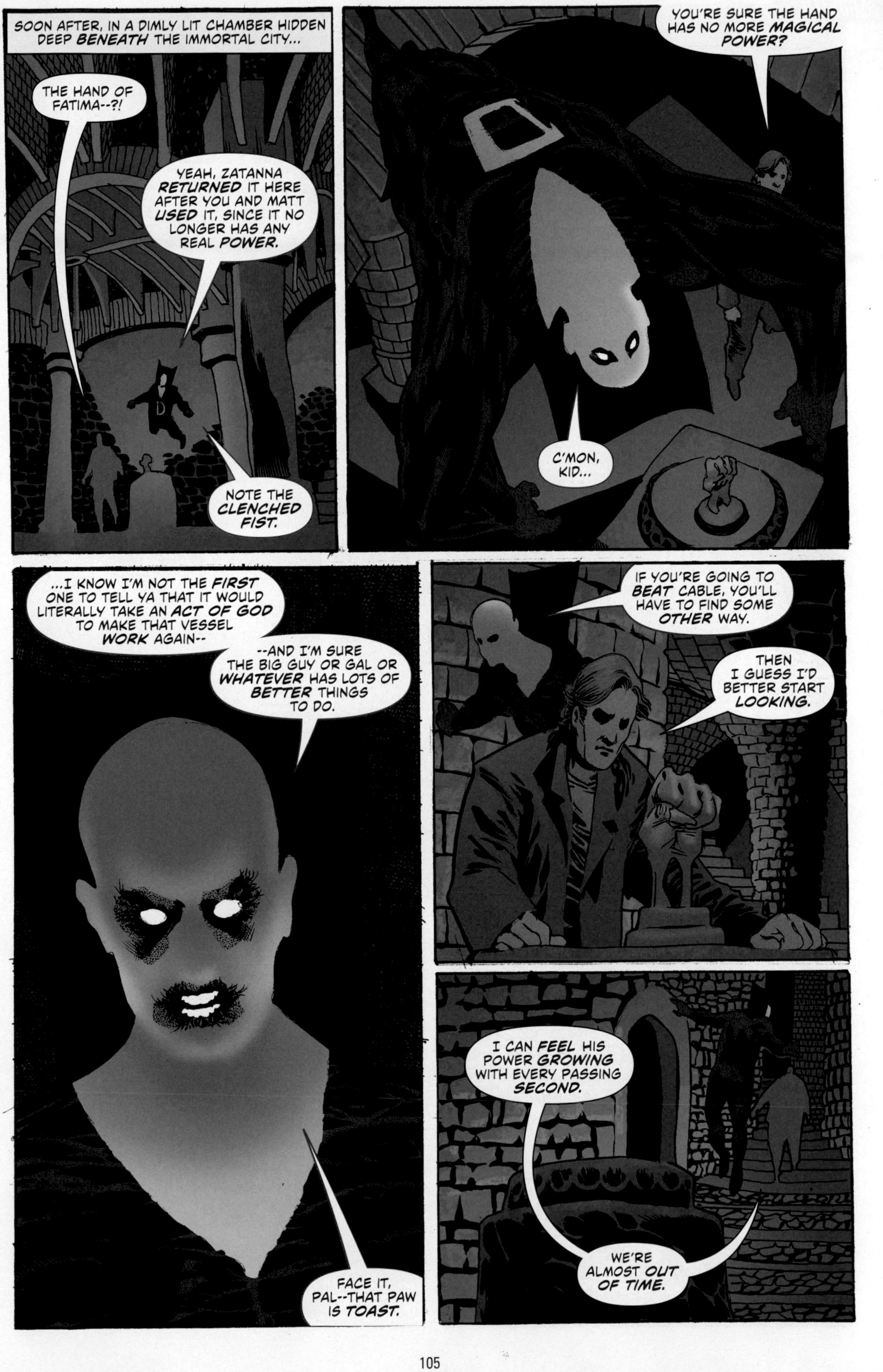
SOON AFTER, IN A DIMLY LIT CHAMBER HIDDEN DEEP BENEATH THE IMMORTAL CITY...
THE HAND OF FATIMA--?!
YEAH, ZATANNA RETURNED IT HERE AFTER YOU AND MATT USED IT, SINCE IT NO LONGER HAS ANY REAL POWER.
NOTE THE CLENCHED FIST.
YOU'RE SURE THE HAND HAS NO MORE MAGICAL POWER?
C'MON, KID...
...I KNOW I'M NOT THE FIRST ONE TO TELL YA THAT IT WOULD LITERALLY TAKE AN ACT OF GOD TO MAKE THAT VESSEL WORK AGAIN--
--AND I'M SURE THE BIG GUY OR GAL OR WHATEVER HAS LOTS OF BETTER THINGS TO DO.
FACE IT, PAL--THAT PAW IS TOAST.
IF YOU'RE GOING TO BEAT CABLE, YOU'LL HAVE TO FIND SOME OTHER WAY.
THEN I GUESS I'D BETTER START LOOKING.
I CAN FEEL HIS POWER GROWING WITH EVERY PASSING SECOND.
WE'RE ALMOST OUT OF TIME.

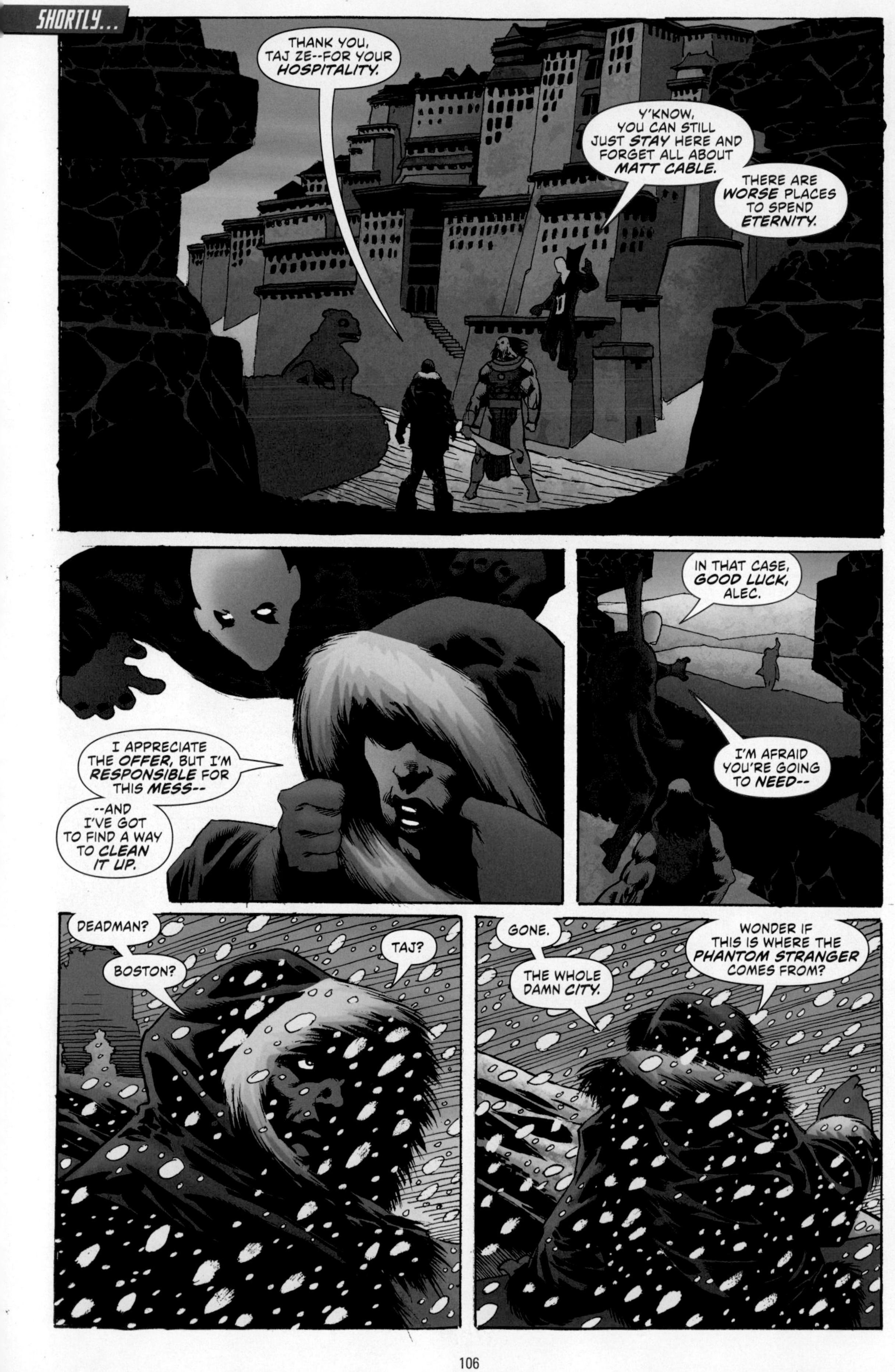
SHORTLY...
THANK YOU, TAJ ZE--FOR YOUR HOSPITALITY.
Y'KNOW, YOU CAN STILL JUST STAY HERE AND FORGET ALL ABOUT MATT CABLE.
THERE ARE WORSE PLACES TO SPEND ETERNITY.
I APPRECIATE THE OFFER, BUT I'M RESPONSIBLE FOR THIS MESS--
--AND I'VE GOT TO FIND A WAY TO CLEAN IT UP.
IN THAT CASE, GOOD LUCK, ALEC.
I'M AFRAID YOU'RE GOING TO NEED--
DEADMAN?
BOSTON?
TAJ?
GONE.
THE WHOLE DAMN CITY.
WONDER IF THIS IS WHERE THE PHANTOM STRANGER COMES FROM?

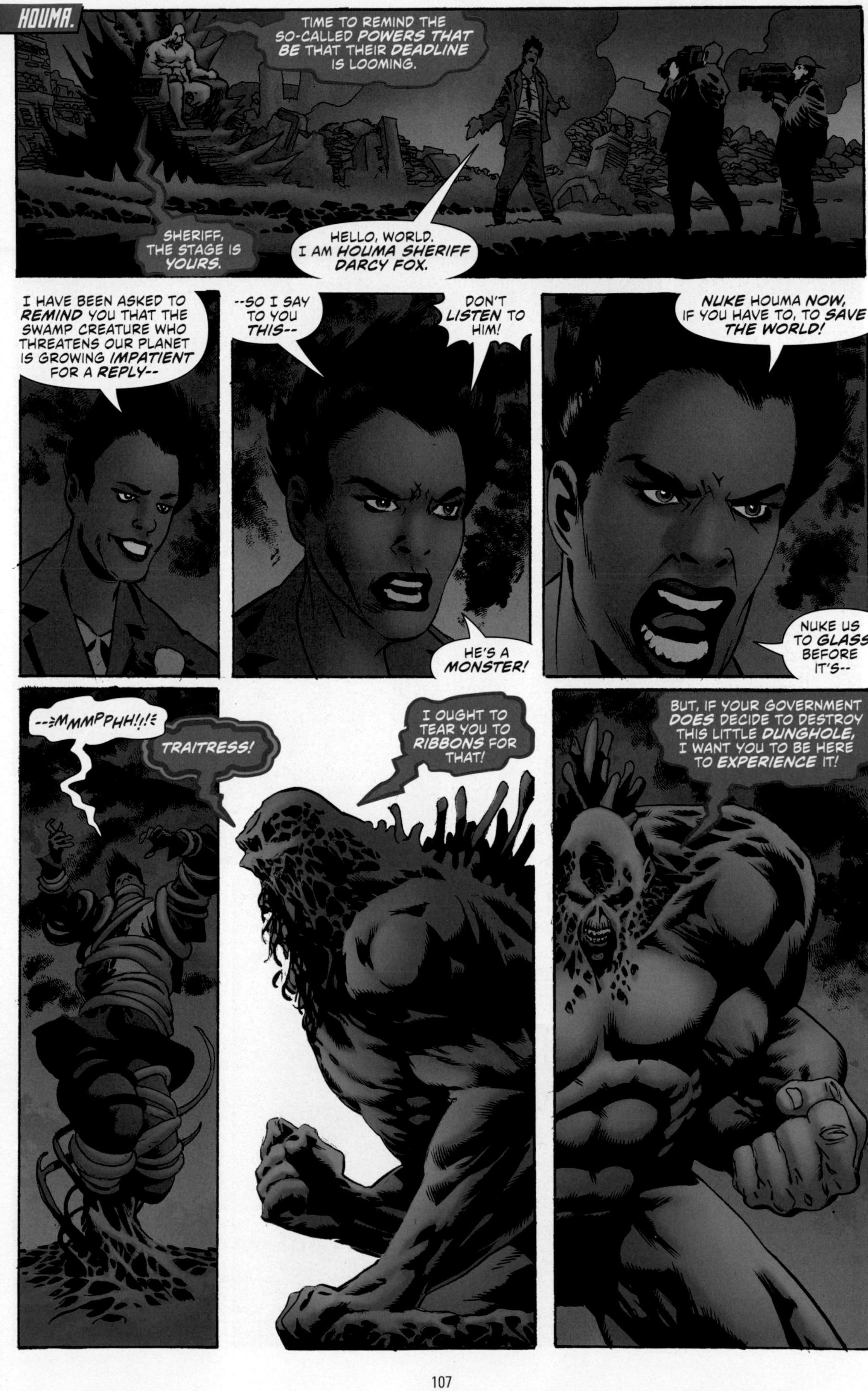
HOUMA.
TIME TO REMIND THE SO-CALLED POWERS THAT BE THAT THEIR DEADLINE IS LOOMING.
SHERIFF, THE STAGE IS YOURS.
HELLO, WORLD. I AM HOUMA SHERIFF DARCY FOX.
I HAVE BEEN ASKED TO REMIND YOU THAT THE SWAMP CREATURE WHO THREATENS OUR PLANET IS GROWING IMPATIENT FOR A REPLY--
--SO I SAY TO YOU THIS--
DON'T LISTEN TO HIM!
HE'S A MONSTER!
NUKE HOUMA NOW, IF YOU HAVE TO, TO SAVE THE WORLD!
NUKE US TO GLASS BEFORE IT'S--
--MMMPPHH!!!
TRAITRESS!
I OUGHT TO TEAR YOU TO RIBBONS FOR THAT!
BUT, IF YOUR GOVERNMENT DOES DECIDE TO DESTROY THIS LITTLE DUNGHOLE, I WANT YOU TO BE HERE TO EXPERIENCE IT!

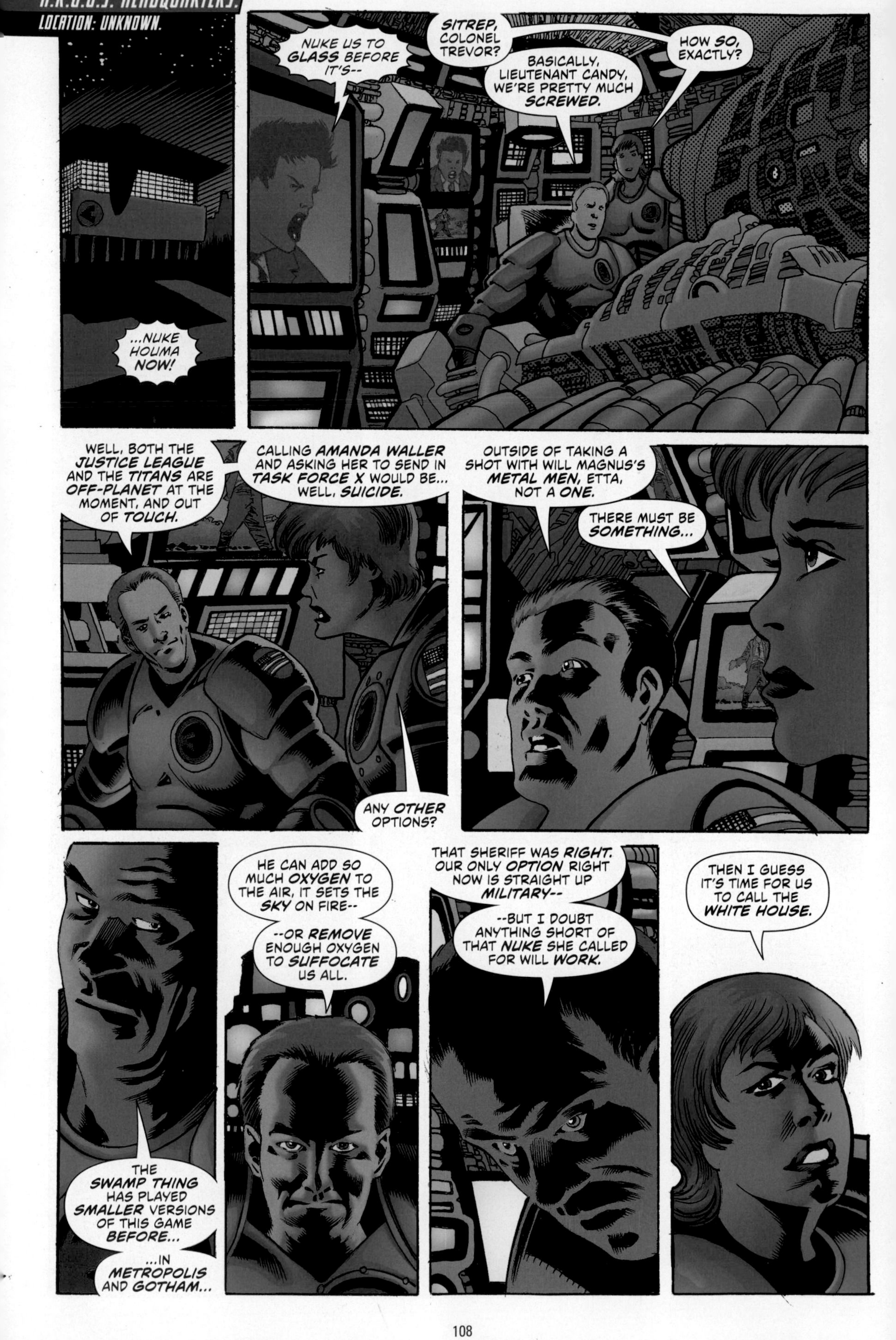
A.R.G.U.S. HEADQUARTERS.
LOCATION: UNKNOWN.
...NUKE HOUMA NOW!
NUKE US TO GLASS BEFORE IT'S--
SITREP, COLONEL TREVOR?
BASICALLY, LIEUTENANT CANDY, WE'RE PRETTY MUCH SCREWED.
HOW SO, EXACTLY?
WELL, BOTH THE JUSTICE LEAGUE AND THE TITANS ARE OFF-PLANET AT THE MOMENT, AND OUT OF TOUCH.
CALLING AMANDA WALLER AND ASKING HER TO SEND IN TASK FORCE X WOULD BE... WELL, SUICIDE.
ANY OTHER OPTIONS?
OUTSIDE OF TAKING A SHOT WITH WILL MAGNUS'S METAL MEN, ETTA, NOT A ONE.
THERE MUST BE SOMETHING...
THE SWAMP THING HAS PLAYED SMALLER VERSIONS OF THIS GAME BEFORE...
...IN METROPOLIS AND GOTHAM...
HE CAN ADD SO MUCH OXYGEN TO THE AIR, IT SETS THE SKY ON FIRE--
--OR REMOVE ENOUGH OXYGEN TO SUFFOCATE US ALL.
THAT SHERIFF WAS RIGHT. OUR ONLY OPTION RIGHT NOW IS STRAIGHT UP MILITARY--
--BUT I DOUBT ANYTHING SHORT OF THAT NUKE SHE CALLED FOR WILL WORK.
THEN I GUESS IT'S TIME FOR US TO CALL THE WHITE HOUSE.

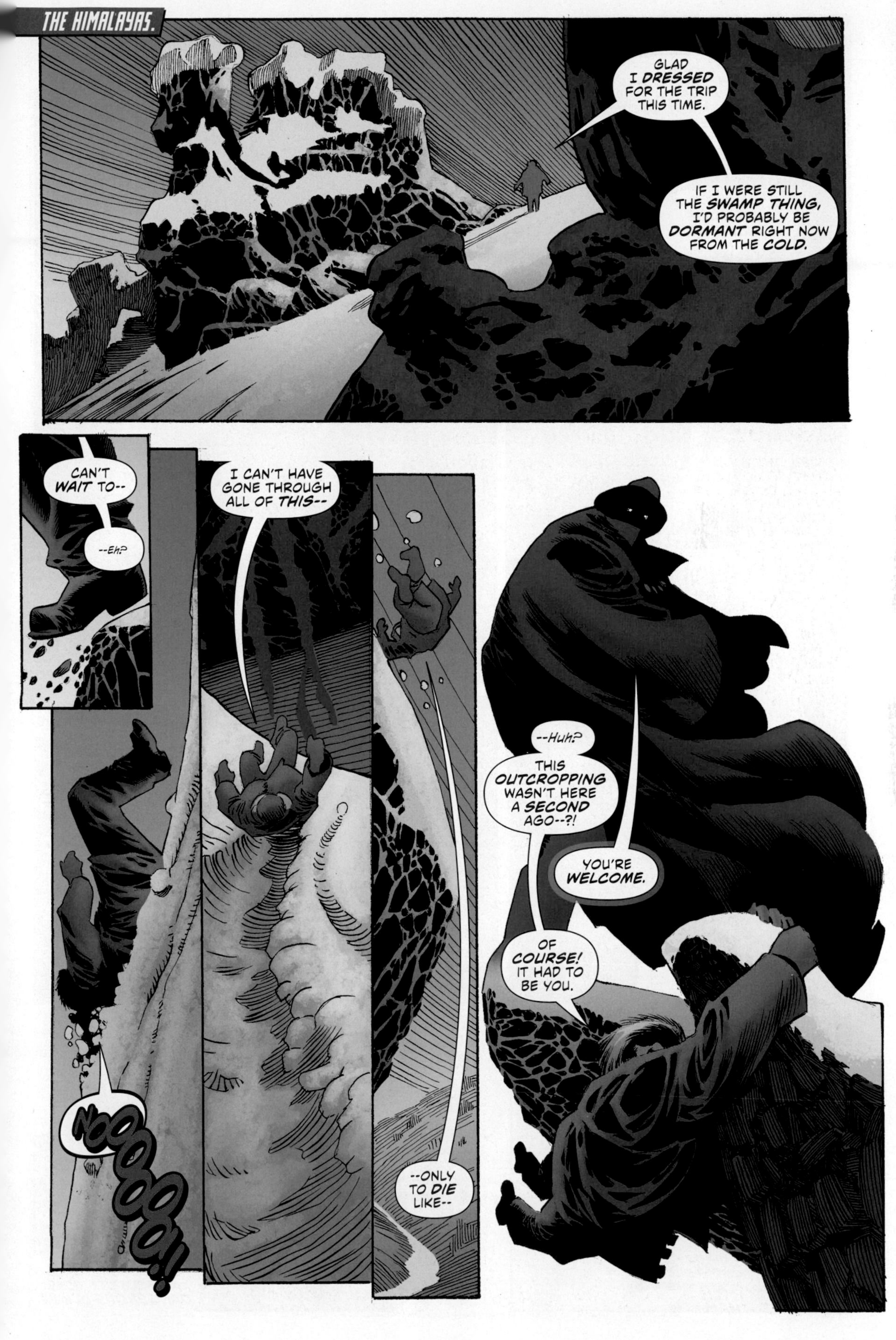
THE HIMALAYAS.
GLAD I DRESSED FOR THE TRIP THIS TIME.
IF I WERE STILL THE SWAMP THING, I'D PROBABLY BE DORMANT RIGHT NOW FROM THE COLD.
CAN'T WAIT TO--
--EH?
NOOOOOOO!!
I CAN'T HAVE GONE THROUGH ALL OF THIS--
--ONLY TO DIE LIKE--
--HUH?
THIS OUTCROPPING WASN'T HERE A SECOND AGO--?!
YOU'RE WELCOME.
OF COURSE! IT HAD TO BE YOU.

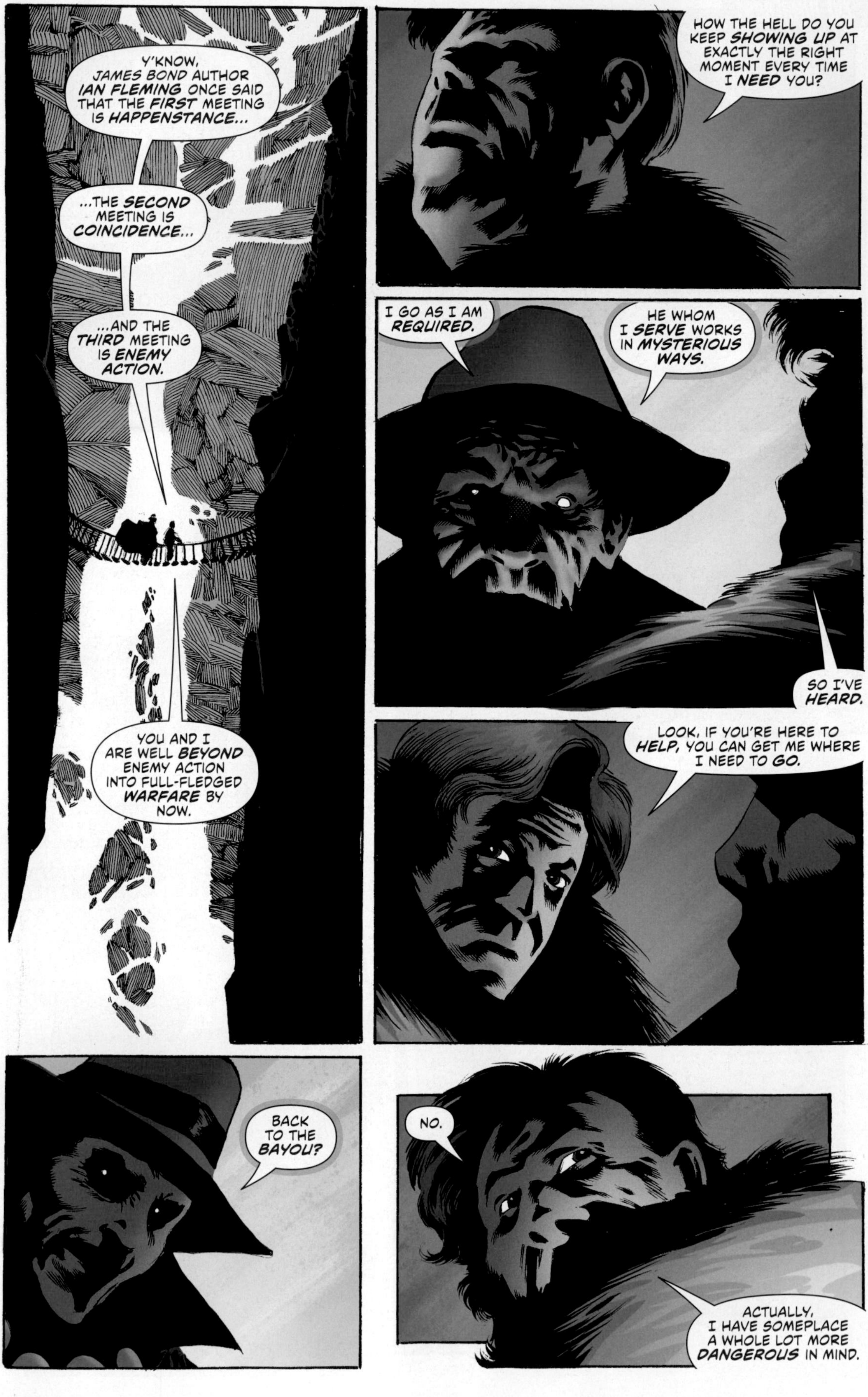

Y'KNOW, JAMES BOND AUTHOR IAN FLEMING ONCE SAID THAT THE FIRST MEETING IS HAPPENSTANCE...
...THE SECOND MEETING IS COINCIDENCE...
...AND THE THIRD MEETING IS ENEMY ACTION.
YOU AND I ARE WELL BEYOND ENEMY ACTION INTO FULL-FLEDGED WARFARE BY NOW.
HOW THE HELL DO YOU KEEP SHOWING UP AT EXACTLY THE RIGHT MOMENT EVERY TIME I NEED YOU?
I GO AS I AM REQUIRED.
HE WHOM I SERVE WORKS IN MYSTERIOUS WAYS.
SO I'VE HEARD.
LOOK, IF YOU'RE HERE TO HELP, YOU CAN GET ME WHERE I NEED TO GO.
BACK TO THE BAYOU?
NO.
ACTUALLY, I HAVE SOMEPLACE A WHOLE LOT MORE DANGEROUS IN MIND.

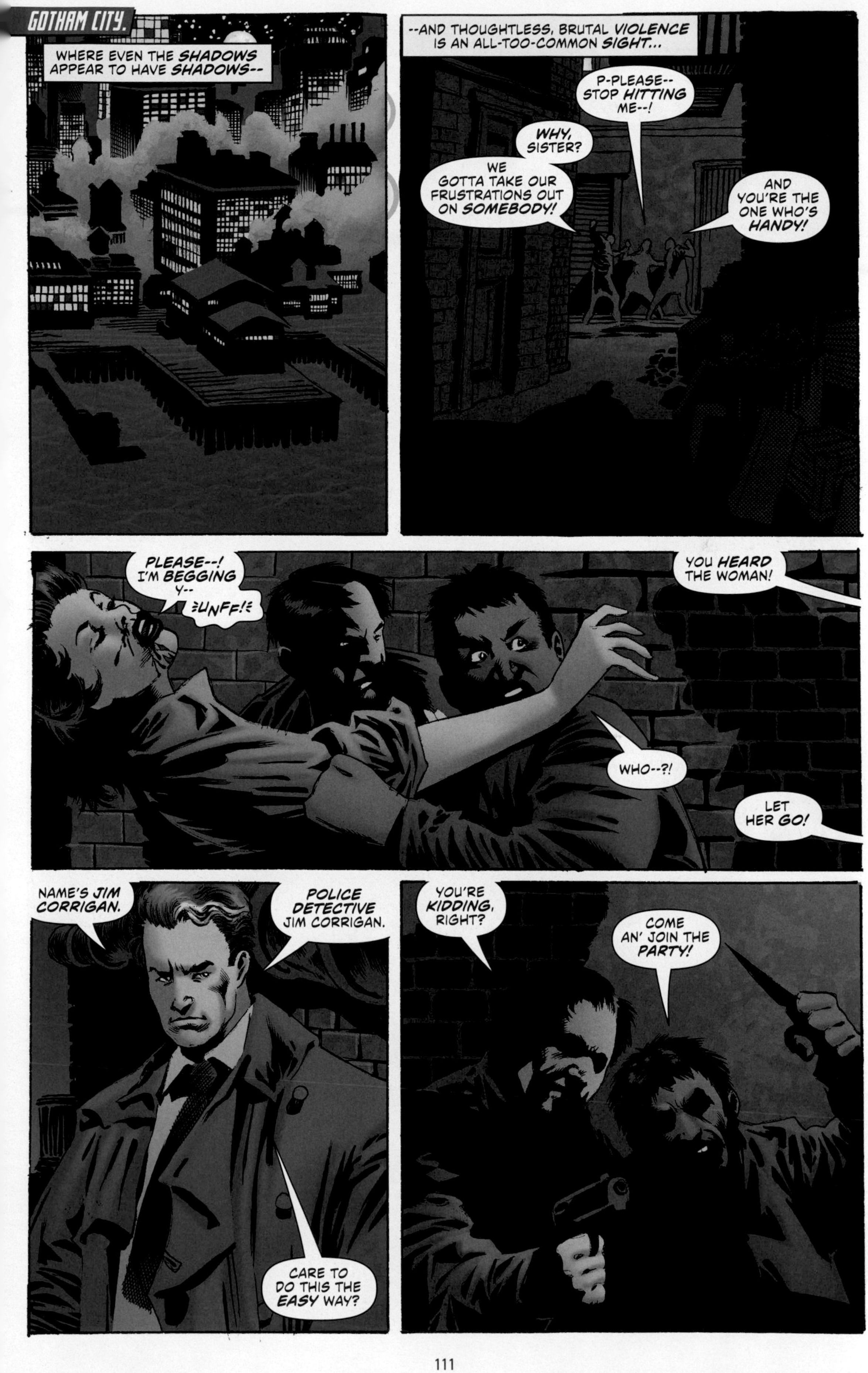
GOTHAM CITY.
WHERE EVEN THE SHADOWS APPEAR TO HAVE SHADOWS--
--AND THOUGHTLESS, BRUTAL VIOLENCE IS AN ALL-TOO-COMMON SIGHT...
P-PLEASE-- STOP HITTING ME--!
WHY, SISTER?
WE GOTTA TAKE OUR FRUSTRATIONS OUT ON SOMEBODY!
AND YOU'RE THE ONE WHO'S HANDY!
PLEASE--! I'M BEGGING Y--
UNFF!
YOU HEARD THE WOMAN!
WHO--?!
LET HER GO!
NAME'S JIM CORRIGAN.
POLICE DETECTIVE JIM CORRIGAN.
CARE TO DO THIS THE EASY WAY?
YOU'RE KIDDING, RIGHT?
COME AN' JOIN THE PARTY!

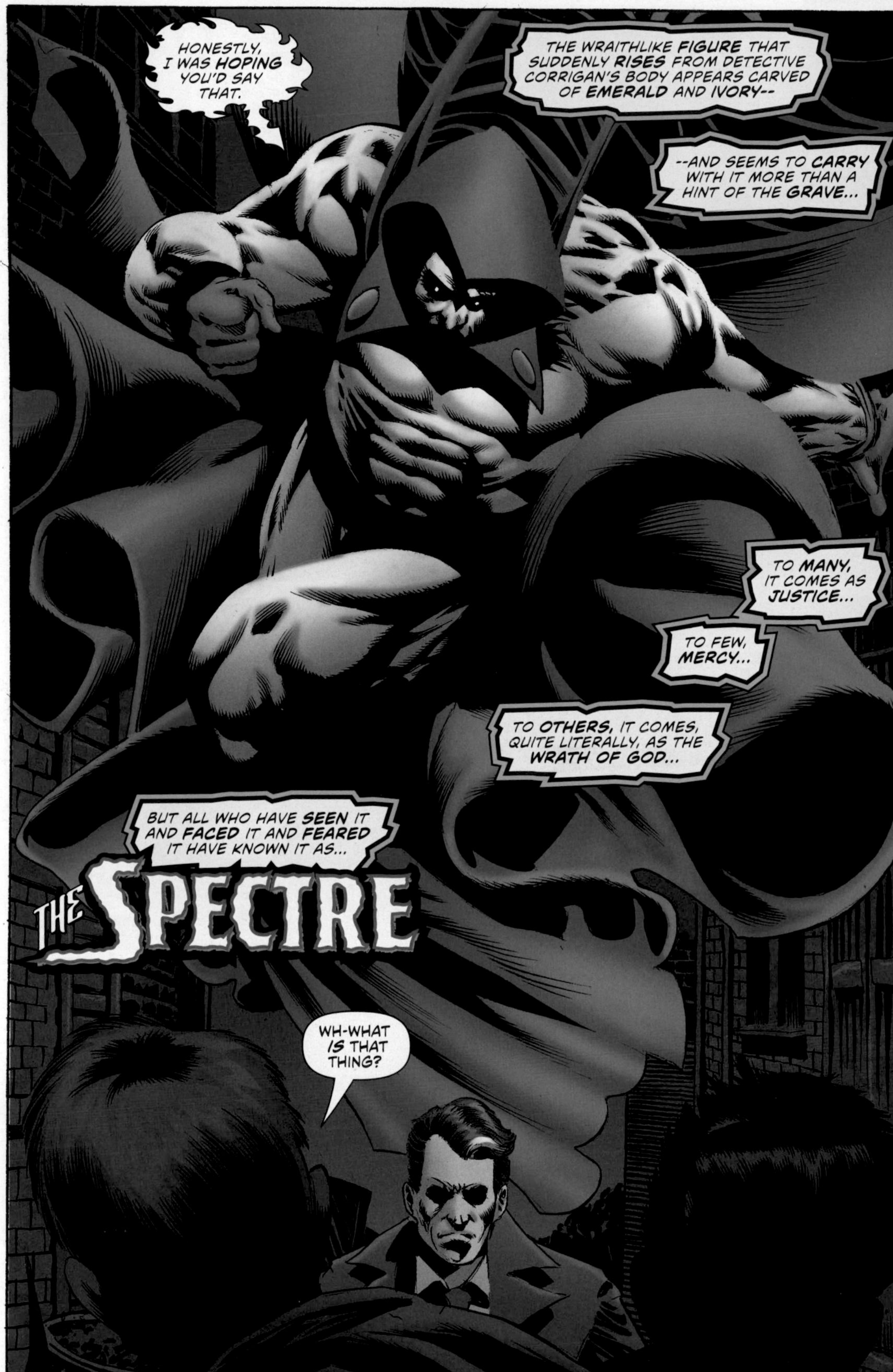

HONESTLY, I WAS HOPING YOU'D SAY THAT.
THE WRAITHLIKE FIGURE THAT SUDDENLY RISES FROM DETECTIVE CORRIGAN'S BODY APPEARS CARVED OF EMERALD AND IVORY--
--AND SEEMS TO CARRY WITH IT MORE THAN A HINT OF THE GRAVE...
TO MANY, IT COMES AS JUSTICE...
TO FEW, MERCY...
TO OTHERS, IT COMES, QUITE LITERALLY, AS THE WRATH OF GOD...
BUT ALL WHO HAVE SEEN IT AND FACED IT AND FEARED IT HAVE KNOWN IT AS...
THE SPECTRE
WH-WHAT IS THAT THING?

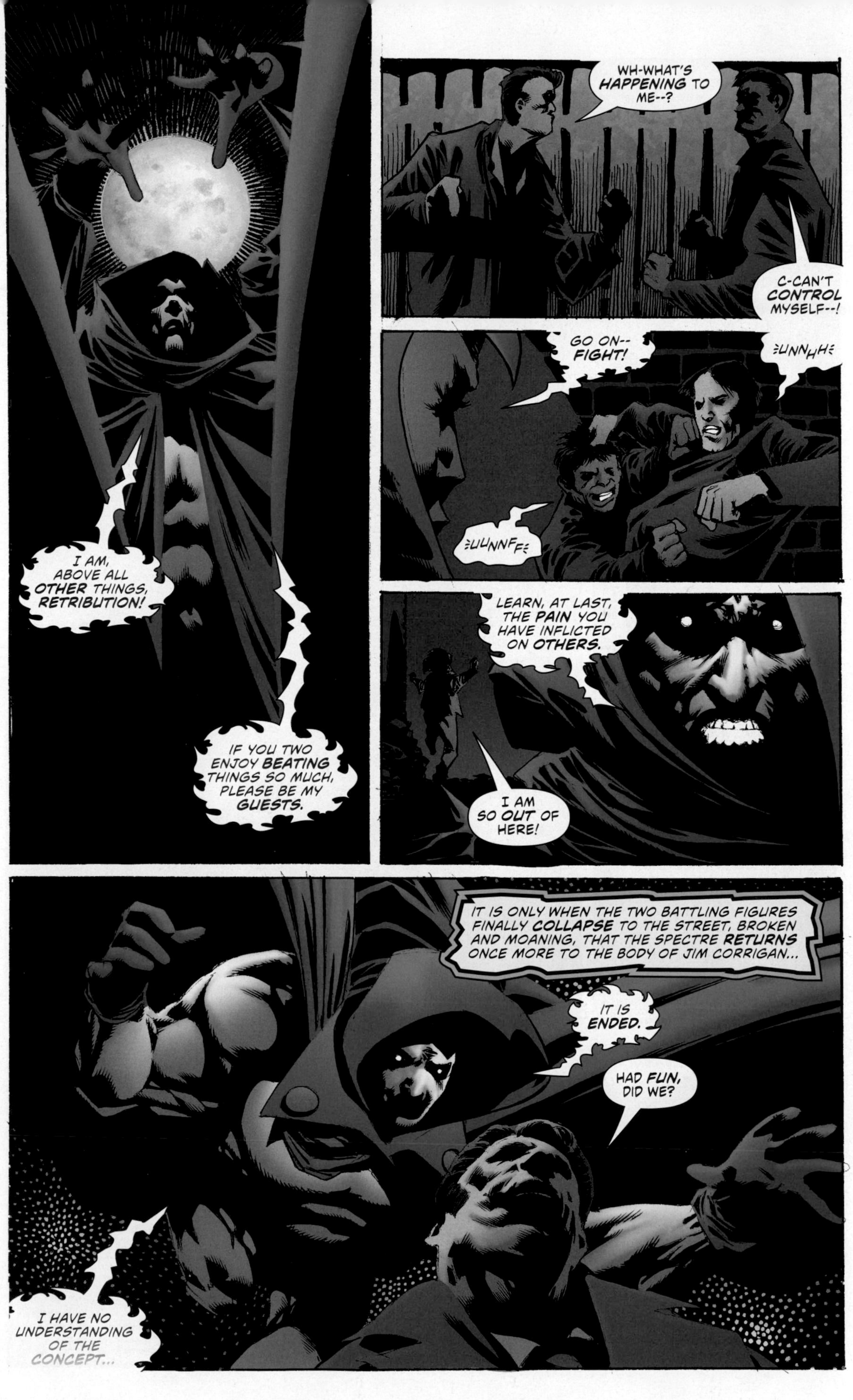

I AM, ABOVE ALL OTHER THINGS, RETRIBUTION!
IF YOU TWO ENJOY BEATING THINGS SO MUCH, PLEASE BE MY GUESTS.
WH-WHAT'S HAPPENING TO ME--?
C-CAN'T CONTROL MYSELF--!
GO ON-- FIGHT!
UNNHH
UUNNFF
LEARN, AT LAST, THE PAIN YOU HAVE INFLICTED ON OTHERS.
I AM SO OUT OF HERE!
IT IS ONLY WHEN THE TWO BATTLING FIGURES FINALLY COLLAPSE TO THE STREET, BROKEN AND MOANING, THAT THE SPECTRE RETURNS ONCE MORE TO THE BODY OF JIM CORRIGAN...
IT IS ENDED.
HAD FUN, DID WE?
I HAVE NO UNDERSTANDING OF THE CONCEPT...

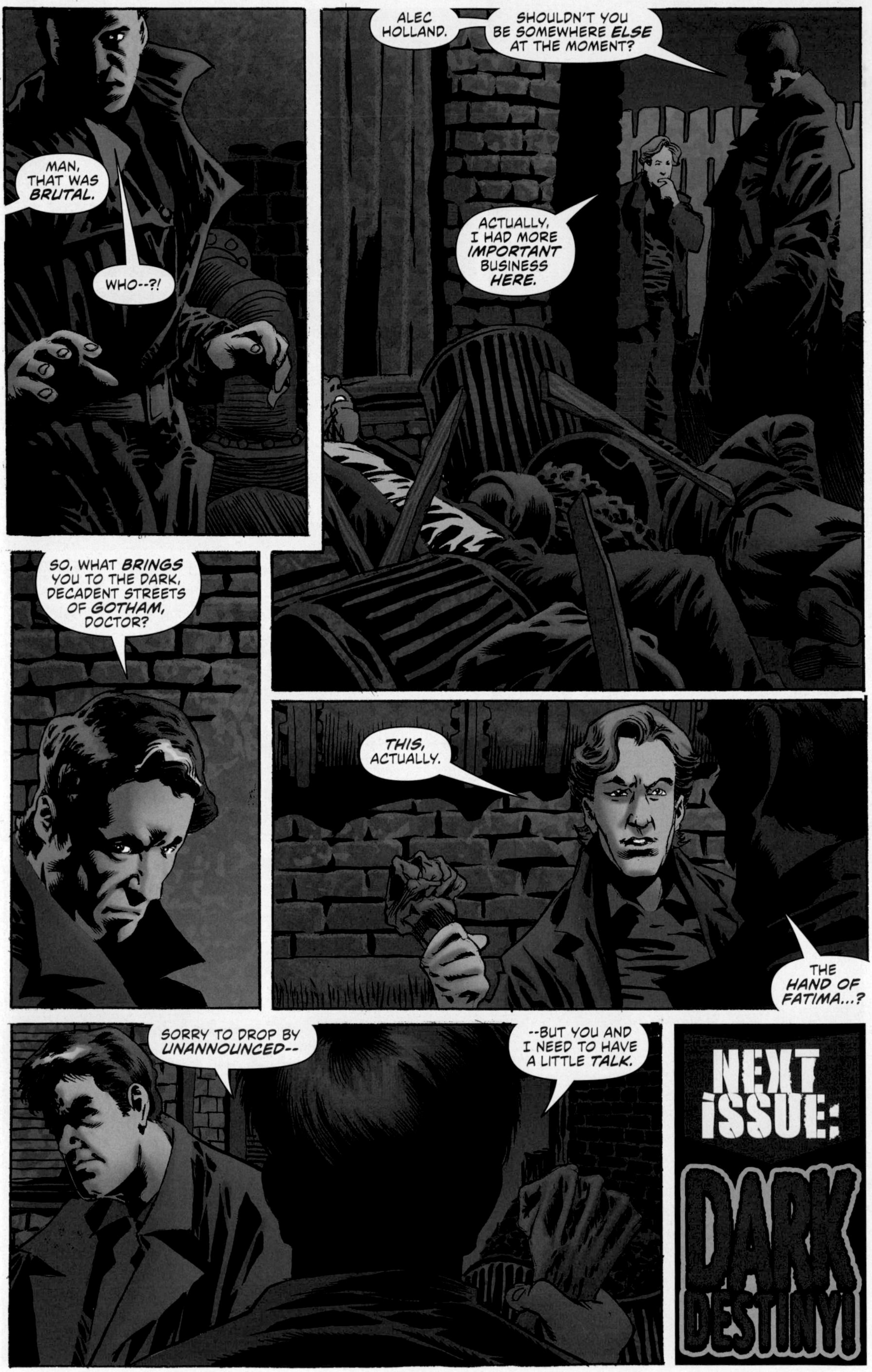
MAN, THAT WAS BRUTAL.
WHO--?!
ALEC HOLLAND.
SHOULDN'T YOU BE SOMEWHERE ELSE AT THE MOMENT?
ACTUALLY, I HAD MORE IMPORTANT BUSINESS HERE.
SO, WHAT BRINGS YOU TO THE DARK, DECADENT STREETS OF GOTHAM, DOCTOR?
THIS, ACTUALLY.
THE HAND OF FATIMA...?
SORRY TO DROP BY UNANNOUNCED--
--BUT YOU AND I NEED TO HAVE A LITTLE TALK.
NEXT ISSUE:
DARK DESTINY!

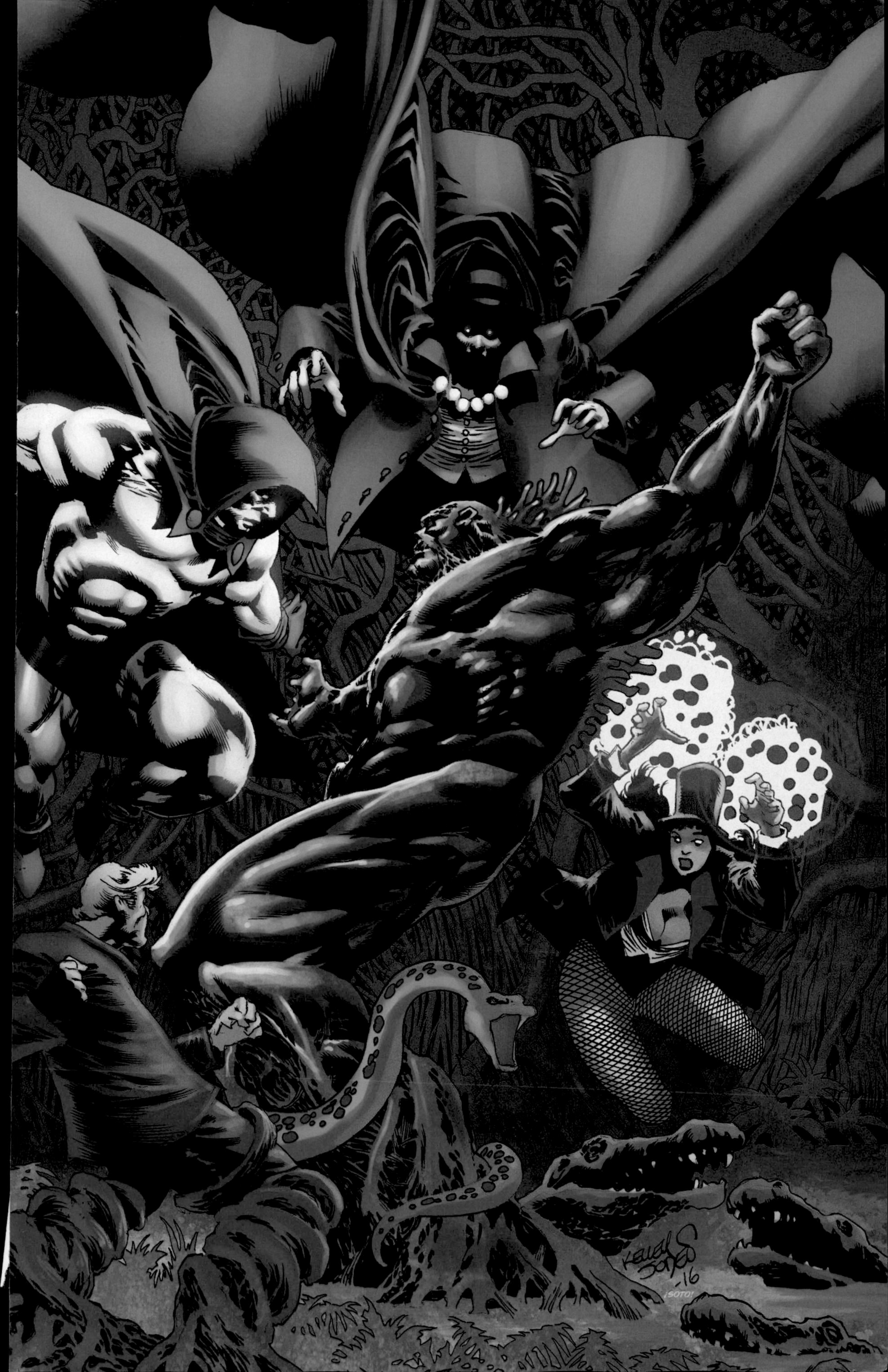

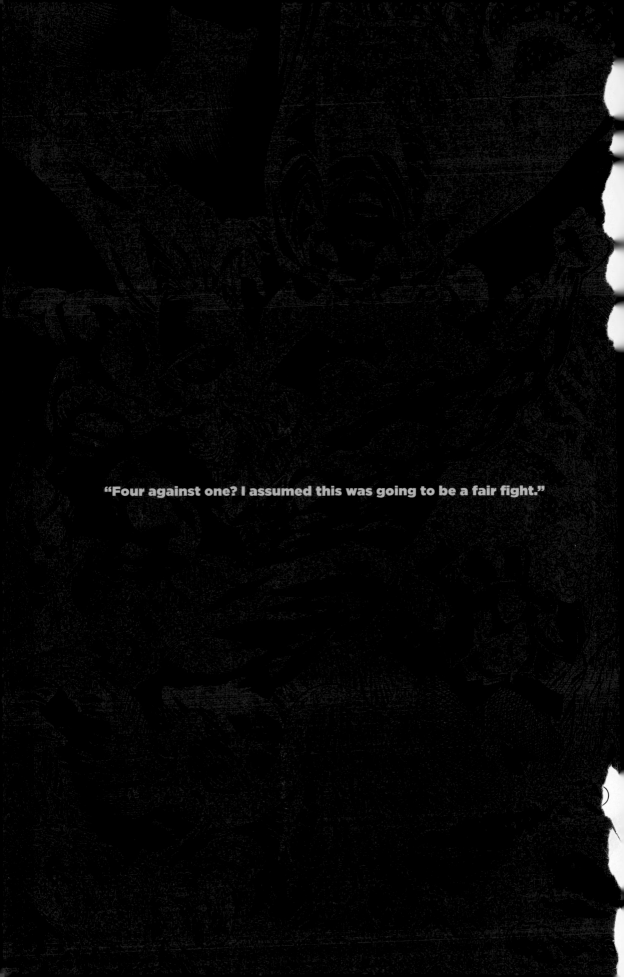

"Four against one? I assumed this was going to be a fair fight."

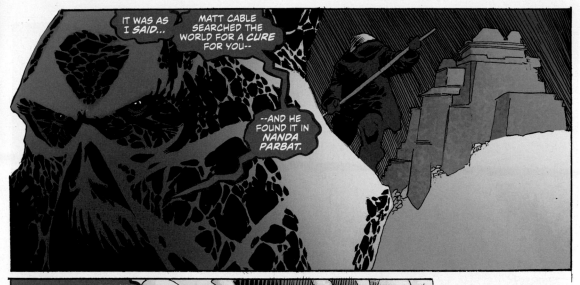

IT WAS AS I *SAID*...

MATT CABLE SEARCHED THE WORLD FOR A *CURE* FOR YOU--

--AND HE FOUND IT IN *NANDA PARBAT.*

BUT, ON HIS WAY *DOWN* THE MOUNTAIN, HE WAS CAUGHT IN A TERRIBLE *AVALANCHE*--

--AND ALMOST *DIED.*

WHILE HE LAY THERE, BATTERED AND BROKEN, SUFFERING *TERRIBLY,* A *VOICE* CAME TO HIM--

--AND OFFERED HIM *LIFE* IN EXCHANGE FOR *POWER.*

A DEAL WITH *WHOM?*

AND WHY DO YOU KEEP SPEAKING ABOUT YOURSELF IN THE *THIRD PERSON?*

WHAT CAN I *SAY?* CABLE WAS A *COWARD.*

IN THE END, HE TOOK THE *DEAL.*

MY GOD, YOU REALLY ARE AS THICK AS THE PROVERBIAL *POST,* AREN'T YOU?

WHO DO YOU *THINK* OFFERED HIM THE DEAL, ALEC?

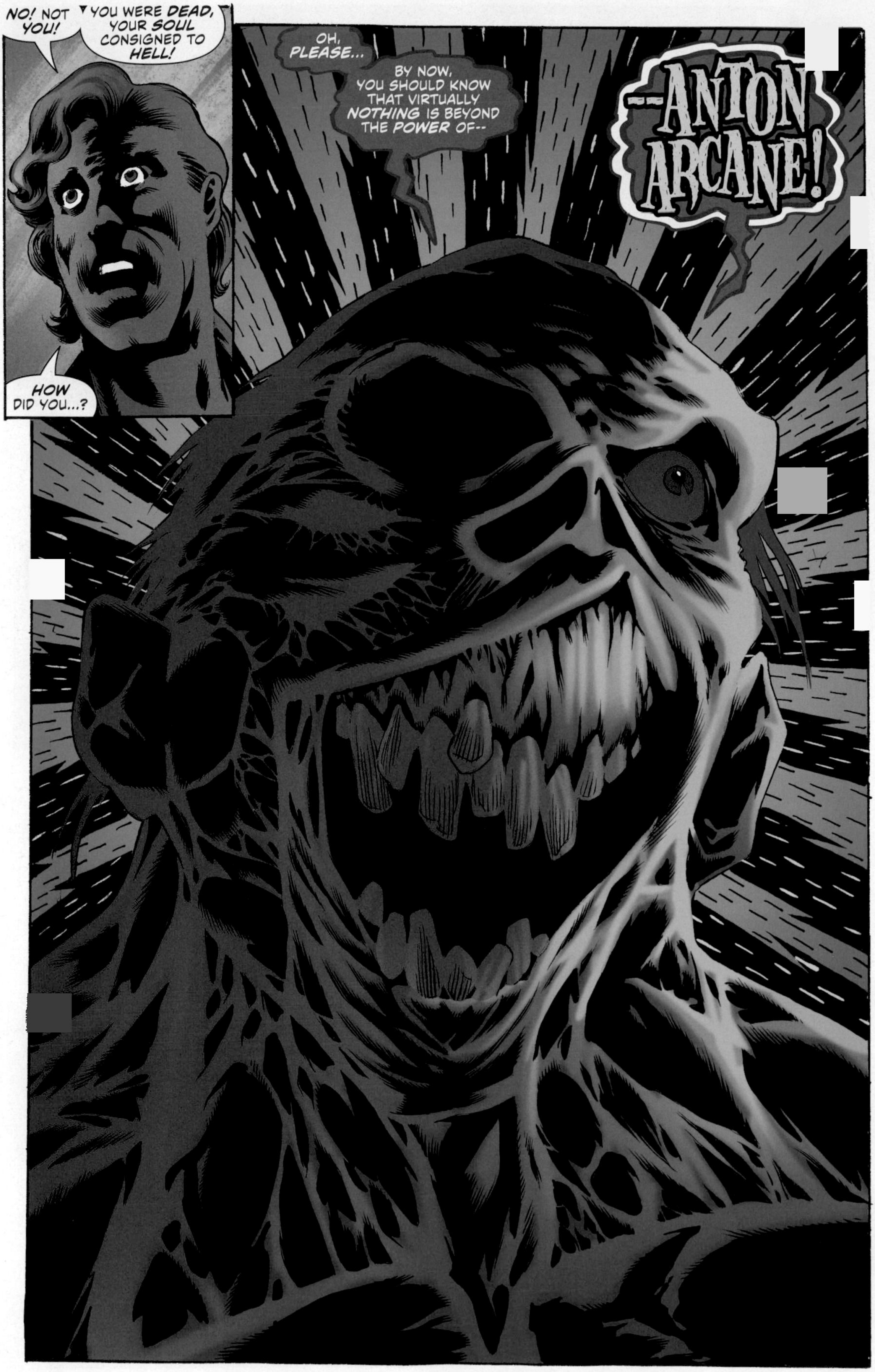
NO! NOT YOU!
YOU WERE DEAD, YOUR SOUL CONSIGNED TO HELL!
HOW DID YOU...?
OH, PLEASE...
BY NOW, YOU SHOULD KNOW THAT VIRTUALLY NOTHING IS BEYOND THE POWER OF--
--ANTON ARCANE!

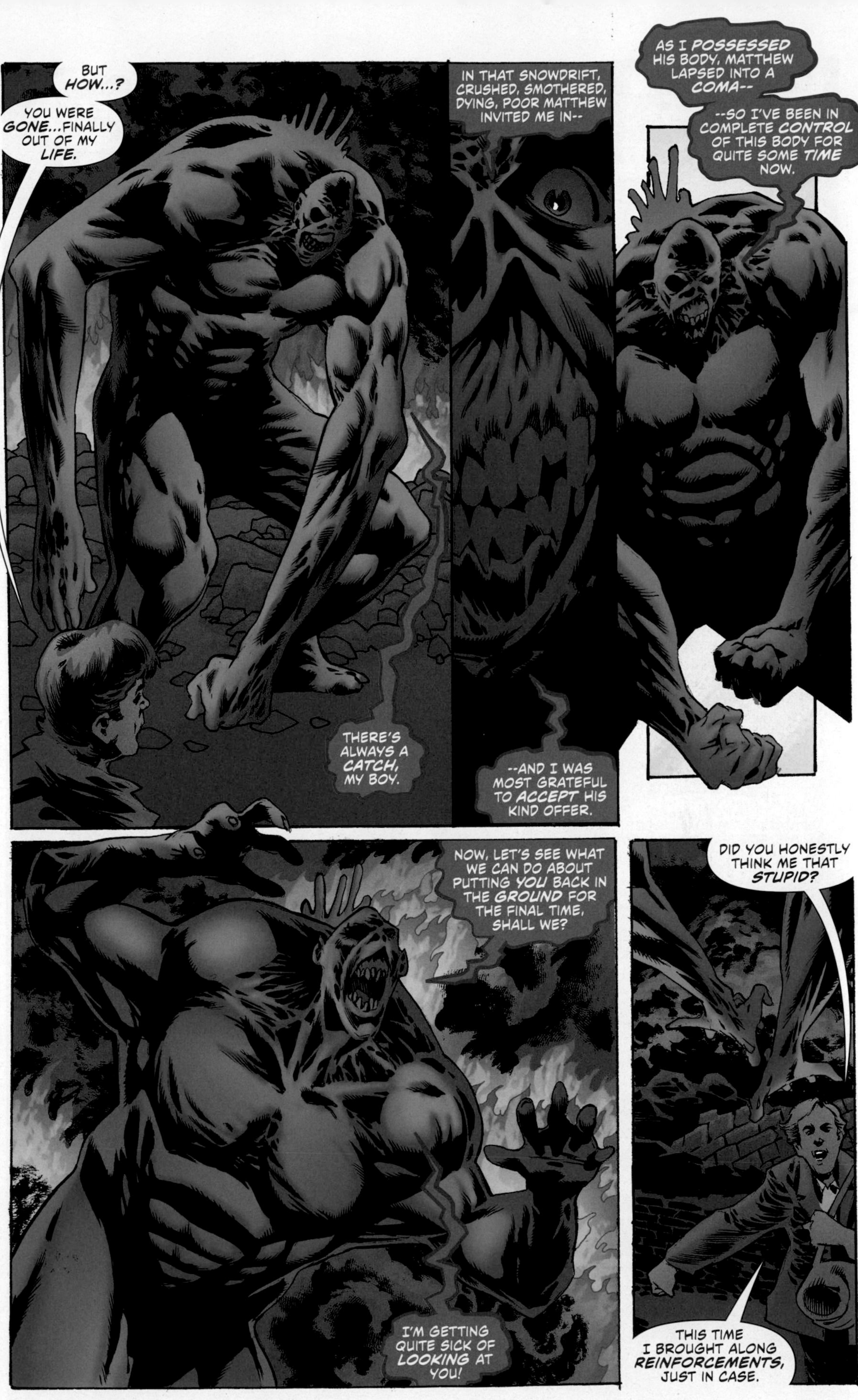
BUT HOW...?
YOU WERE GONE...FINALLY OUT OF MY LIFE.
THERE'S ALWAYS A CATCH, MY BOY.
IN THAT SNOWDRIFT, CRUSHED, SMOTHERED, DYING, POOR MATTHEW INVITED ME IN--
--AND I WAS MOST GRATEFUL TO ACCEPT HIS KIND OFFER.
AS I POSSESSED HIS BODY, MATTHEW LAPSED INTO A COMA--
--SO I'VE BEEN IN COMPLETE CONTROL OF THIS BODY FOR QUITE SOME TIME NOW.
NOW, LET'S SEE WHAT WE CAN DO ABOUT PUTTING YOU BACK IN THE GROUND FOR THE FINAL TIME, SHALL WE?
I'M GETTING QUITE SICK OF LOOKING AT YOU!
DID YOU HONESTLY THINK ME THAT STUPID?
THIS TIME I BROUGHT ALONG REINFORCEMENTS, JUST IN CASE.

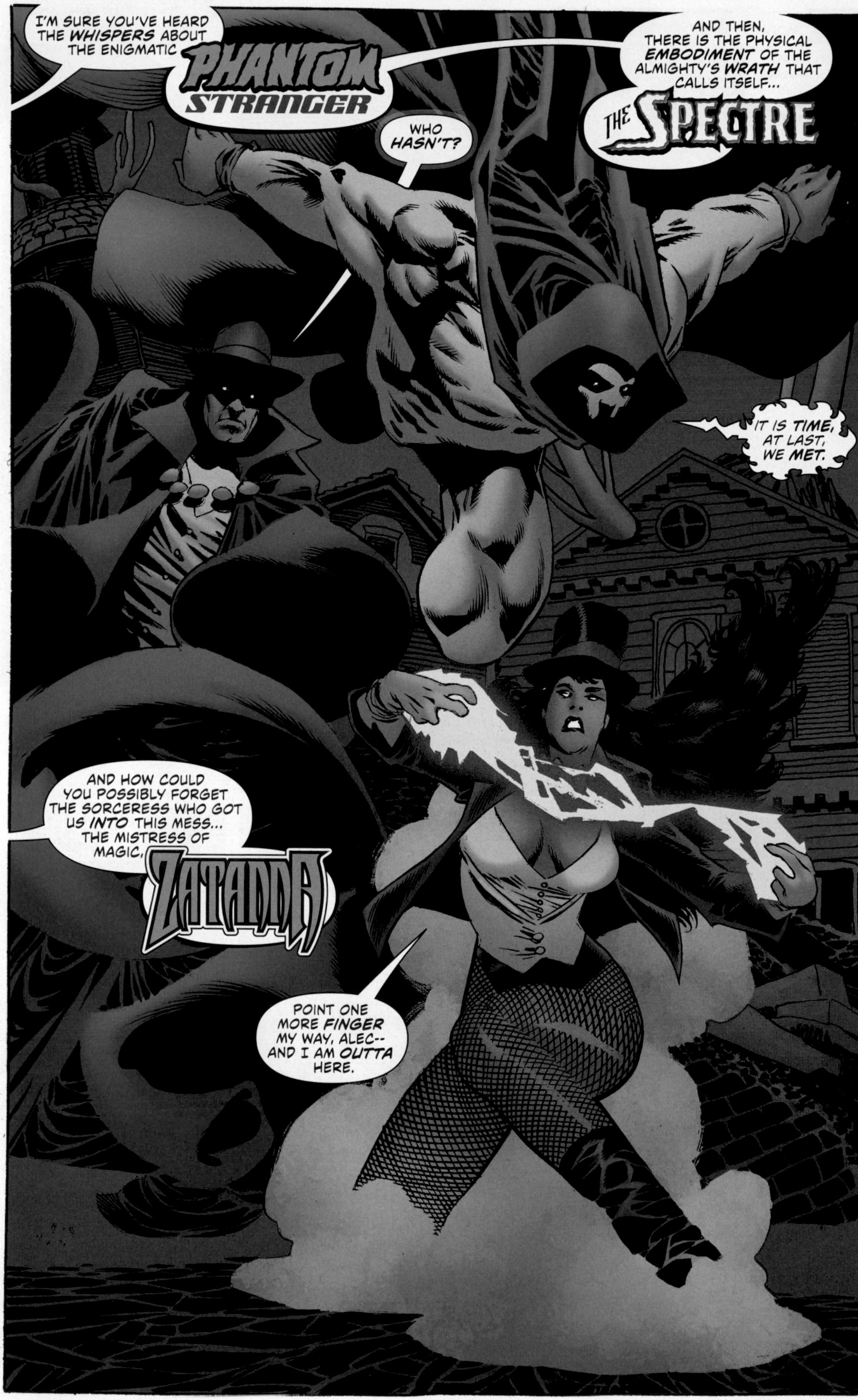
I'M SURE YOU'VE HEARD THE WHISPERS ABOUT THE ENIGMATIC
PHANTOM STRANGER
WHO HASN'T?
AND THEN, THERE IS THE PHYSICAL EMBODIMENT OF THE ALMIGHTY'S WRATH THAT CALLS ITSELF...
THE SPECTRE
IT IS TIME, AT LAST, WE MET.
AND HOW COULD YOU POSSIBLY FORGET THE SORCERESS WHO GOT US INTO THIS MESS... THE MISTRESS OF MAGIC,
ZATANNA
POINT ONE MORE FINGER MY WAY, ALEC-- AND I AM OUTTA HERE.

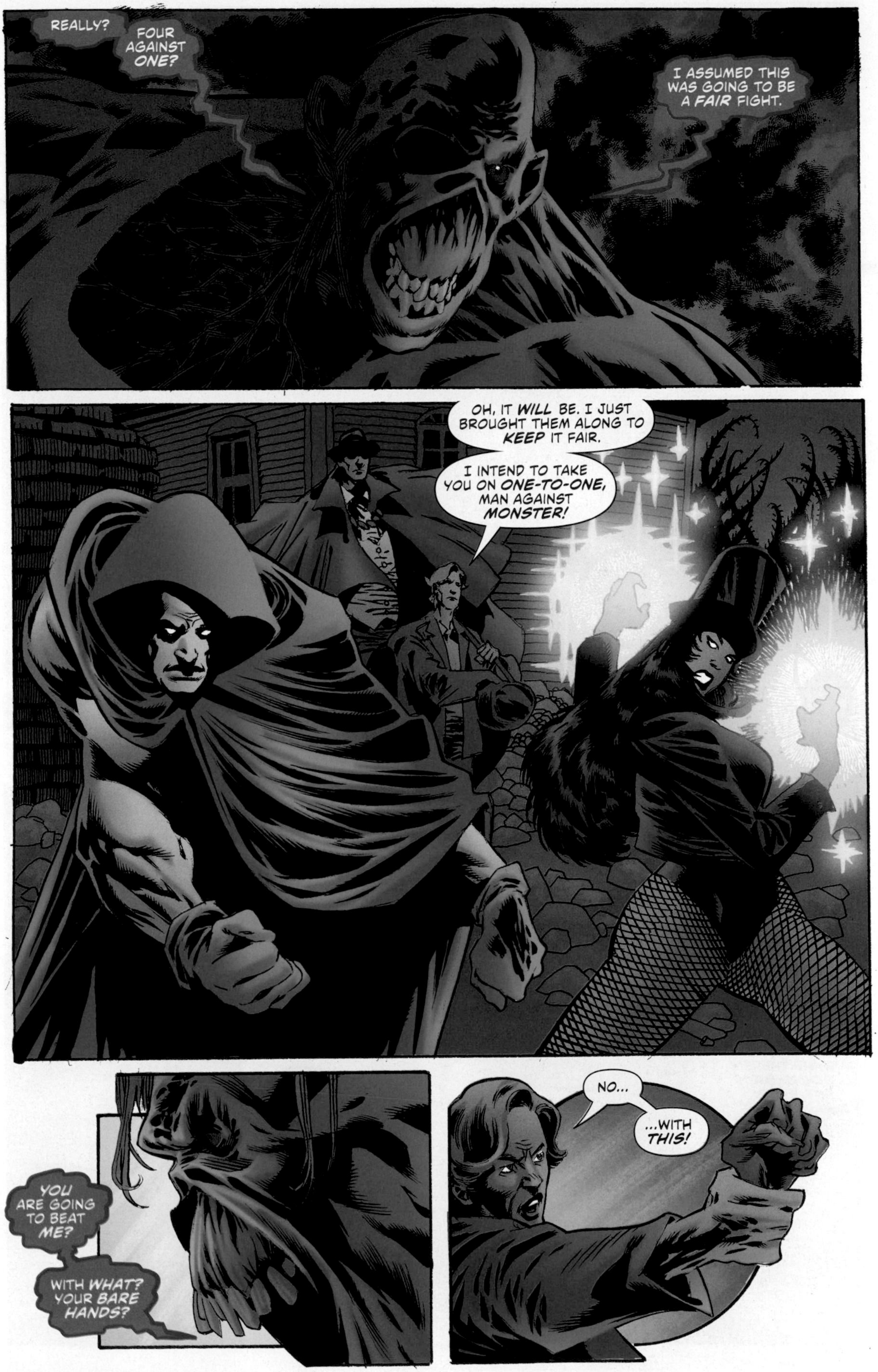
REALLY?
FOUR AGAINST ONE?
I ASSUMED THIS WAS GOING TO BE A FAIR FIGHT.
OH, IT WILL BE. I JUST BROUGHT THEM ALONG TO KEEP IT FAIR.
I INTEND TO TAKE YOU ON ONE-TO-ONE, MAN AGAINST MONSTER!
YOU ARE GOING TO BEAT ME?
WITH WHAT? YOUR BARE HANDS?
NO...
...WITH THIS!

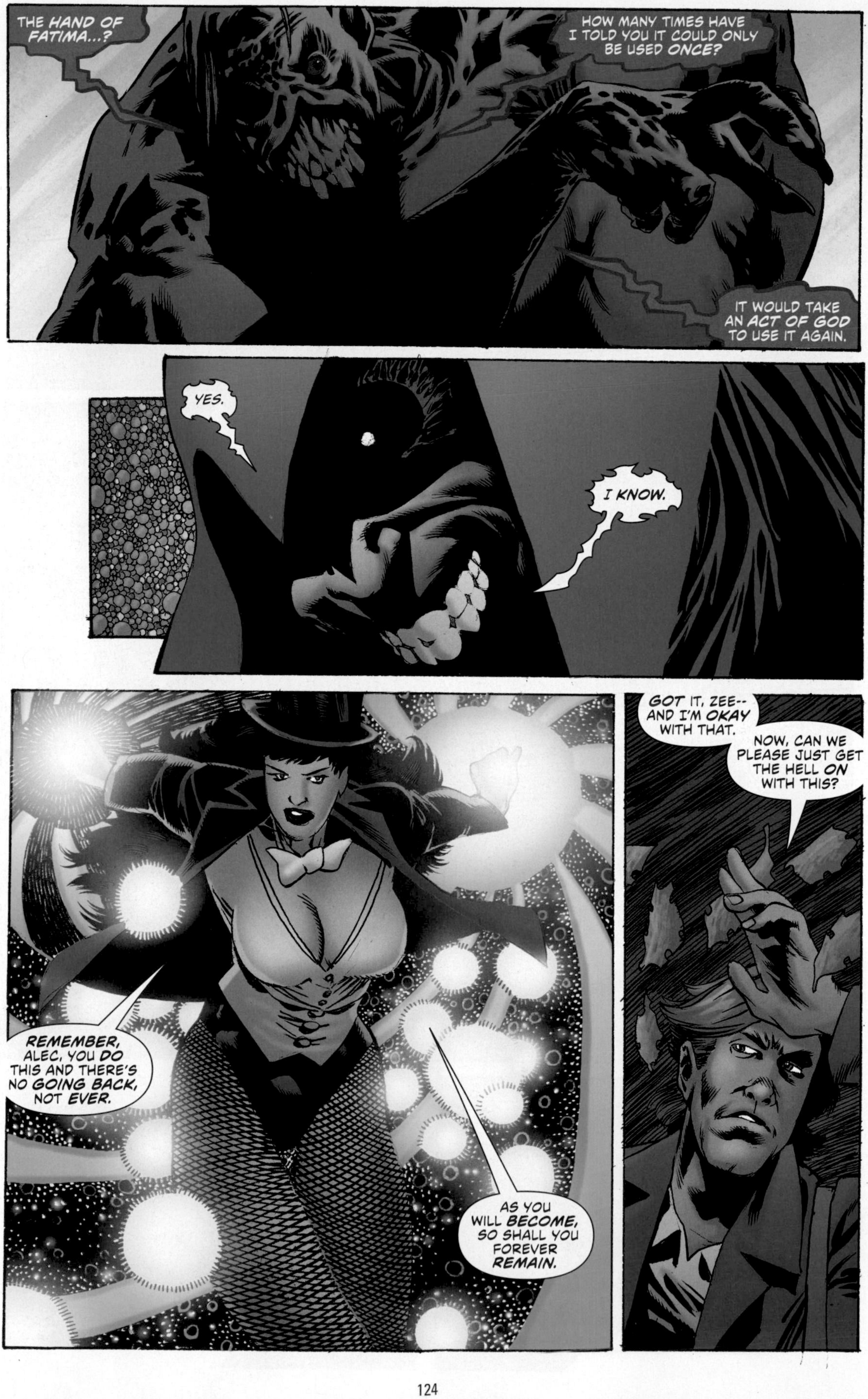
THE HAND OF FATIMA...?
HOW MANY TIMES HAVE I TOLD YOU IT COULD ONLY BE USED ONCE?
IT WOULD TAKE AN ACT OF GOD TO USE IT AGAIN.
YES.
I KNOW.
REMEMBER, ALEC, YOU DO THIS AND THERE'S NO GOING BACK, NOT EVER.
AS YOU WILL BECOME, SO SHALL YOU FOREVER REMAIN.
GOT IT, ZEE-- AND I'M OKAY WITH THAT.
NOW, CAN WE PLEASE JUST GET THE HELL ON WITH THIS?

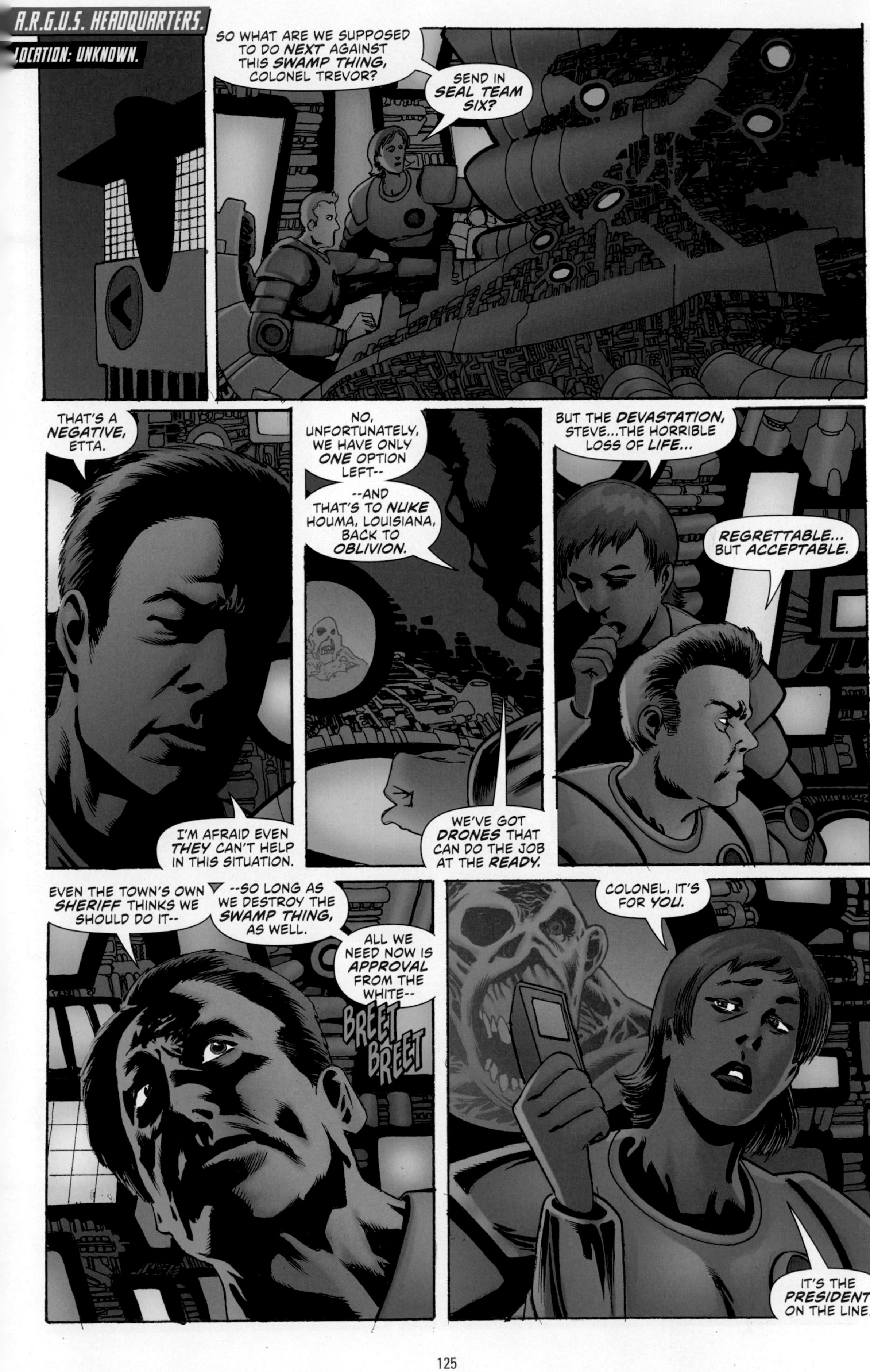
A.R.G.U.S. HEADQUARTERS.
LOCATION: UNKNOWN.
SO WHAT ARE WE SUPPOSED TO DO NEXT AGAINST THIS SWAMP THING, COLONEL TREVOR?
SEND IN SEAL TEAM SIX?
THAT'S A NEGATIVE, ETTA.
I'M AFRAID EVEN THEY CAN'T HELP IN THIS SITUATION.
NO, UNFORTUNATELY, WE HAVE ONLY ONE OPTION LEFT--
--AND THAT'S TO NUKE HOUMA, LOUISIANA, BACK TO OBLIVION.
WE'VE GOT DRONES THAT CAN DO THE JOB AT THE READY.
BUT THE DEVASTATION, STEVE...THE HORRIBLE LOSS OF LIFE...
REGRETTABLE... BUT ACCEPTABLE.
EVEN THE TOWN'S OWN SHERIFF THINKS WE SHOULD DO IT--
--SO LONG AS WE DESTROY THE SWAMP THING, AS WELL.
ALL WE NEED NOW IS APPROVAL FROM THE WHITE--
BREET BREET
COLONEL, IT'S FOR YOU.
IT'S THE PRESIDENT ON THE LINE.

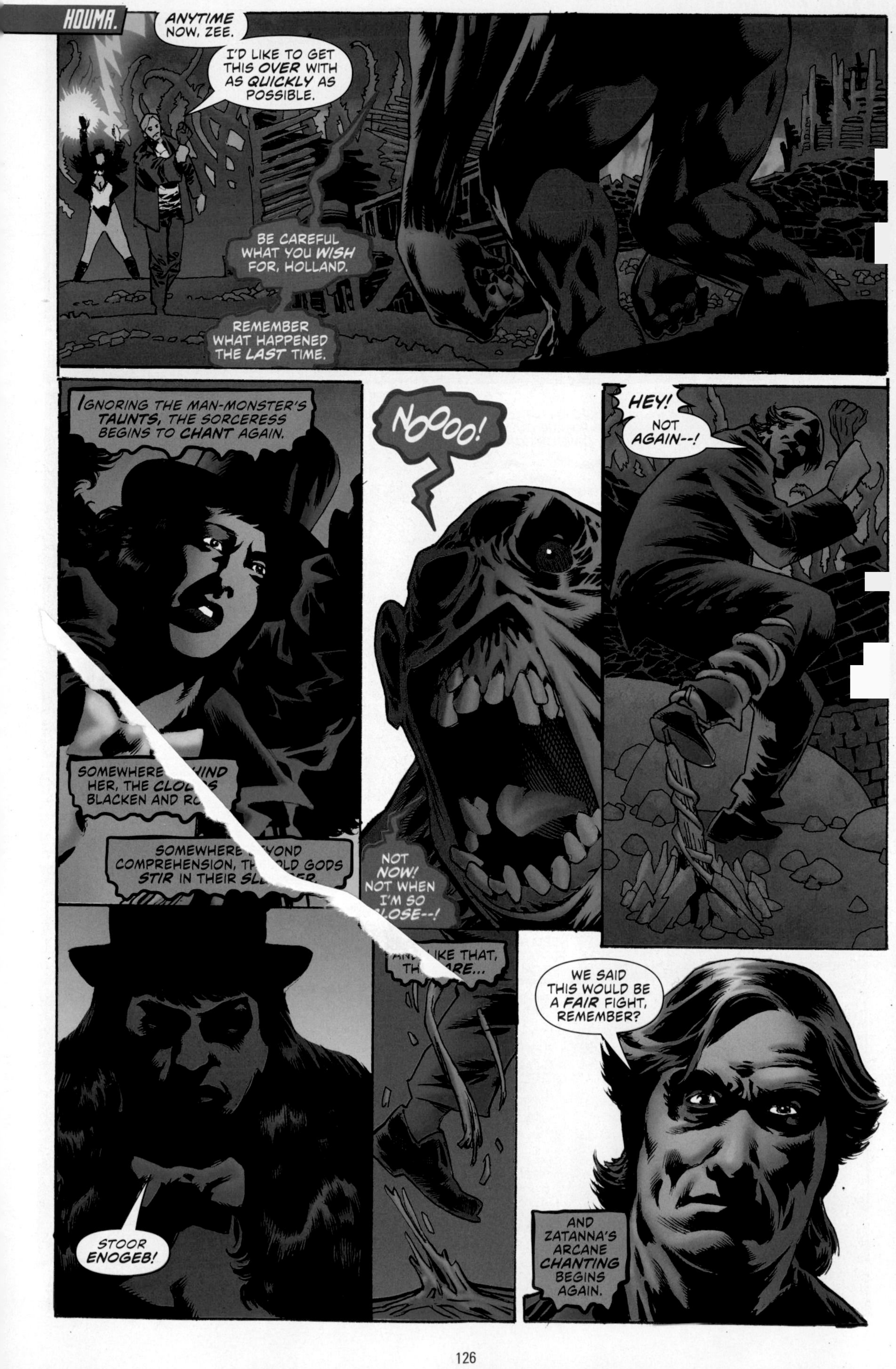

HOUMA.
ANYTIME NOW, ZEE.
I'D LIKE TO GET THIS OVER WITH AS QUICKLY AS POSSIBLE.
BE CAREFUL WHAT YOU WISH FOR, HOLLAND.
REMEMBER WHAT HAPPENED THE LAST TIME.
IGNORING THE MAN-MONSTER'S TAUNTS, THE SORCERESS BEGINS TO CHANT AGAIN.
SOMEWHERE
HER, THE
BLACKEN AND
SOMEWHERE
COMPREHENSION,
STIR IN THEIR
NOOOO!
NOT NOW! NOT WHEN I'M SO
HEY! NOT AGAIN--!
STOOR ENOGEB!
LIKE THAT,
ARE...
WE SAID THIS WOULD BE A FAIR FIGHT, REMEMBER?
AND ZATANNA'S ARCANE CHANTING BEGINS AGAIN.

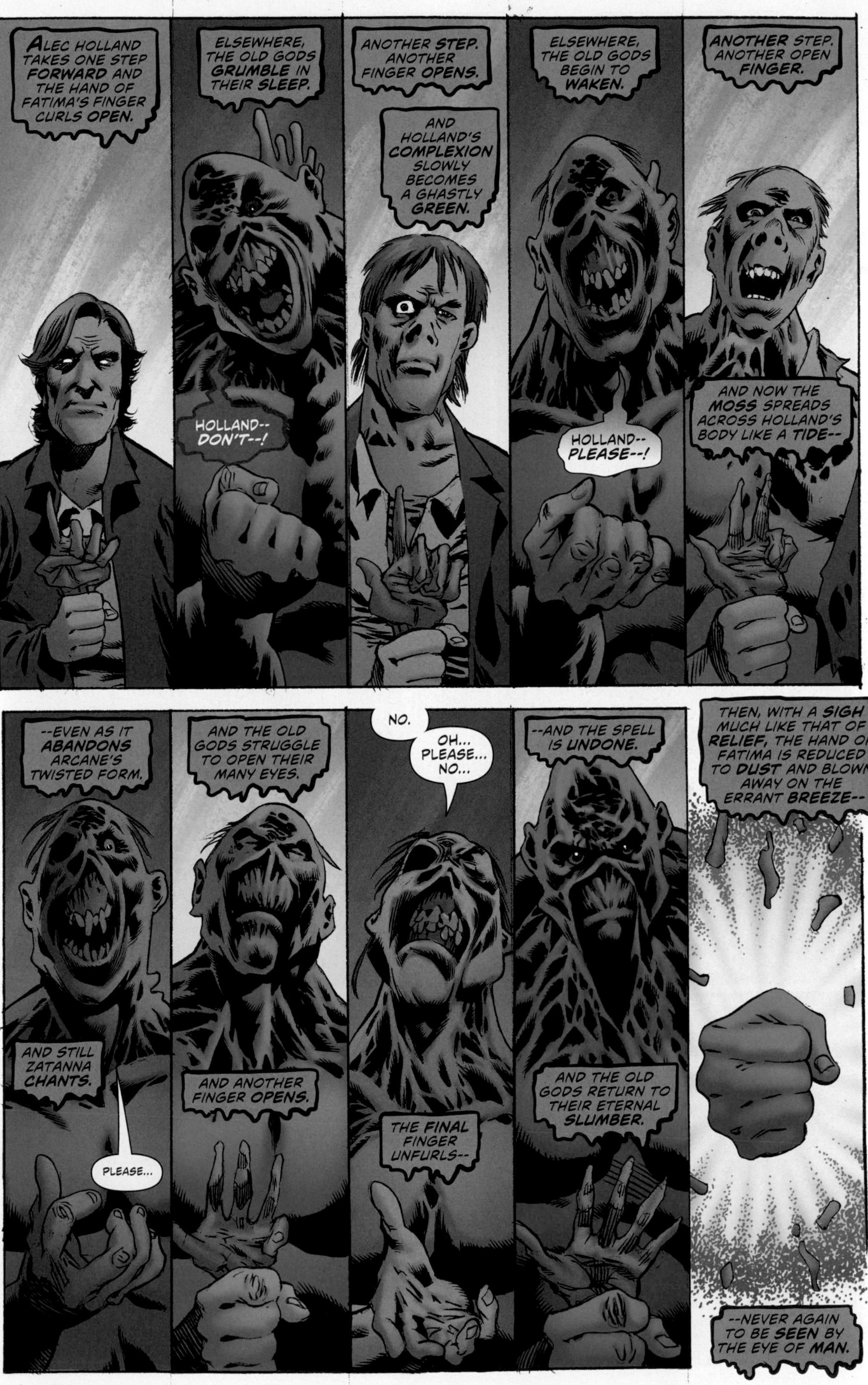
ALEC HOLLAND TAKES ONE STEP FORWARD AND THE HAND OF FATIMA'S FINGER CURLS OPEN.
ELSEWHERE, THE OLD GODS GRUMBLE IN THEIR SLEEP.
HOLLAND-- DON'T--!
ANOTHER STEP. ANOTHER FINGER OPENS.
AND HOLLAND'S COMPLEXION SLOWLY BECOMES A GHASTLY GREEN.
ELSEWHERE, THE OLD GODS BEGIN TO WAKEN.
HOLLAND-- PLEASE--!
ANOTHER STEP. ANOTHER OPEN FINGER.
AND NOW THE MOSS SPREADS ACROSS HOLLAND'S BODY LIKE A TIDE--
--EVEN AS IT ABANDONS ARCANE'S TWISTED FORM.
AND STILL ZATANNA CHANTS.
PLEASE...
AND THE OLD GODS STRUGGLE TO OPEN THEIR MANY EYES.
AND ANOTHER FINGER OPENS.
NO.
OH... PLEASE... NO...
THE FINAL FINGER UNFURLS--
--AND THE SPELL IS UNDONE.
AND THE OLD GODS RETURN TO THEIR ETERNAL SLUMBER.
THEN, WITH A SIGH MUCH LIKE THAT OF RELIEF, THE HAND OF FATIMA IS REDUCED TO DUST AND BLOWN AWAY ON THE ERRANT BREEZE--
--NEVER AGAIN TO BE SEEN BY THE EYE OF MAN.

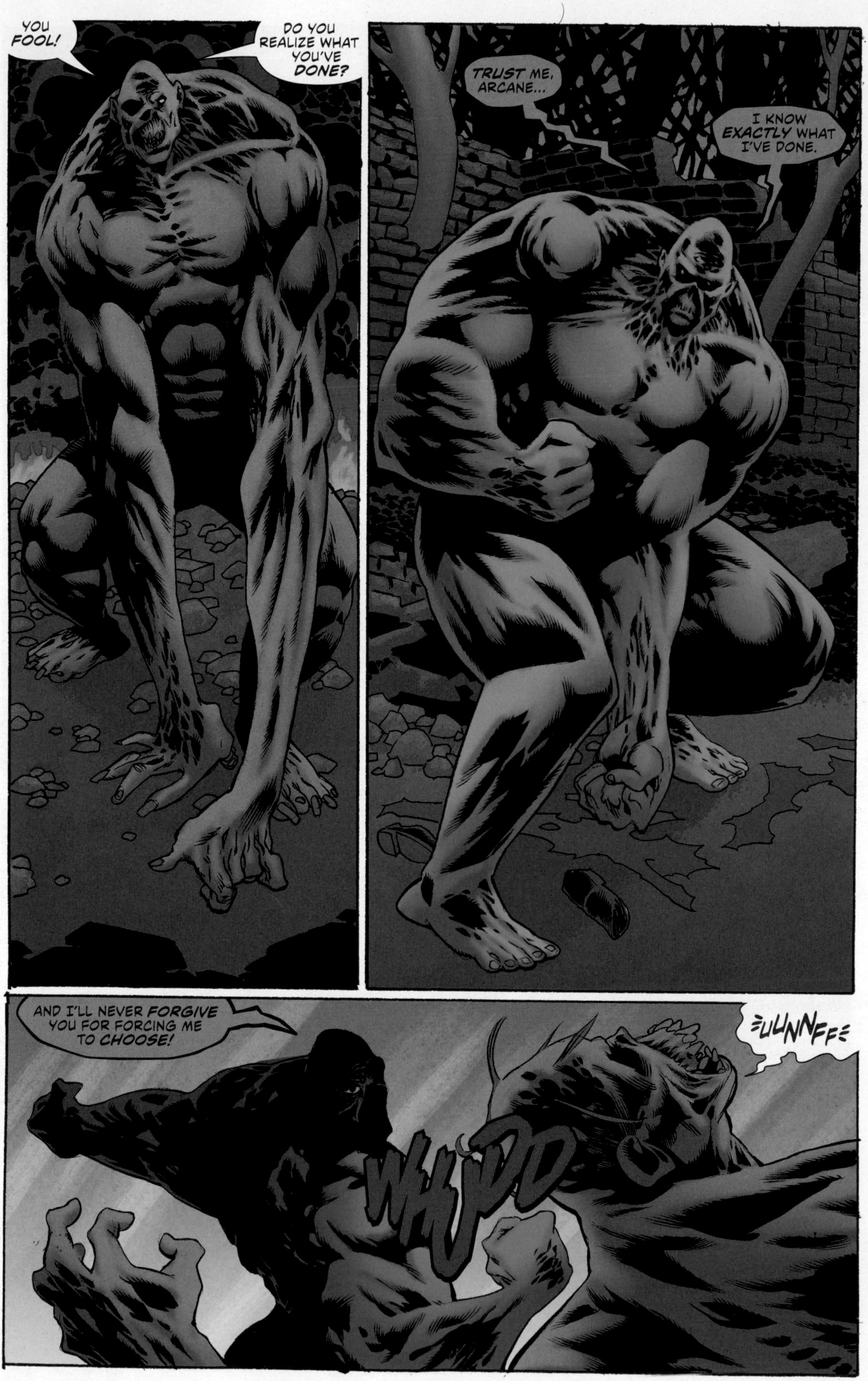

YOU FOOL!
DO YOU REALIZE WHAT YOU'VE DONE?
TRUST ME, ARCANE...
I KNOW EXACTLY WHAT I'VE DONE.
AND I'LL NEVER FORGIVE YOU FOR FORCING ME TO CHOOSE!
UUNNFF
WHUDD

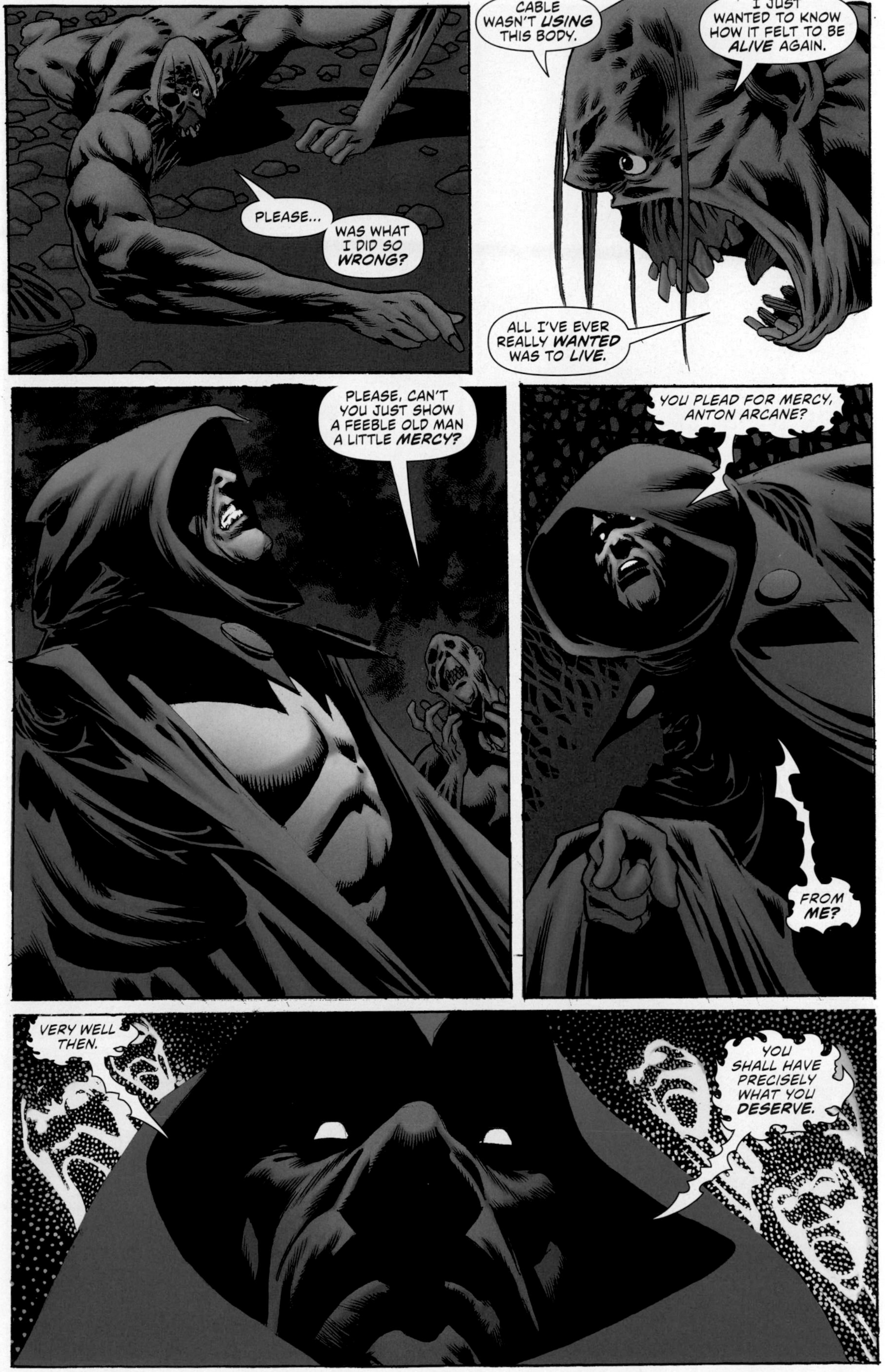
PLEASE...
WAS WHAT I DID SO WRONG?
CABLE WASN'T USING THIS BODY.
I JUST WANTED TO KNOW HOW IT FELT TO BE ALIVE AGAIN.
ALL I'VE EVER REALLY WANTED WAS TO LIVE.
PLEASE, CAN'T YOU JUST SHOW A FEEBLE OLD MAN A LITTLE MERCY?
YOU PLEAD FOR MERCY, ANTON ARCANE?
FROM ME?
VERY WELL THEN.
YOU SHALL HAVE PRECISELY WHAT YOU DESERVE.

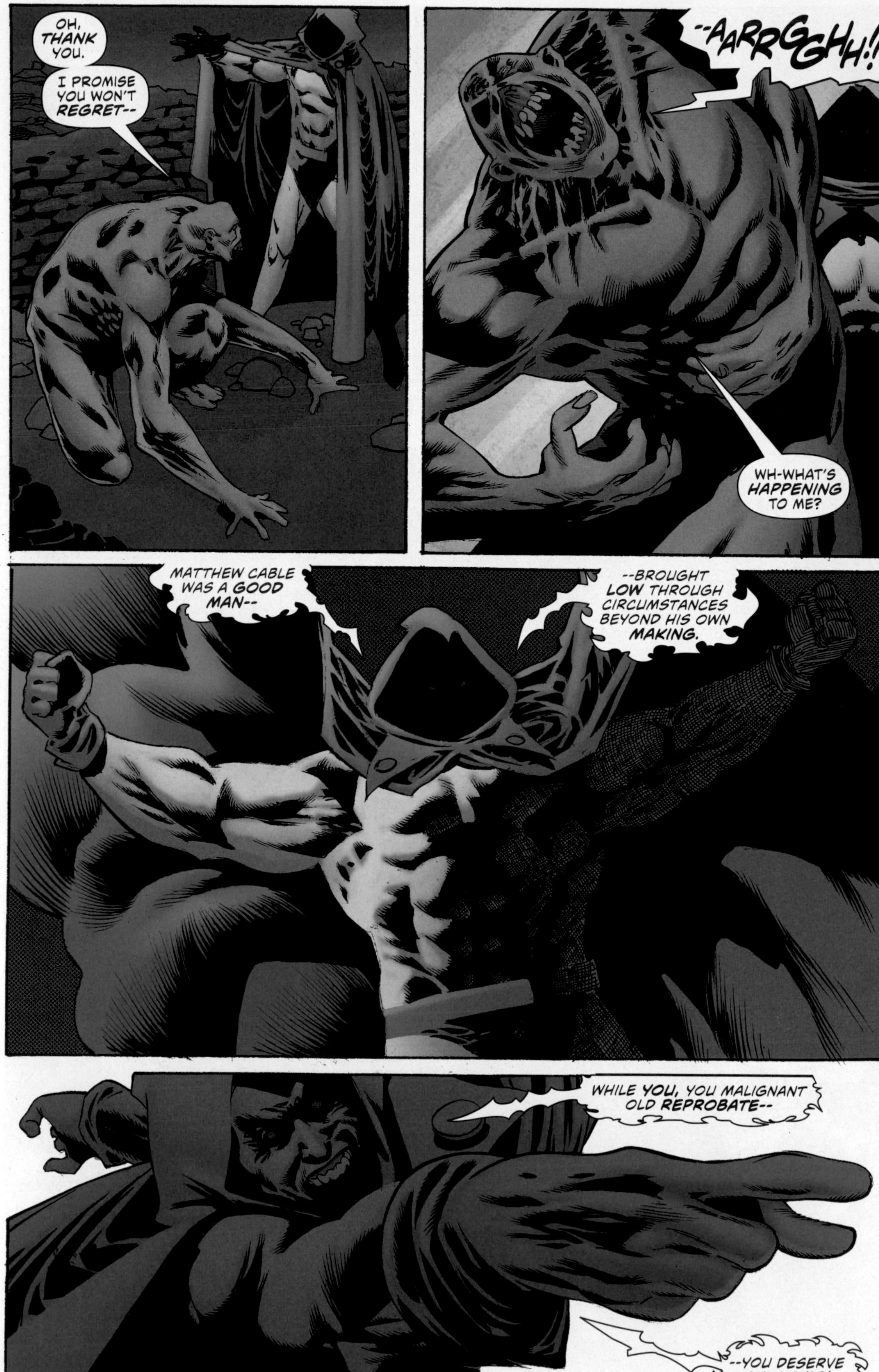
OH, THANK YOU.
I PROMISE YOU WON'T REGRET--
--AARRGGHH!!
WH-WHAT'S HAPPENING TO ME?
MATTHEW CABLE WAS A GOOD MAN--
--BROUGHT LOW THROUGH CIRCUMSTANCES BEYOND HIS OWN MAKING.
WHILE YOU, YOU MALIGNANT OLD REPROBATE--
--YOU DESERVE ONLY THIS!

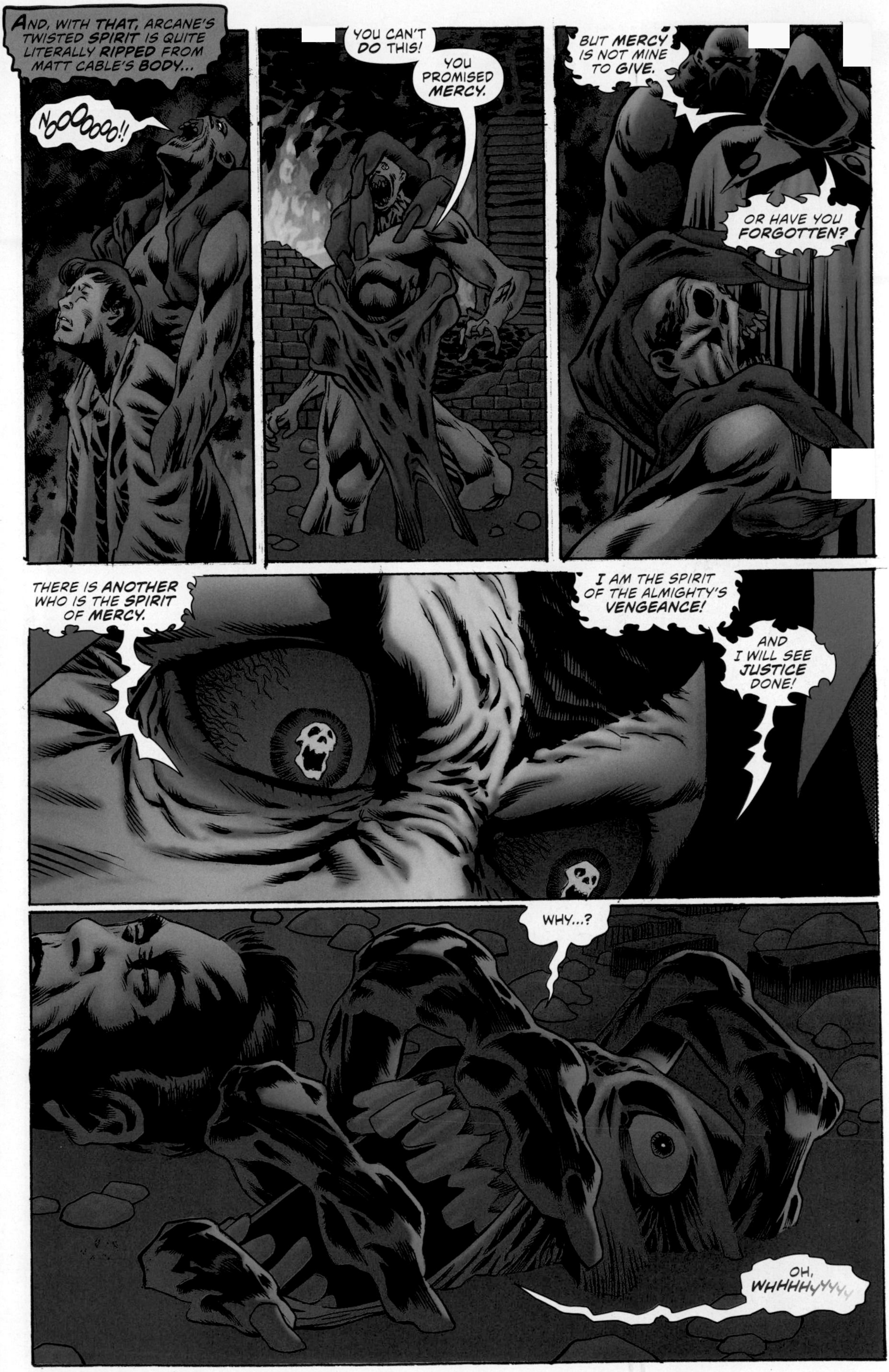
AND, WITH THAT, ARCANE'S TWISTED SPIRIT IS QUITE LITERALLY RIPPED FROM MATT CABLE'S BODY...
NOOOOOOO!!
YOU CAN'T DO THIS!
YOU PROMISED MERCY.
BUT MERCY IS NOT MINE TO GIVE.
OR HAVE YOU FORGOTTEN?
THERE IS ANOTHER WHO IS THE SPIRIT OF MERCY.
I AM THE SPIRIT OF THE ALMIGHTY'S VENGEANCE!
AND I WILL SEE JUSTICE DONE!
WHY...?
OH, WHHHHYYYY

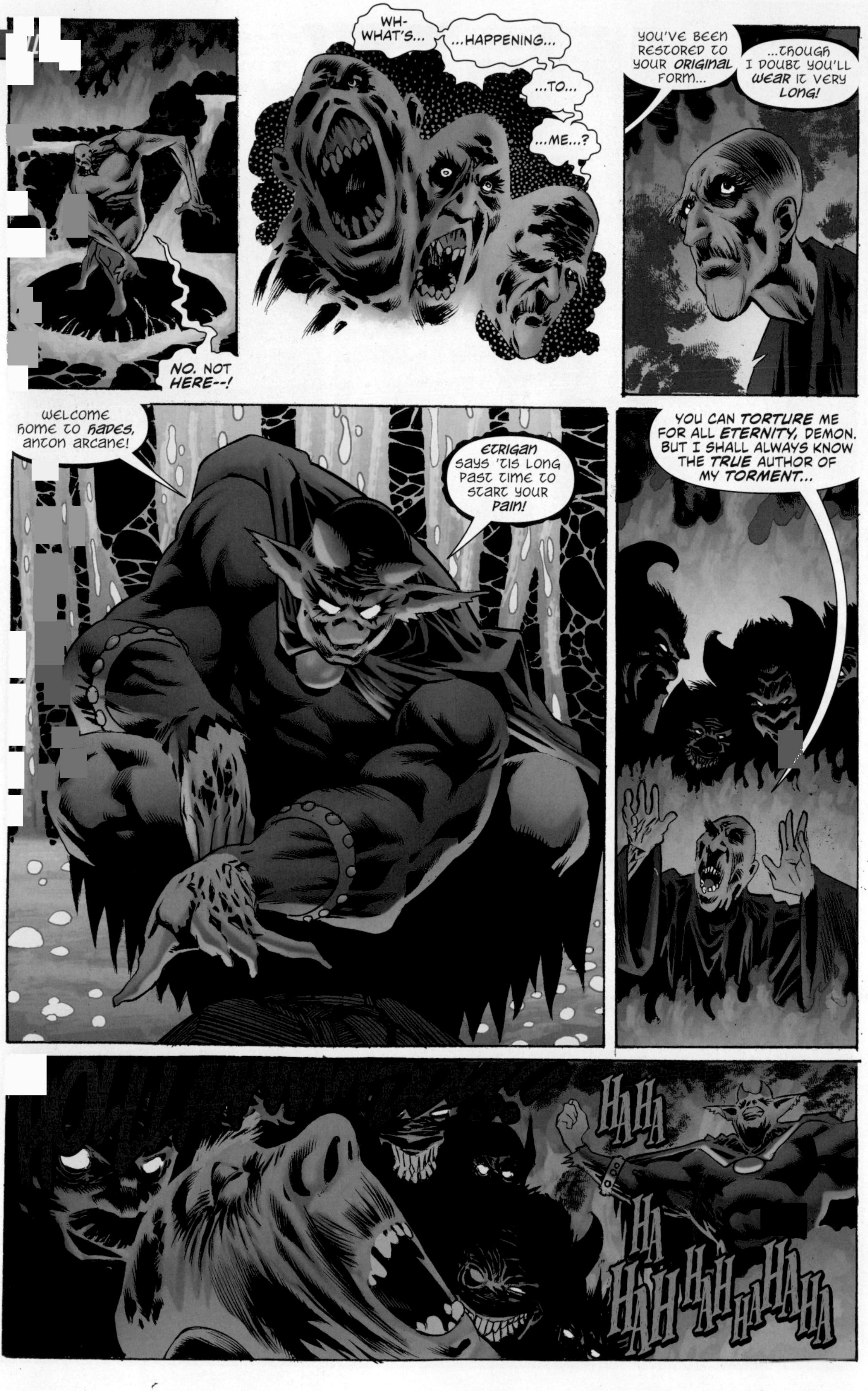
NO. NOT HERE--!
WH-WHAT'S...
...HAPPENING...
...TO...
...ME...?
YOU'VE BEEN RESTORED TO YOUR ORIGINAL FORM...
...THOUGH I DOUBT YOU'LL WEAR IT VERY LONG!
WELCOME HOME TO HADES, ANTON ARCANE!
ETRIGAN SAYS 'TIS LONG PAST TIME TO START YOUR PAIN!
YOU CAN TORTURE ME FOR ALL ETERNITY, DEMON. BUT I SHALL ALWAYS KNOW THE TRUE AUTHOR OF MY TORMENT...
HAHA
HA
HAH HAH HAHAHA

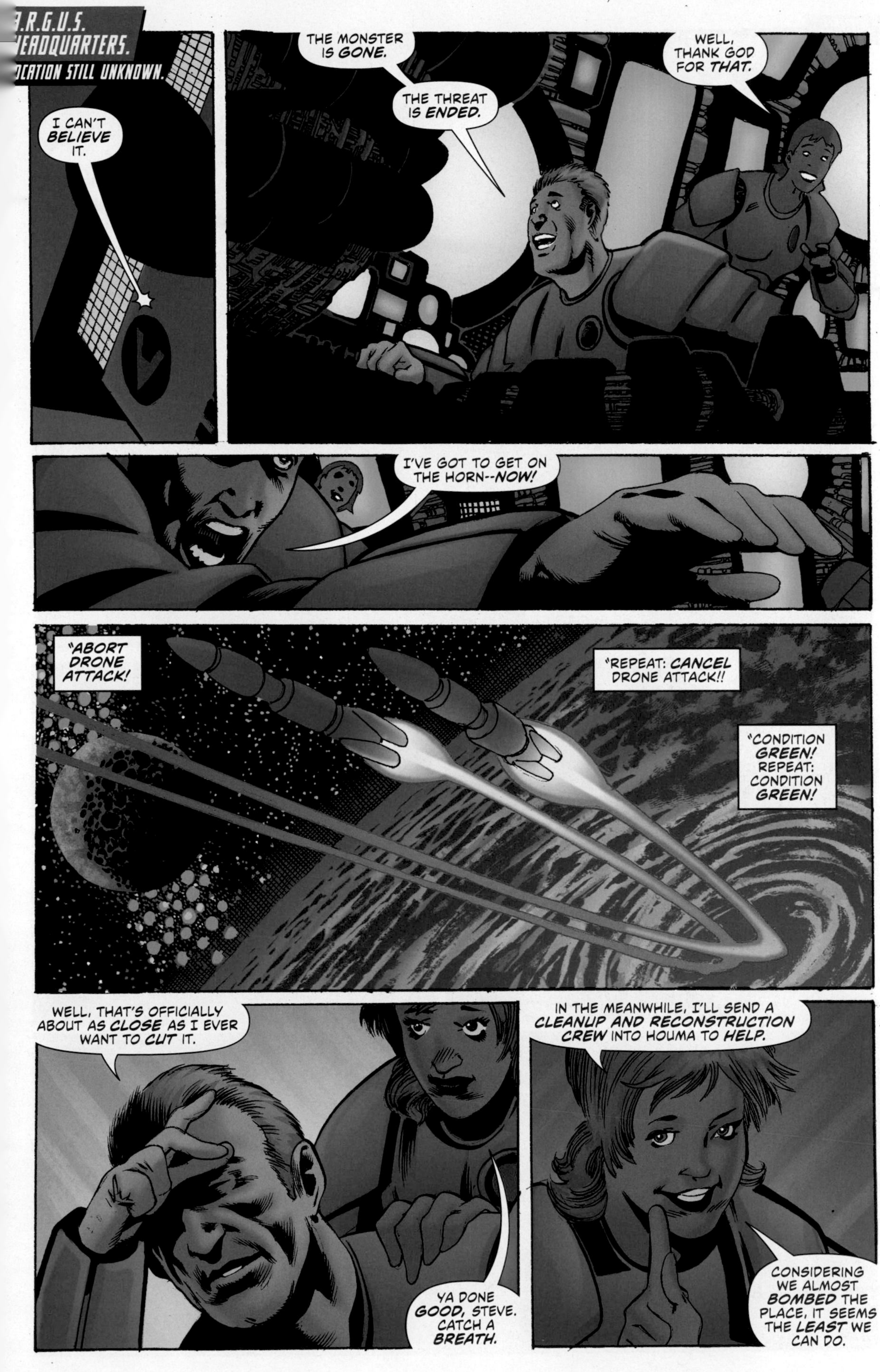
A.R.G.U.S. HEADQUARTERS. LOCATION STILL UNKNOWN.
I CAN'T BELIEVE IT.
THE MONSTER IS GONE.
THE THREAT IS ENDED.
WELL, THANK GOD FOR THAT.
I'VE GOT TO GET ON THE HORN--NOW!
"ABORT DRONE ATTACK!
"REPEAT: CANCEL DRONE ATTACK!!
"CONDITION GREEN! REPEAT: CONDITION GREEN!
WELL, THAT'S OFFICIALLY ABOUT AS CLOSE AS I EVER WANT TO CUT IT.
YA DONE GOOD, STEVE. CATCH A BREATH.
IN THE MEANWHILE, I'LL SEND A CLEANUP AND RECONSTRUCTION CREW INTO HOUMA TO HELP.
CONSIDERING WE ALMOST BOMBED THE PLACE, IT SEEMS THE LEAST WE CAN DO.

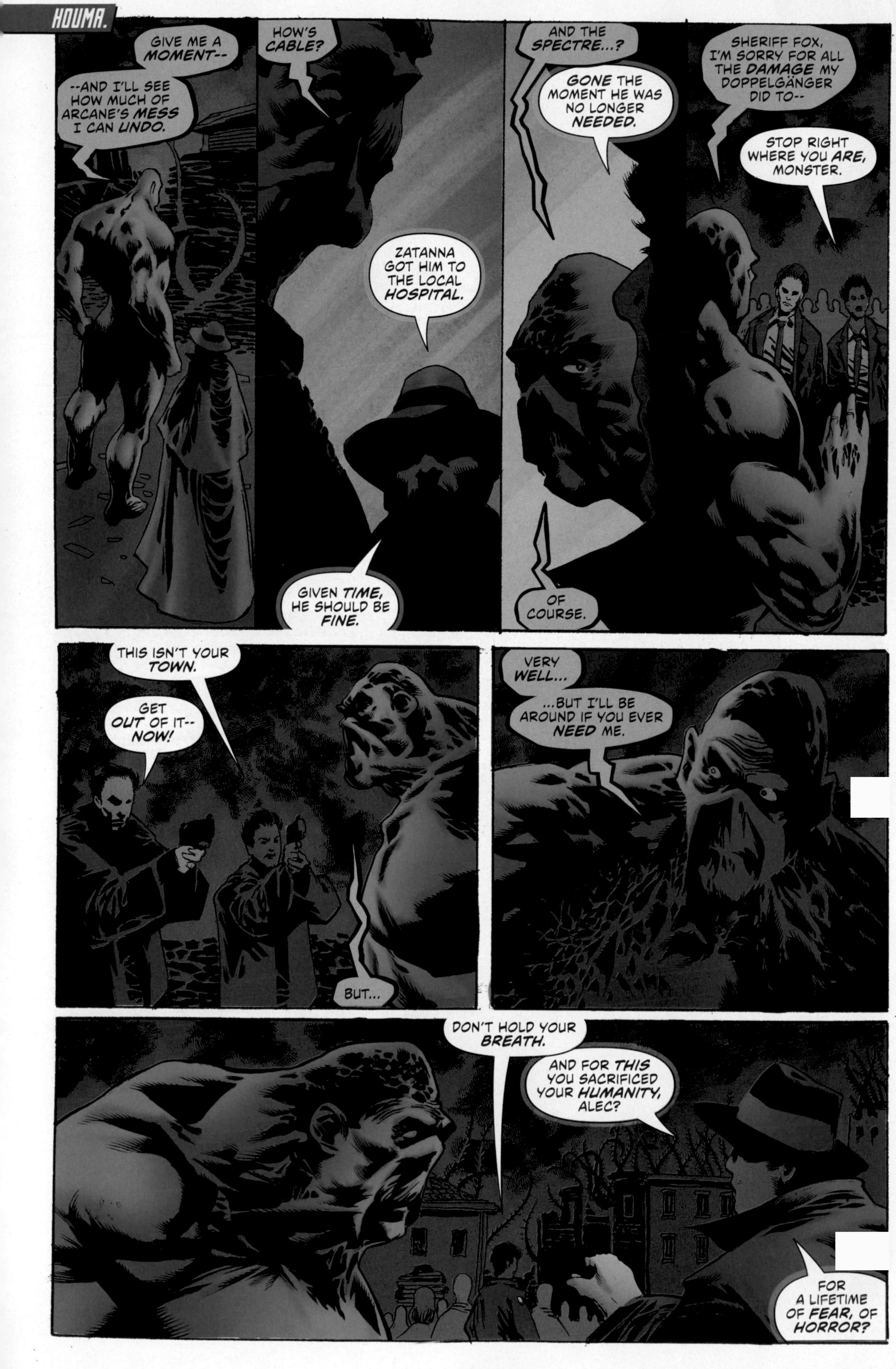
HOUMA.
GIVE ME A MOMENT--
--AND I'LL SEE HOW MUCH OF ARCANE'S MESS I CAN UNDO.
HOW'S CABLE?
ZATANNA GOT HIM TO THE LOCAL HOSPITAL.
GIVEN TIME, HE SHOULD BE FINE.
AND THE SPECTRE...?
GONE THE MOMENT HE WAS NO LONGER NEEDED.
OF COURSE.
SHERIFF FOX, I'M SORRY FOR ALL THE DAMAGE MY DOPPELGÄNGER DID TO--
STOP RIGHT WHERE YOU ARE, MONSTER.
THIS ISN'T YOUR TOWN.
GET OUT OF IT-- NOW!
BUT...
VERY WELL...
...BUT I'LL BE AROUND IF YOU EVER NEED ME.
DON'T HOLD YOUR BREATH.
AND FOR THIS YOU SACRIFICED YOUR HUMANITY, ALEC?
FOR A LIFETIME OF FEAR, OF HORROR?

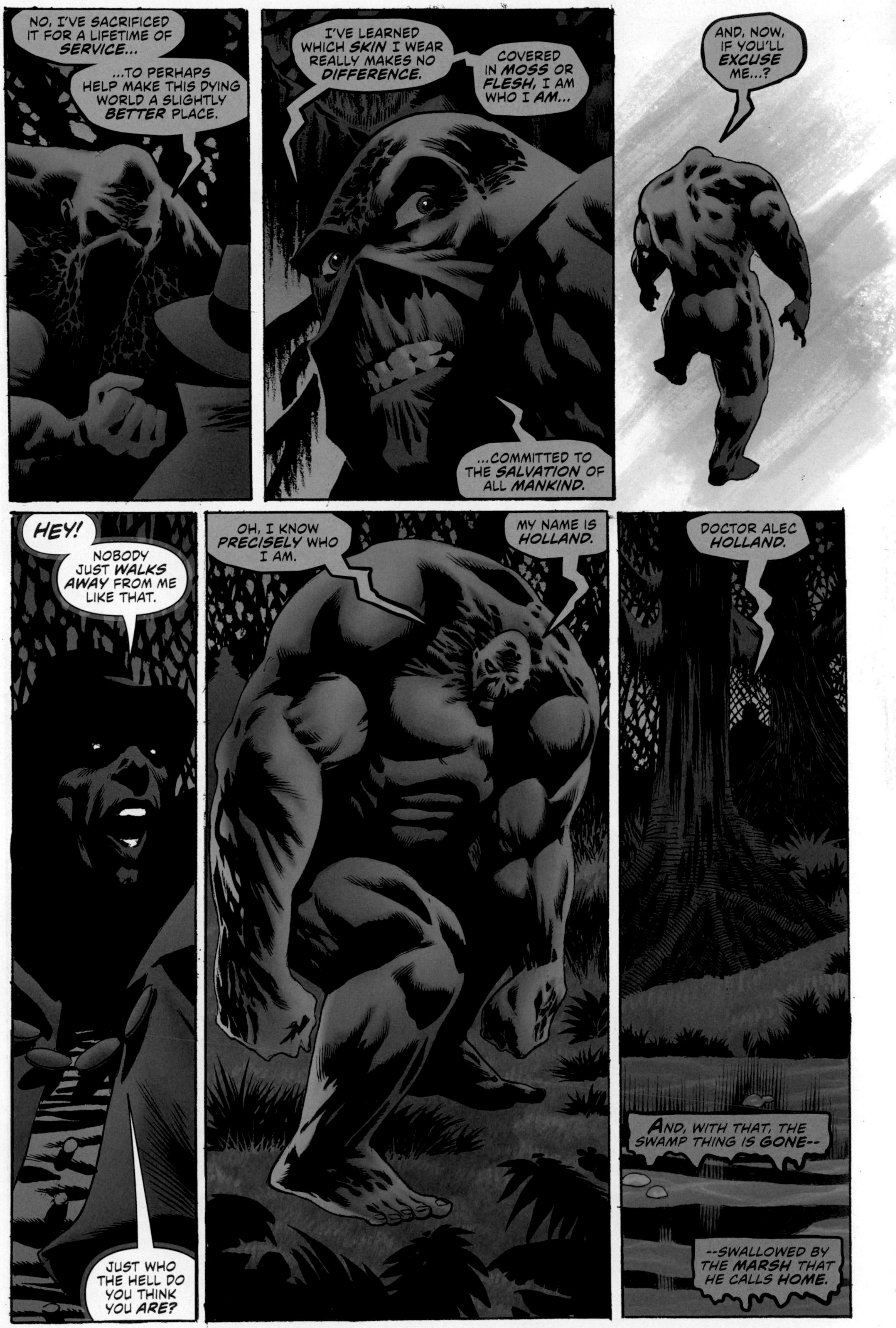
NO, I'VE SACRIFICED IT FOR A LIFETIME OF SERVICE...
...TO PERHAPS HELP MAKE THIS DYING WORLD A SLIGHTLY BETTER PLACE.
I'VE LEARNED WHICH SKIN I WEAR REALLY MAKES NO DIFFERENCE.
COVERED IN MOSS OR FLESH, I AM WHO I AM...
...COMMITTED TO THE SALVATION OF ALL MANKIND.
AND, NOW, IF YOU'LL EXCUSE ME...?
HEY!
NOBODY JUST WALKS AWAY FROM ME LIKE THAT.
JUST WHO THE HELL DO YOU THINK YOU ARE?
OH, I KNOW PRECISELY WHO I AM.
MY NAME IS HOLLAND.
DOCTOR ALEC HOLLAND.
AND, WITH THAT, THE SWAMP THING IS GONE--
--SWALLOWED BY THE MARSH THAT HE CALLS HOME.

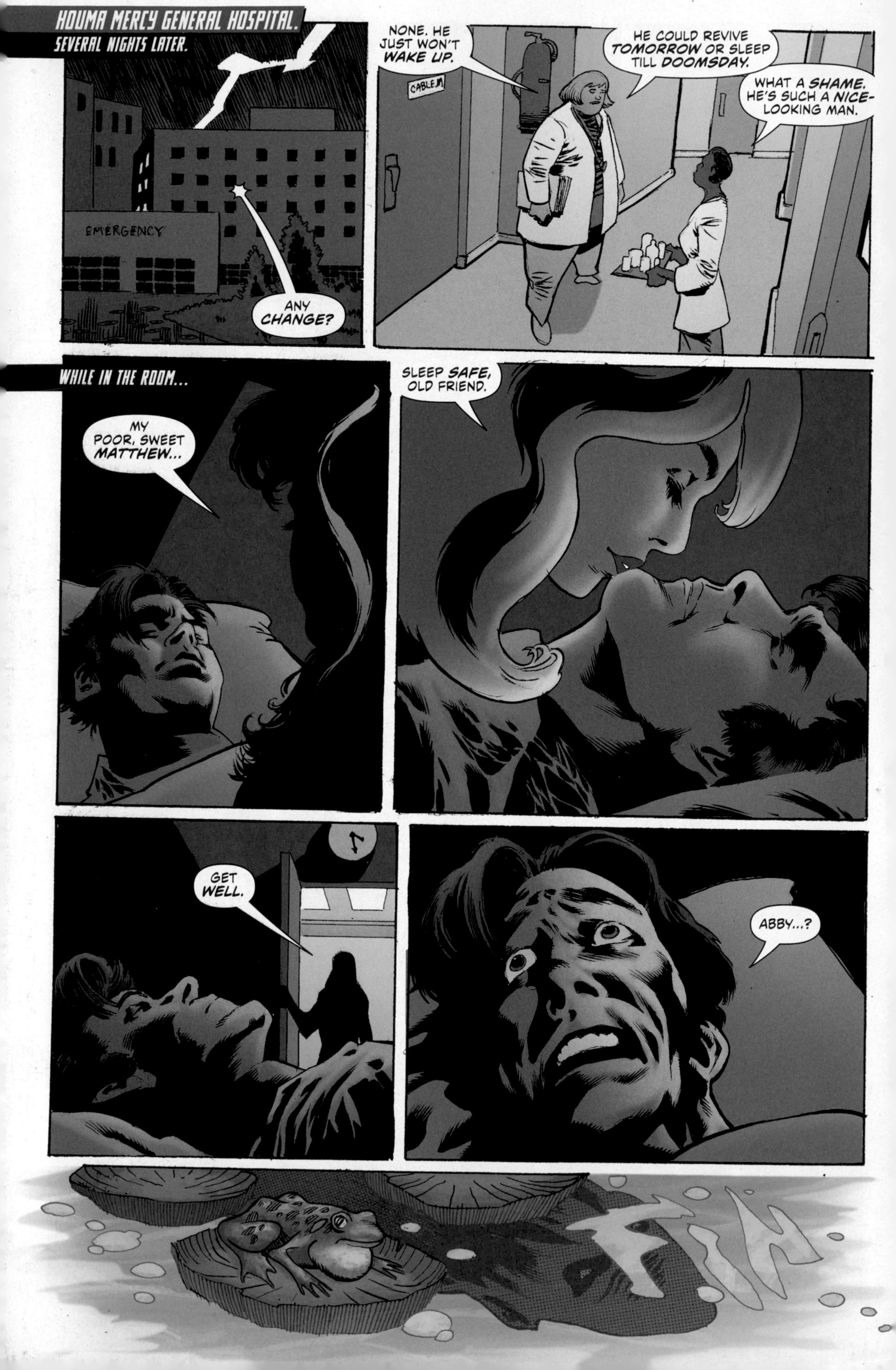
HOUMA MERCY GENERAL HOSPITAL.
SEVERAL NIGHTS LATER.
EMERGENCY
ANY CHANGE?
NONE. HE JUST WON'T WAKE UP.
HE COULD REVIVE TOMORROW OR SLEEP TILL DOOMSDAY.
WHAT A SHAME. HE'S SUCH A NICE-LOOKING MAN.
WHILE IN THE ROOM...
MY POOR, SWEET MATTHEW...
SLEEP SAFE, OLD FRIEND.
GET WELL.
ABBY...?
FIN

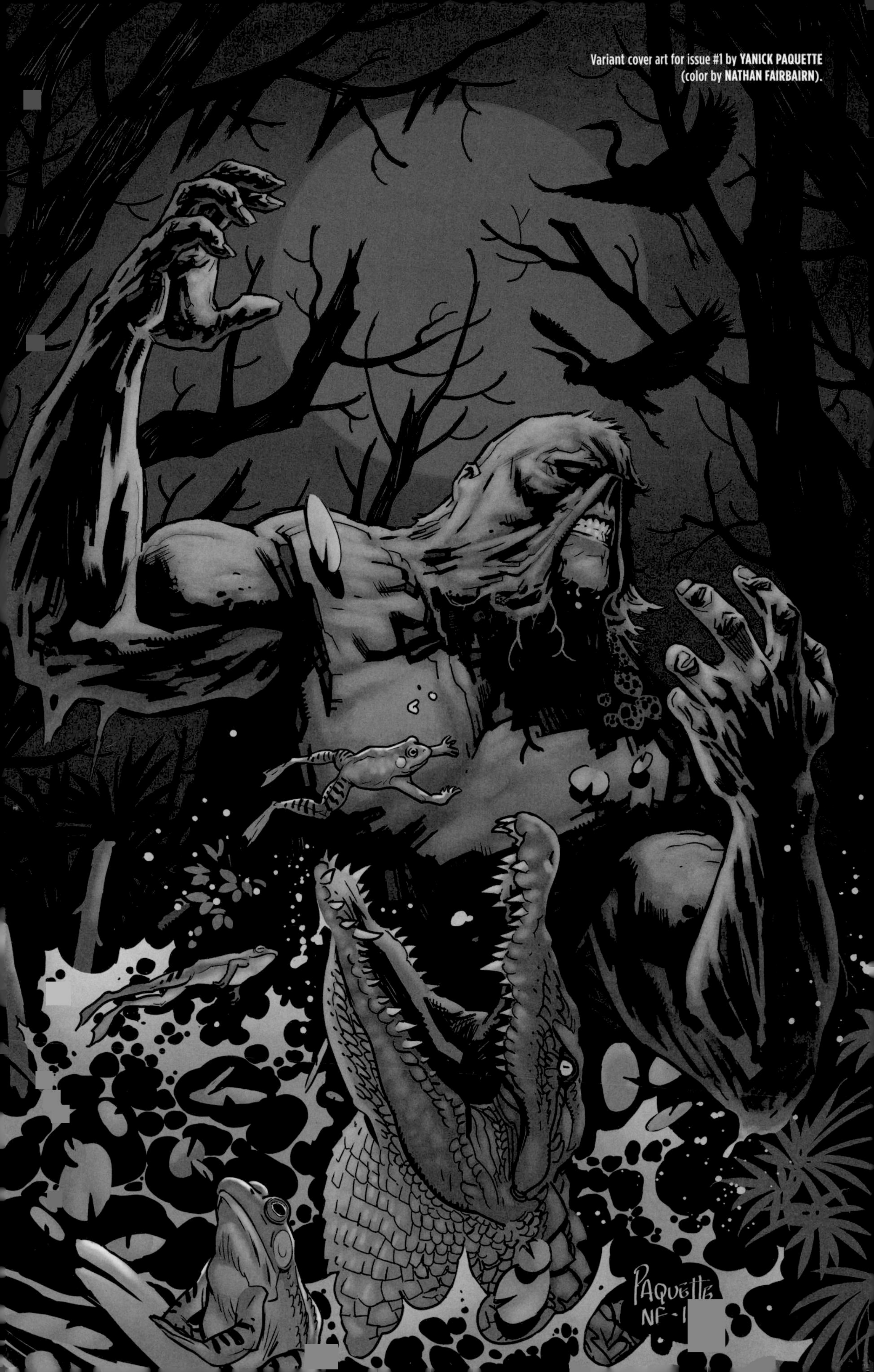

Variant cover art for issue #1 by **YANICK PAQUETTE**
(color by **NATHAN FAIRBAIRN**).

UP FROM THE MIRE

Character sketches by **KELLEY JONES**

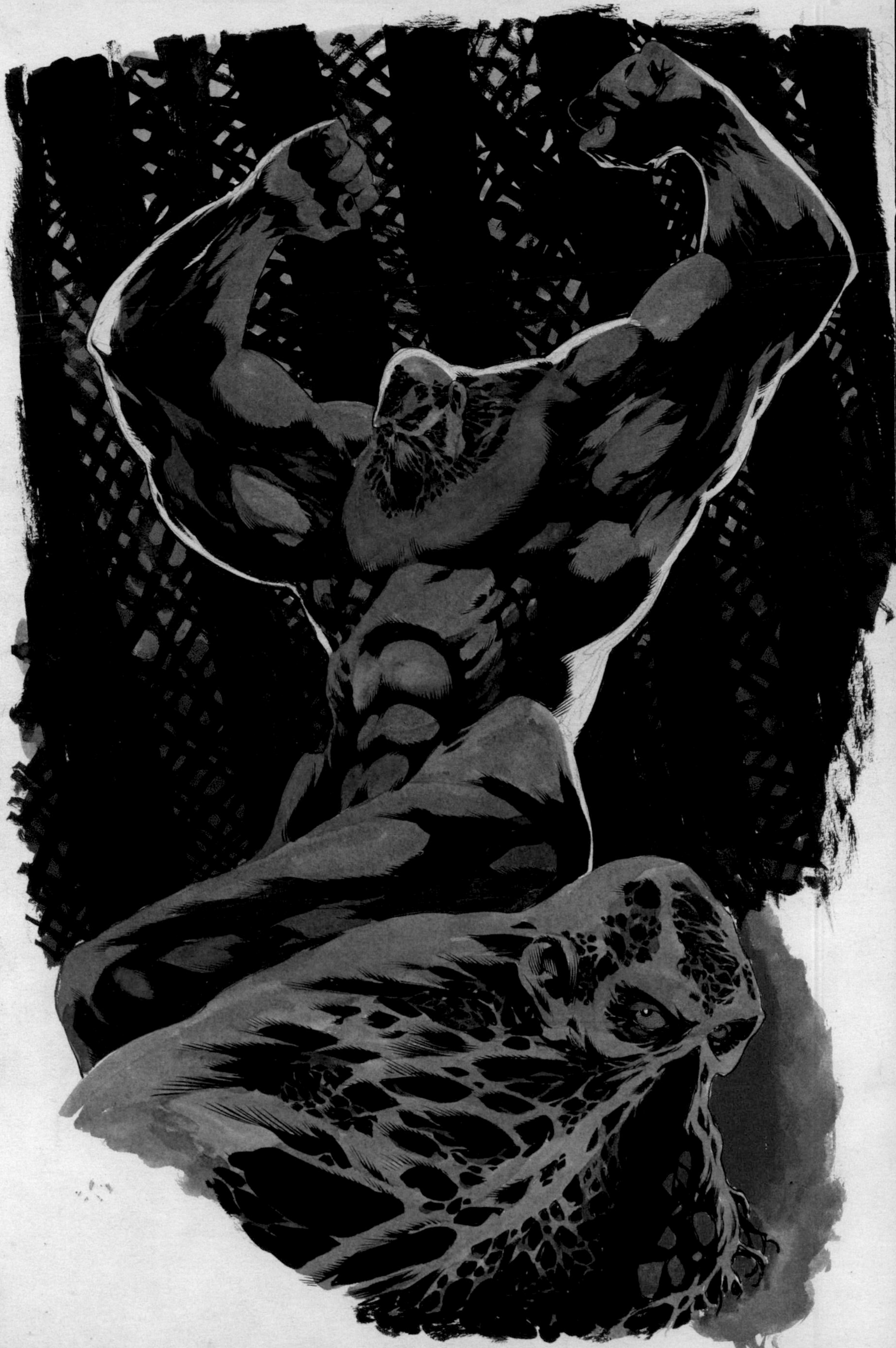

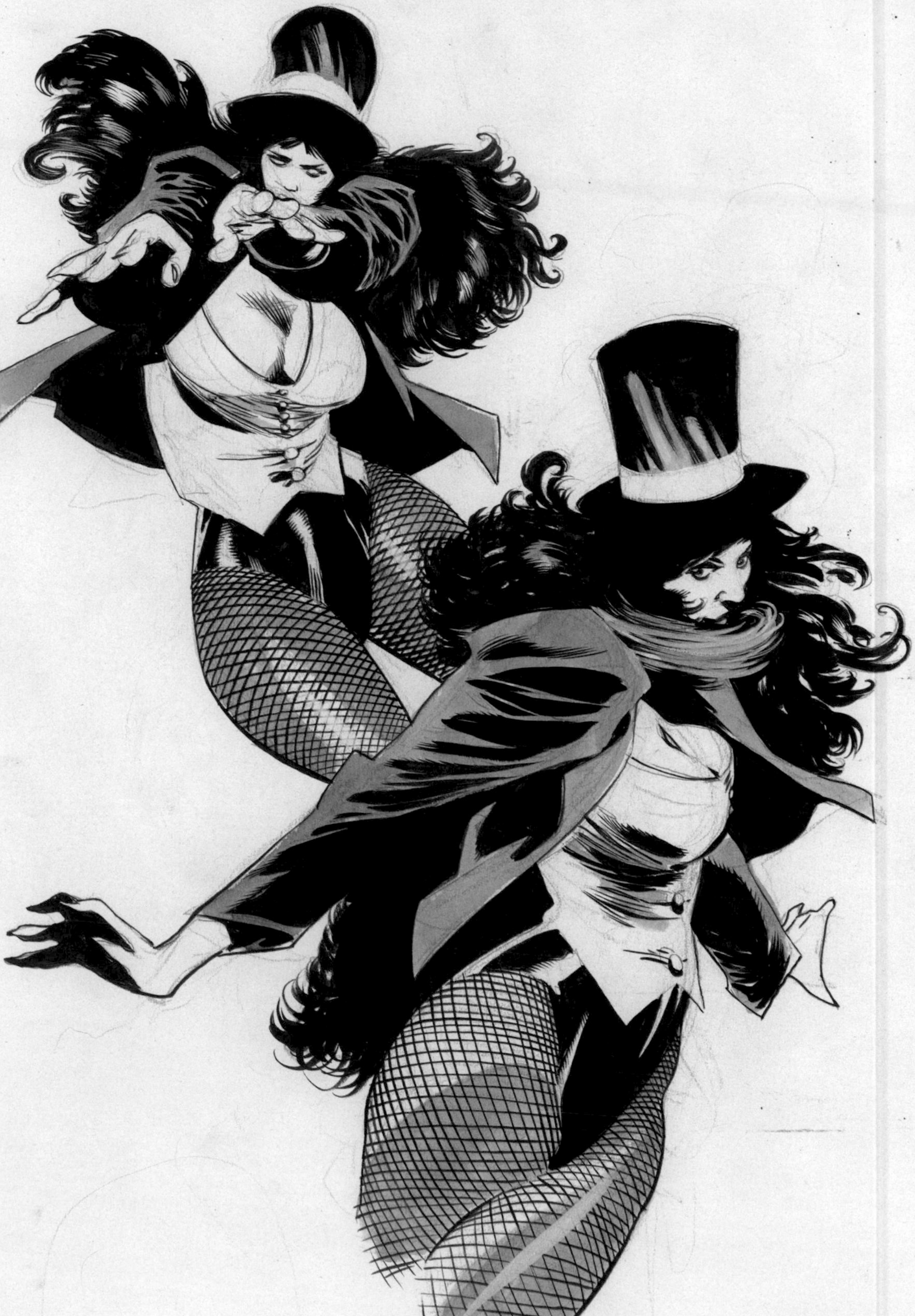

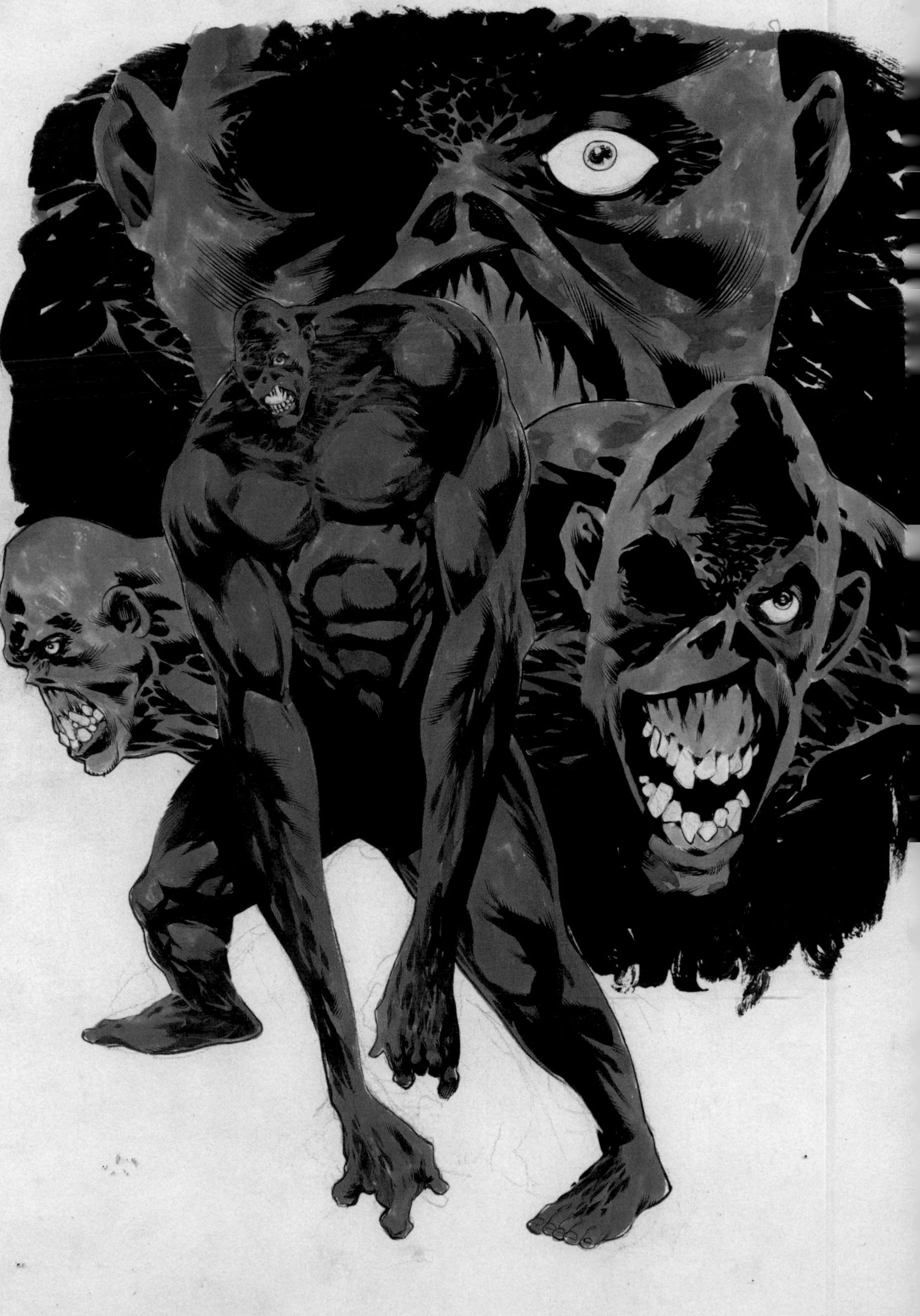

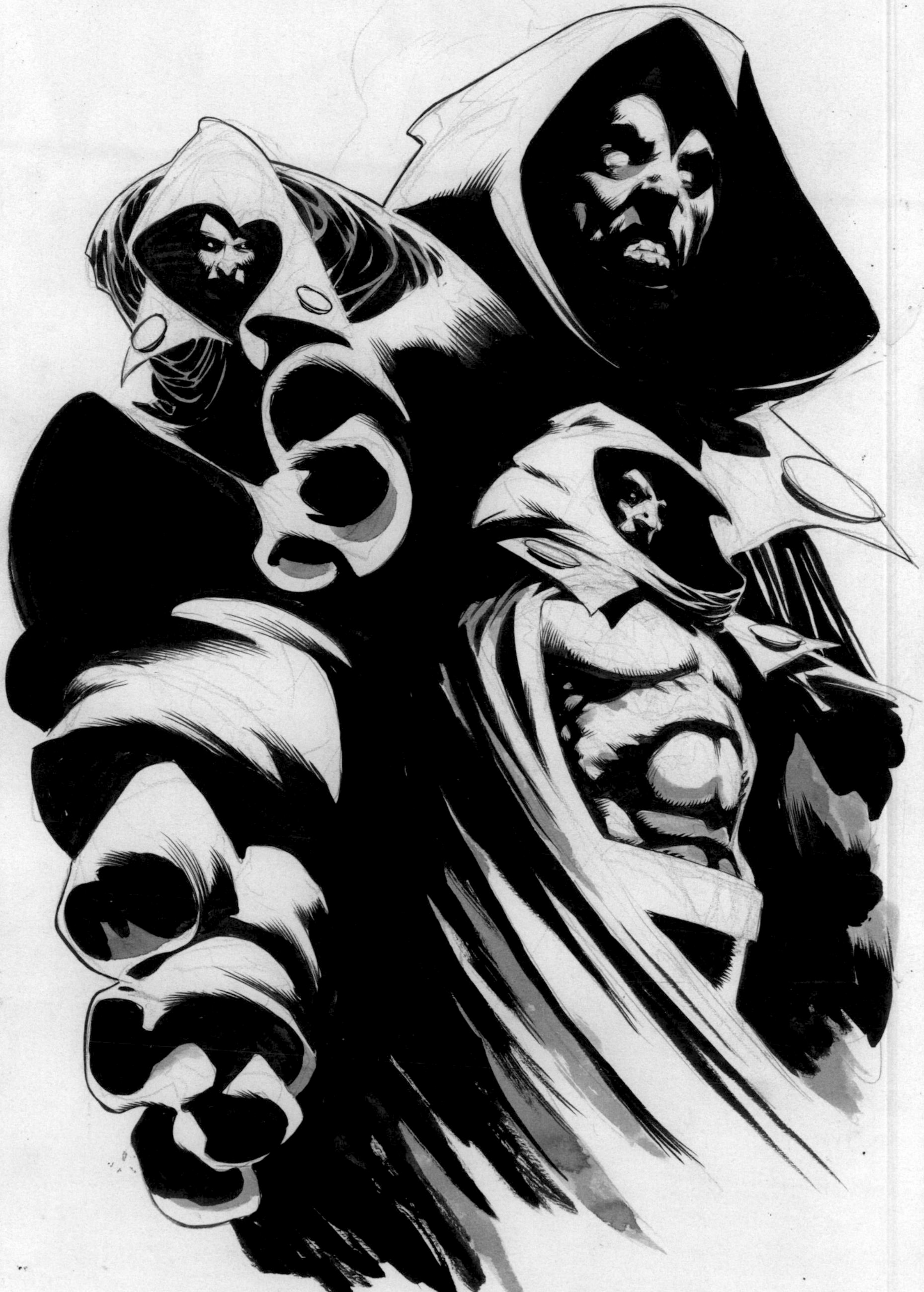

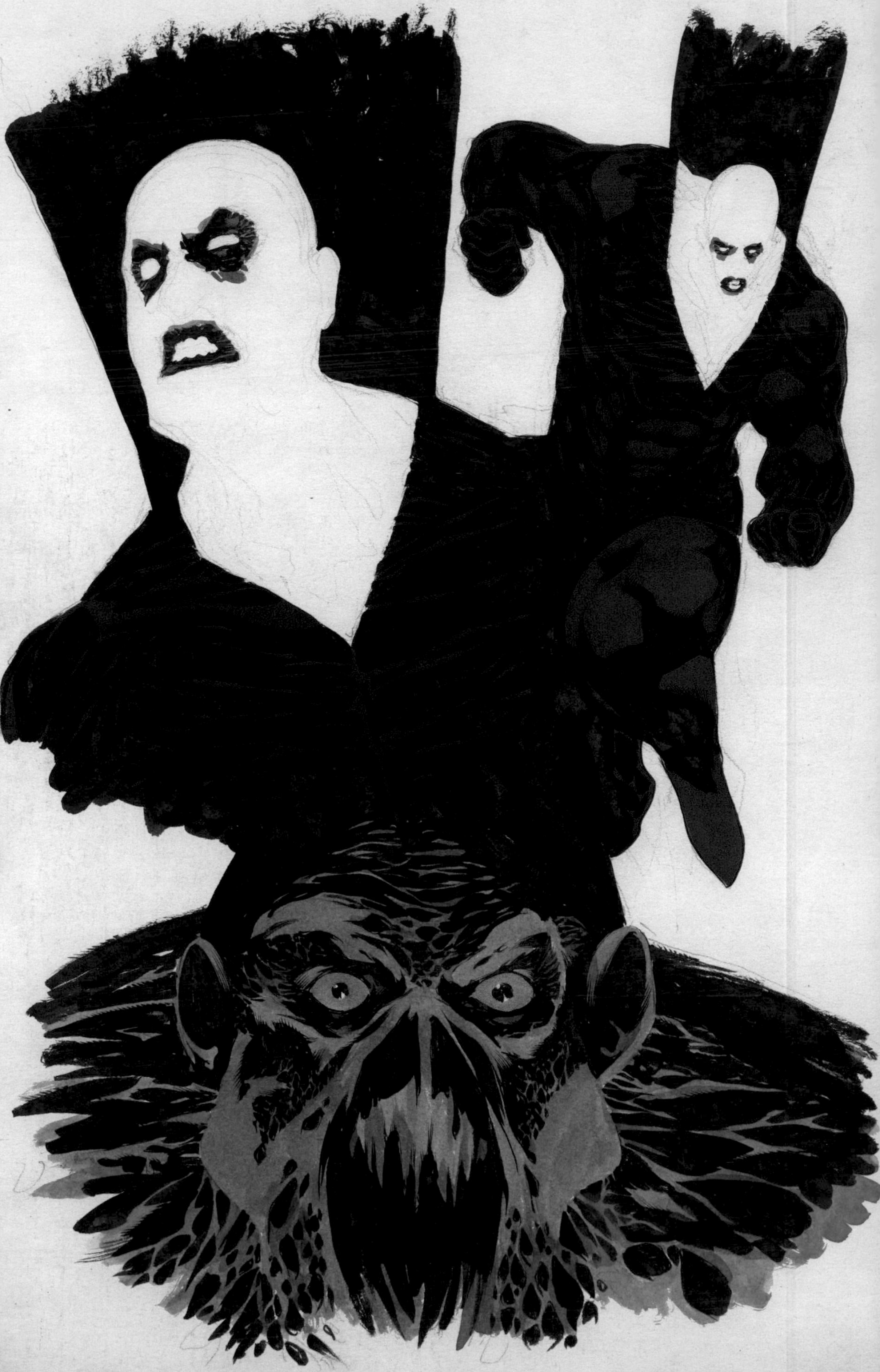